Keepers of the Central Fire

Issues in Ecology for Indigenous Peoples

LORELEI ANNE LAMBERT COLOMEDA, PhD., R.N.

D1552632

JONES AND BARTLETT PUBLISHERS
Sudbury, Massachusetts
BOSTON   TORONTO   LONDON   SINGAPORE

DEC 1998

ELMHURST COLLEGE LIBRARY

World Headquarters
Jones and Bartlett Publishers
40 Tall Pine Drive
Sudbury, MA 01776
978-443-5000

info@jbpub.com
www.jbpub.com

Jones and Bartlett Publishers International
Barb House, Barb Mews
London W6 7PA
UK

Jones and Bartlett Publishers Canada
P.O. Box 19020
Toronto, ON M5S 1X1
CANADA

Copyright © 1999 by Jones and Bartlett Publishers, Inc.

A portion of the royalties from this work will be donated to grassroots organizations working on environmental issues with Aboriginal People.

All rights reserved. No part of the material protected by this copyright notice may be reproduced or utilized in any form, electronic or mechanical, including photocopying, recording, or by any other information storage and retrieval system, without written permission from the copyright owner.

The views expressed in this publication represent the views of the authors and do not necessarily reflect the official views of the National League for Nursing.

Lambert Colomeda, Lorelei Anne.
    Keepers of the central fire : issues in ecology for indigenous
peoples / Lorelei (Lori) A. Lambert Colomeda.
        p.   cm.
    Includes bibliographical references and index.
    ISBN 0-7637-0923-9
    1. Indians of North America—Health and hygiene.   2. Ecology—
Environmental aspects.   I. Title.
    [DNLM: 1. Environmental Health.   2. Indians, North American.
3. Ethnology—North America.   4. Ecology.   WA 30 L222k 1998]
RA448.5.I5L36 1998
613'.089'97—DC21
DNLM/DLC
for Library of Congress   97-51179
                                                                CIP

Printed in the United States of America
02 01 00 99 98   10 9 8 7 6 5 4 3 2 1

ELMHURST COLLEGE LIBRARY

*This work is dedicated to
the children of the
Next Seven Generations
and Eric who wrote:*

*I like the warm sun because
the sun helps things grow.
I like the way it feels when
the sun melts the snow.*

FOREWORD

Public health is not a science, rather an art or even better, a craft. It applies scientific concepts, strategies, and methods, which it borrows from disciplines like sociology, ecology, epidemiology, psychology, or economy. It integrates sections of these disciplines according to its particular problem definitions and comes up with its own flavor of objectives, goals, implementation strategies, and evaluation approaches.

In short, public health is involved with the real world—its structures, power players (or gamblers?), bureaucracies, cultures, communities, people, environmental and economic conditions and, probably most important, with all the prejudices and attitudes we have developed in the course of our lives, and those of the people we will be working with.

Someone working in public health leads an interesting life. Never boring, always exciting, and more often than not, it's simply life on the edge because the problems of public health are too many and sometimes too complex for a casual approach. This is particularly true when it comes to public health policy formation, a process full of miracles good and bad. Who would have thought that reasonable people could stand up against public health? Who would have thought that policy formation in others than the health sector deliberately takes into account the endangerment of the human species and Mother Earth? Who would have thought that we value money higher than the well-being of our fellow-humans?

The westernized model of public health imposes its concepts and methods globally, just like westernized economies or electronic communication.

Foreword

We are witness of the *McDonaldization* (Ritzer, 1996) of society and all its sectors. We lose diversity with increasing speed and uniformity lurks around the corner more often than not. Sociologists talk about *globalization*, referring to the process of Western domination over the "rest of the world" in terms of economy, culture, politics, and subsequently in terms of shaping all public and private places of human interaction according to the dominant patterns of taste and power. Public health is not excluded, neither in terms of morbidity and mortality patterns nor in terms of environmental degradation in remote areas due to the export of pollution and waste from so-called developed countries.

In the past decades, the gap between so-called developed and developing countries has been widened with regard to almost all indicators used by the United Nations Statistical Office. Recently, we find that within societies the world over, the gap between rich and poor is widening as well. The key concept that describes the current state of the world precisely is called *inequality*. As our societies become more unhealthy (Wilkinson, 1996), so does the global ecosystem.

It's strange to write that people live in an environment. It seems so obvious that we live in an ecological system in which we are connected to many other species, functions, and modes of energy exchange that the notion of environment in the context of public health seems almost superfluous. However, if one takes a closer look at public health books and studies, one will find that the environment plays a rather neglected role. Public health and the environment present a pair of concepts, which only recently caught the attention of agencies such as the World Health Organization (1992). The environment—the biological and chemical context of human life including such diverse aspects as climate, agriculture, human settlements or water and air—provides the frame of reference of life on Mother Earth. We seem to take it for granted, but it represents a very long process of what Western political philosophy calls development, which has led to some serious degradation of our ecosystem.

Despite all lip-service paid to environmental protection, the condition of Mother Earth is worsening. In a few days, the international conference on climate change will begin in Kyoto (Japan). Governments will discuss measures to control global warming. We will listen to political leaders emphatically stating how much they are concerned with the environment—and we will also see how reluctantly they will take active steps to reduce environmental pollution nationally and internationally. Australia will be on the forefront of those who claim that ecological concerns are second to economic ones. The pattern of Western economical thought will prevail against all other statistics and reports presented by environmental scientists and organizations.

Here is the starting point for Lori Colomeda's unique studies. She is not satisfied with sitting at her desk and looking into governmental statistics and published epidemiological and environmental research, analyzing their methodological consistencies and drawing conclusions. She seems to mistrust these figures, knowing that they report only on what is perceivable on the surface and which is calculable by sophisticated statistical software packages. Theodor W. Adorno (1974) comes to mind here, especially when he stated, "When all actions are mathematically calculated, they also take on a stupid quality."

Colomeda's understanding of science involves humans rather than numbers, conversations rather than correlations, encounters rather than experiments. She enlightens through her practice of getting involved in her subject, becoming part of the settings she studies and reporting back how it felt having been part of other humans' lives and their particular living conditions. Her capacity for observation is excellently developed and her insight into others as well as into herself is sometimes stunning, to say the least.

Reading the manuscript of *Keepers of the Central Fire* presented a constant challenge to me, as the presentation of the content does not follow well-established paths of "scientific writing." Colomeda finds her own way of presenting her case, weaving all kinds of material together to a sometimes horrific, sometimes beautiful picture of current environmental issues and concerns among Indigenous people and non-Indigenous people. This manuscript has not left me untouched. It presents a rollercoaster ride through hundreds of years of manmade environmental degradation; that is, degradation caused by Western men's greed for resources and wealth.

Lori Colomeda is a champion of public health. *Keepers of the Central Fire* is a book about a person getting involved in public health as much as it is a book about public health itself, that is, the Westernized model of public health and its limited role within governmental policies. The rich texture of Colomeda's report is the result of her unique capability to blend scientific information with Indigenous knowledge and wisdom.

Eberhard Wenzel, PhD
Griffith University
Australian School of Environmental Studies
Nathan, Australia

REFERENCES

Adorno, T. W. (1974). *Minima moralia. Reflections from damaged life.* London: NLB. (Original work published in German 1951)

Ritzer, G. (1996). *The McDonaldization of society. An investigation into the changing character of contemporary social life* (rev. ed). Thousand Oaks, CA.: Pone Forge Press.

Wilkinson, R. G. (1996). *Unhealthy societies. The afflictions of inequality.* London/New York: Routledge.

World Health Organization. (1992). *Our planet, our health.* Geneva: WHO.

Acknowledgments

This book was born out of my love for the natural world and a sense of responsibility to American Indian students in courses of *Environmental Health and Justice* and *Social and Environmental Ethics* at Salish Kootenai College, Montana. No current text includes issues of health as it relates to ecology and environmental change for American Indians; no text encompasses the feelings of environmental health and injustice issues that American Indian students wrestle with on a daily basis. I hope this book will support that need.

This book is meant not to romanticize nor perpetuate the 1800s stereotyped images of First Nations exploited in the media, but to demonstrate that modern tribal sovereignty is strong in the face of harassment from megabusiness and federal government policies, and that Native People can assert themselves in solving issues of land conflict that compromise health.

Many individuals helped drive this work: My thanks to all of the students at Salish Kootenai College. These words are meant to honor them, their ideas, their devotion to learning, to one another, and to the Earth. They are the hope for the Next Seven Generations. It is an honor to be part of their lives. My deepest appreciation and thanks to all of the people who told me stories about tribal issues affecting their environment and health, who welcomed me into their lives and their homes. Without them there would be no book. Thank you to Anne Dunn, White Earth Reservation, Minnesota, for the use of her beautiful creation story *Before the Beginning*. My appreciation to Navajo Nation member Jeff Brown, Window Rock,

Acknowledgments

Arizona, for permission to use his paper developed for the course, *Social and Environmental Ethics* at Salish Kootenai College; JoEllen Koerner, MSN, Sioux Valley Hospital, Sioux Falls, South Dakota, and Jacque Dolberry, MSN, Director of the Nursing Program at Salish Kootenai College, for providing me with the opportunity to visit with Maori elders passing through the Lakota Nation; thanks also is due to my Maori sisters in Aukland, New Zealand: Tania Pompallier, MSN, Olive Pompallier, RN, Bella and Phillip Hutchinson, and Ngaire Kaika Stevens who work with Te Awhi Limited, an Indigenous health care company, and who helped gather information from Maori people on the lands of Aukland; to Bella Wikaira, a social worker with Aukland Hospital in Aukland, New Zealand, for conversations regarding the health of adolescents in New Zealand; to Roy BigCrane, one of the producers at the Salish Kootenai College Teleproductions Center, for his insight into issues resulting from the construction of the Kerr Dam; thanks to the Bush Foundation of Salish Kootenai College, Dr. Tim Olson, Chair, for faculty support to travel to Finland; thanks also to Dr. Marlene Ryan Warner of the Union Institute for her friendship, boundless energy, and masses of taped packages of resource information; to Dr. Eberhard Wenzel, faculty of environmental science at Griffith University, Queensland, Australia, for in-depth professorial discussions, his friendship via the Web, and his global insight into health promotion, public health, and public health policy; to Padma Guidi, doctoral candidate at the Union Institute Graduate School for her connections with and interviews of Upper Skagit Tribal members in Washington State; to Wendy Griswald, Haskell Indian Nations University, for her assistance in securing permission from Haskell Environmental Research Studies Center (HERS) to present Rose Main's issues at Fort Belknap; to John Honskey, BSN, MA, Ed, Salish Kootenai College, for turning me toward Gregory Cajete's work; to Cindy Rossmith, MSN for theoretical discussions.

My deep appreciation to the former Director of NLN Press, Allan Graubard, Brother Beaver, for his belief in the message of this work and his editorial leadership in guiding the process. Like Spirit Beaver bringing fire to his people, hiding it in wood so people could find it, so too, hidden in the pages of this book are Allan Graubard's many editorial talents . . . pooyai! Finally, love and gratitude to my husband, Frank Tyro, for his tireless efforts in editing endless drafts, his encouragement, his photographs, and love of the natural world.

About the Author

Lori Colomeda is the Curriculum Coordinator for the Distance Education Department at Salish Kootenai College in Pablo, Montana, where she teaches courses in Environmental Health, Social and Environmental Ethics, and Personal, Community and Tribal-cultural Health. A descendent of French Canadians and Micmac Indians, Dr. Colomeda grew up in Boston, Massachusetts, where she graduated from Nursing School. She holds a B.S. and a Master equivalency degree in therapeutic recreation from Temple University, Philadelphia, and a M.S. in environmental science education from Beaver College, Glenside, Pennsylvania. Before coming to Montana, she taught for twelve years at the Schuylkill Center for Environmental Education, a satellite campus of the Beaver College graduate program in Environmental Science Education. She also taught classes for Pennsylvania State University and Temple University. Her Ph.D. in Medical Ecology: Northern Studies is from the Union Institute Graduate School, Cincinnati, Ohio.

An internationally known researcher and conference presenter, Dr. Colomeda recently presented at The World Breast Cancer Conference, Kingston, Ontario, The Barents Nord-Plus Conference: Environment and Health, Bodo, Norway, and The Nursing Conference in Polar Twilight: People, Environmental Conditions and Health in the Arctic Region, Rovaniemi, Finland.

About the Author

One of her greatest passions is living in the mountains of western Montana with her husband, Frank Tyro, two Siberians, a Dalmation, a Daschund, and a cat named Kit. She is interested in many seemingly diverse issues: the Arctic, the North, Indigenous people, women, the environment, health, and the cultural survival of the world's Indigenous people.

CONTENTS

Contents

PREFACE

Dr. Lori Colomeda has produced a unique contribution toward a more complete understanding of the nature of health and ecology among Indigenous peoples. *Keepers of the Fire* raises the consciousness of healthcare professionals with regard to tradition, environment, and sense of place among Indigenous peoples. Her focus on the themes of identity, health, and relationship to the environment as part of a greater interrelated worldview is strategic to understanding the nature of contemporary Indigenous health issues.

As a health educator at the Salish Kooteni Community College, Lori's work presents the kind of community health education that is truly transformative. The work of the community health educator many times goes unnoticed yet, it is the most essential kind of education. Lori Colomeda's work should not only be noticed but actively applied in the education of health professionals. Indeed, Lori has provided the beginnings of a foundation for the revitalization of Indigenous health education and its traditional emphasis on living a consciously healthy, whole, and meaningful life.

Keepers of the Fire presents an underlying "ecology" of Indigenous health in terms of the ways it was historically expressed, its current state of disruption, and possibilities for a more ideal and revitalized future. She calls for us to collectively reclaim our human and Indigenous heritage of caring for our "home fires," a metaphor that promotes re-engendering our "biophilic" or innate sensibility for affiliating with other living things and with life-giving relationships. Lori combines an exploration of applied "biophilic" sensibility as expressed in the traditional Indigenous sense for and understanding of natural connections with a view of "health in its broadest perspective through the medical ecology model." In this way, she honors the paradigm of Indigenous health succinctly stated in the phrase "healthy environment, healthy culture, healthy people." (p. 7, Ch. 1). It is this paradigm which she views as paramount and around which she weaves the presentation of the various and complex issues of environmental health and ecological theory as it applies to the practice of healthcare and environmental justice for Indigenous people.

Dr. Colomeda advocates for an environmental perspective that has inherently been a part of the practice of nursing since the time of Florence Nightingale but has been relatively latent as a realm of serious discussion and research since then. In addition, Lori advocates for the medical ecology model in the training of healthcare professionals. She talks about the contributions of Suzy Walking Bear Yellowtail—one of the first American Indian RNs. She talks about the various theories that parallel the Indigenous view of interactive relationship and interdependence.

She demonstrates how contemporary nursing theorists (such as Martha Rogers) and ecologically based theorists of environmental health (such as Rose Marie Parse) parallel traditional American Indian views of relationship and "natural democracy" or the inherent right of all living things to exist.

Lori emphasizes the importance of including a comprehensive view of environmental health in the education of nurses. For her the question is not whether nursing education should include Environmental Health, but how it should be included. At the same time, she explores the relationship of several First Nations People with their land, relating the history of how this human–land relationship is important to health. She also describes the effects of European contact and values and the inherent struggle with First Nations philosophies, health, balance, and the environment.

In various chapters, she paints a portrait of the state of health among not only American Indians but other Indigenous populations that have a similar history of oppression and who are also facing similar struggles with environmental health issues. Lori is candid in her assertion that the European mind set has never been able to integrate a true understanding of the Indian view of land and relationship. Her observation that the essential contrast between First Nations and European views of relationship to the land is that of anthropocentrism vs. nonanthropocentrism touches the very core of the conflict between world views.

She also sheds light on the difference between Indigenous Healing and Western Medicine. This tenuous relationship has historically been fraught with misunderstanding. It is only within the last 30 years, with rise of interest in alternative healing, that the wisdom of Indigenous healing has begun to be given credibility. Yet, recognition continues to be slow in coming from mainstream western medicine.

Her analysis of the inadequacy of the Year 2000 Objectives for Healthy Indian People, issued under the auspice of the PHS Indian Health Service, which espouses admirable goals but neglects consideration of a holistic view of Indian health and the interrelationship of environmental health problems, is both astute and telling of the usual shortsightedness of federal health programs. Environmental health issues resulting from pollution, culture clash, loss of identity, poverty, and biosocial epidemiology such as diabetes, alcoholism, spousal abuse, and suicide are all related symptoms of ethnostress caused by culture loss and loss of land base. As such, federal initiatives which fail to consider the context of Indian health are doomed to be little more than stop-gap measures which have little promise of addressing the deeper issues of maintenance and revitalization. Regarding such deeper issues, Lori advocates for the development of interdisciplinary research teams comprised of Indigenous community educators, medical ecology, and health professionals as a means to begin to realistically assess the health problems of Indigenous communities. In addition, she advocates for a serious look at how the medicine wheel model, medical ecology model, feminist methodologies, and applied qualitative research can found a comprehensive program for addressing and restoring the health of Indian communities.

"Expanding consciousness for health care professionals" provides an essential impetus for writing *Keepers of the Central Fire*. For this book is first and foremost a health education text "of an alternative kind," a treatise that presents a vision and advocates for a change in the mind set of healthcare relative to Indigenous peoples. Lori Colomeda provides an invaluable text and overview of essential information, theory, philosophical discussion, case studies, methodology, interview forms, and appendices all of which provide an invaluable resource for students, community health workers, researchers, and health practitioners as they attempt to address the challenges of Indigenous healthcare in the 21st century.

In the final analysis, *Keepers of the Central Fire* is a book of vision. It is a book of what can be if health educators and practitioners open themselves to creative possibilities inherent in the Indigenous metaphor, "healthy environment, healthy culture, healthy people." And in doing this, they also expand the possibilities of a more comprehensive and meaningful paradigm of healthcare for all people. May the Good Spirits Guide and Keep You as you read *Keepers of the Central Fire,* for you too are called to be a keeper of that fire. Be With Life!

Before the Beginning

Long ago when the Earth was new Anishinabe* was told by the Creator that he must walk the Earth and name all of the plants, animals, mountains, and lands that have been created . . . he went everywhere. There was not a place that he did not touch. Anishinabe identified the plants, what was good to eat, what was good for medicine and for purposes. He saw that the Earth produced much food. He named all of the waters. He found that some rivers ran underground . . . the arteries and veins of Mother Earth. Water cleanses and restores life. He also named all of the animals and found that each had their own wisdom. He noticed that animals were in pairs and asked the Creator to send him a helper, because he felt alone. Creator sent him Wolf. In this journey Wolf and Anishinabe became brothers. ". . . what happens to one will happen to the other. Each of you will be feared, respected, and misunderstood by the people."

What the Creator said has come to pass. Both mate for life; both have had their land taken; both have been hunted toward destruction. But the wolf is returning and gaining strength where he was once destroyed. Anishinabe will also return and gain strength to teach and lead the way to respect Mother Earth and live by the perfect law of nature. (Dunne, 1993)

---

*Used with permission from Anne Dunne and Midwest Traditions, Inc., P.O. Box 320, Mt. Horeb, WI 53572. Anishnabe: The Ojibwe People of the Great Lakes Region also known as Chippewa and Ojibway.

Introduction

THE CENTRAL FIRE

In most cultures, it is women who tend fires and keep them burning for warmth, cooking, and ceremonies. In my grandmother's time, men and women who participated in World War I felt that keeping the home fires burning was an important endeavor for the people left behind. Home fires connotate our home, our *Ekos,** our sense of warmth, health, culture, protection, and life. In this work, the Central Fire burns in the hearts and minds of all Indigenous people, reflecting their love of, and connection to, the land. The Central Fire is meant to illuminate the wisdom from the ancient path of our ancestors, a path on which all people must travel to answer the ecological crises that plague our planet.

American Indian culture is rich with myths and legends about how the Earth first received the gift of fire. The majority of such myths relate the integral role of the animals in Distant Time who brought the fire to Earth. In the North, among the Athabascan people, Raven, the trickster and Creator, is credited with bringing the "Sun" to the people. The Apache nation credits Fox for playing a trick on the fireflies to bring fire to the

---

Ekos: From the Greek, meaning home or ecosystem; ecology, the study of homes.

Introduction

Earth. Some Plains tribes feel it is Coyote, trickster, prankster, and Creator, who brought fire to the Earth. People of the Columbia River Valley feel it was Beaver who hid fire in sticks so the people could find it. But in numerous cultures, Grandmother Spider is honored and remembered for bringing fire to the Earth. Each Grandmother Spider legend is a variation on a similar theme, but this is the one I remember:

> In the beginning, there was no fire and the world was cold. It was the time before humans came to Earth and when animals all spoke the same language. The animals held a council and planned to bring back a piece of the Sun to Earth. Every animal that could fly or swim attempted the challenge. They all failed. At last, the spider was called, but all of the animals asked how she, being so fragile, would manage to bring back the fire. She spun a thread from her body and wove it into a bowl which she fastened on her back. Eagle carried her to the Sun where she was able to capture a piece of it in her bowl. Eagle flew back to Earth with Grandmother Spider clinging to its back. And that is how fire came to people.

Chapter 1

HEALTH AND CULTURE AMONG INDIGENOUS PEOPLE

O Our mother, the earth, O our father, the sky,
Your children are we, and with tired backs
we bring you gifts that you love.

(from Tewa Pueblo Prayer, Roberts & Amidon, 1991)

*I*n the past as today, First Nations cultures revere the Earth as the Great Mother, a living entity who creates and nurtures life and health (Eisler, 1990). In ancient times, the Earth was one with all of the creatures. The beating of drums was the heartbeat of the Earth in all its mystery, enchantment, and wonder. Everything from the planting of corn to weaving cloth was done in a sacred manner (Eisler, 1990). Culture was linked to the Earth and to spirituality and both were honored in sacred ceremonies. Here, the concept of health is seen in the broadest view, including the health of the land, the people, and cultural continuation:

Traditional Indian beliefs about health . . . revolve around attempting to live in harmony with Nature while developing the ability to survive under exceedingly difficult circumstances. (Cajete, 1994, p. 109)

Oral tradition in the forms of songs, prayers, ceremonies, and story telling transmits language and cultural values in much the same way these have been passed on for centuries. (Walters, 1993, p. 13)

Physical environments also affect the core values of a particular group. As interpreted by each group, nature's laws were also the center of the group's core teachings. Ceremonies involving women, particularly naming ceremonies, puberty rites, marriage ceremonies, funeral ceremonies, and memorial ceremonies, were all part of the women's education in the tribe.

Within the last fifty years, all people have been affected by technological changes such as nuclear power, increased resource extractions, development of dams, housing, shopping malls, video games, life support systems, and computer-based education. In Indian Country technologically literate, modern Native People live on reservations and in cities. Then, as now, conflict over land rights, environmental health, cultural survival, and tribal sovereignty are a significant focus of the relationship between tribes, the federal government, and other organizations. Conflicts arise in the clashing of technological cultures with lifeways and values of those sovereign nations known to the Western World as reservations. Such classic struggles include abuses of land, water, and air, as well as altercations that globally compromise the health of Native People, their land rights, and the guiding principles of Earth as Mother.

In a discussion by the Iroquois concerning the new Americans, the Revolutionary War, and the land known today as North America, Vine Deloria (1973) documents the concept of Earth as Mother as far back as 1776 [the birth of what we modern people call the United States], ". . . for this Big Turtle [Island][1] being our common Mother, we and they are like flesh and blood."

To the Lakota Sioux Nation, White Buffalo Calf Woman gave the Sacred Pipe[2] and the seven rites and ceremonies. Part of her message to the

---

[1] Turtle Island: The Iroquois believed that the Earth (North America) was created on the back of a turtle.

[2] The bowl of the pipe is made of red stone; it is the Earth. Carved in the stone and facing the center is the buffalo calf; it represents all the four leggeds who live upon the Mother. The stem of

people involved the concept of Earth as Mother, "With this Sacred Pipe you will walk upon the Earth; for the Earth is your Grandmother and Mother, and she is sacred. Every step you take upon Her should be a prayer . . . ." (J. Brown, 1989). Lakota people believe White Buffalo Calf Woman came to them in the distant past when human beings and animals were able to talk freely. Roger Black Elk remembers this event as happening a very long time ago, maybe 800 years before his time (Allen, 1991).

T. Weaver (1997) compares the environmental situation of Indigenous people today to the Canary in the coal mine, giving warning to a poisoned world. "Exploitation of the world's resources has caused alarm among ecologists, conservationists, environmentalists, and scientists who study the planet." (Fixico, 1997, p. 42)

This work is about caring for the land, the culture, and the environment as it affects the health of Indigenous, First Nations, American Indians, and Alaskan peoples. It holds an important message for healthcare providers, ecologists, and those who attempt to live their lives in harmony with the planet we call Mother. To guide us in solving our contemporary ecological conflicts, as in the past, we seek out the wisdom of women, Elders, the Old people, the Fragile Ones. They are the repositories of ancient ways and sacred knowledge going back thousands of years. The teachings of the Elders are what centers tribal people and grounds us in the universe rather than in the erratic behavior of other human beings. But throughout this book, we also listen to the voices of the future, young people whose health is affected by the state of their environment and who must act to preserve their environment for the Next Seven Generations.

> We are the mothers of nations . . . . We were born to be guardians of the sacred Earth. That is why the Creator put us here. Guardians of the sacred Earth don't just stand by the rivers and beat the drum and say their prayers. . . . We fight for our people. We are women warriors. (Mililani Trask, speech at the Indigenous Women's Network Conference, 1994)

---

the pipe is made of wood; it represents all things that grow on the Earth. The twelve feathers are from the spotted eagle and they represent all the winged ones. All the people who join in the smoke send their prayers to the Great Spirit (J. Brown, 1989).

As we examine the principles that guide this book, it must be re-membered that although each tribe is culturally, linguistically, and spiri-tually different, most subscribe to the traditional belief that health reflects living in harmony with the Earth and that the Earth itself is a liv-ing organism. Many Indigenous people also believe that a person should treat his or her body with respect, just as the Earth should be treated with respect. The Earth is the giver of all life, food, shelter, and medi-cine. Land belongs to life and life belongs to the land. In order to main-tain health, one must maintain the relationship with the Earth (Spector, 1991). Throughout the course of this work, as we explore environmental health problems affecting Indigenous people, various tribal beliefs con-cerning health will be highlighted. Within the environmental health par-adigm, I will also address current healthcare problems as Healthy Indian People 2000 Objectives.

Yet there are those today who debate the relationship myth of Earth-Mother and Earth Keeper that Native People have with the land; who be-lieve Native People were as exploitive of the natural world and as war-like as Europeans who came seeking gold, silver, slaves, and land. That such views are based more on conjecture than fact, with only few intertribal oral histories including war stories as they exist in First Nations traditions before contact with the Europeans (Sale, 1991), says also something about the need to reinterpret history. To those who hold such views:

> While mistakes were made [in caring for the environment] the fact that the Europeans found the Western Hemisphere to be a natural treasure house indicates that misuses of the environment were not frequent or sustained over long periods of time. (Grinde & Johansen, 1995)

But there will always be those skeptics who argue against the cele-brated, congruent, caring relationship for Mother Earth that we have come to believe as truth; there are those who argue that the concept of Earth as Mother is a recent creation of Indian people going back only to 1805 (J. Weaver, 1996). George Weurthner of Earth First!, for example, argues that the American Indians were the first pillagers and caused the extinc-tion of the woolly mammoth and the desertification of the Sonora Desert (J. Weaver, 1996). Dave Foreman, also a political leader in Earth First!, pronounced Native People as "a threat to the habitat" and advised others to resist the water rights of Indian people (J. Weaver, 1996). W. H. Hutchinson (1972), frontier historian, agrees:

> [The Indian] revered nature because he had no other choice. He perceived nature as being controlled by supernatural forces . . . we ought to dry our eyes and recognize that the Indian was above all a self-centered pragmatist when it came to land use. They were badly exploitive.

In *Keepers of the Game*, Calvin Martin notes that because ". . . hunting tribes were not conservation-minded in the hey day of the fur trade . . . Indian people were ecoterrorists for attempting to exterminate animals in the service of the fur trade (in J. Weaver, 1996). Fortunately, Martin further qualifies his view here, especially in regard to the influence of European contacts: the Indian of post-contact was not the same Indian as pre-contact. The European hunger for furs and the Indian need for technology all contributed to the decimation of game animals. But let the Indian people speak:

> Indian people acknowledge that all living things and non-living things in Nature have important inherent meanings within the context of human life. . . . American Indians symbolically recognize their relationship to plants, animals, stones, trees, mountains, rivers, lakes, streams, and a host of other entities. (Cajete, 1994, p. 74)

> In our religion, we look at this planet as a woman. She is the most important female to us because she keeps us alive. We are nursing off her. (Mary Gopher, Ojibeway, 1993)

> Indigenous women, they're supposed to look at themselves as the Earth. (Carrie Dann, Western Shoshone, 1993)

> What we are fighting is the development. What we are fighting is the greed, corruption, and murder. . . . We are all people of the Earth, the Mother Earth. . . . " (Pat Bellanger, Ojibeway, 1993)

> We are made from Mother Earth and we go back to Mother Earth. We can't own Mother Earth. We're just visiting her. We're the Creator's guests. (Leon Shenandoah, 1993)

Additional references can be found in the teachings of *Women of the Native Struggle* (Walters, 1993).

The Environmental Connection
for Health Professionals

Environmental hazards are everywhere. In 1984, the National Research Council noted that more than 65,000 new chemical compounds have been introduced into the environment since 1950. Worthington and Cary (1993) urge nurses and other health care workers to increase their awareness of environmental risks and issues. The process includes learning about ecological systems, developing skills to recognize and treat environmentally-induced diseases, becoming advocates for a clean healthy environment, and promoting healthy lifestyle behaviors. (Bellack, Musham, Hainer, Graber, & Holmes, 1996)

Several issues of concern arise immediately: How should healthcare professionals define "environment"? In what context should "environment and ecology" be a focus of nursing and domain of nursing knowledge? What are current theories linking ecology and environment to nursing and other health science and healthcare professionals?

Currently, discussions among theorists in nursing and environmental/ecological science clarify one similar aim—to link the two ideologies. Over the years, healthcare providers have come to recognize the connection between a compromised environment and compromised health. However, while Native cultures embrace the environment and Mother Earth when referring to health, in Western culture, health professionals generally view environmental health as synonymous with or rooted in public health. In recent years, however, this confusion has given way to environmental health itself, which has developed into its own discipline. For their part, environmental health professionals and medical ecologists view the discipline specifically as a bridge between biomedical and environmental ethics by virtue of their focus on human health *and* on the health of the larger ecology of which humans are only a part (Chessworth, 1996). In this model, there is no universal methodology for the treatment of disease. Culture- or social-specific knowledge of the nature of man and the universe, and thus of health and illness, will influence greatly any treatment option in any specific culture. Western medical models, on the other hand, via their public/community and environmental health agendas, embrace a variety of micro issues from waste management, toxic chemicals, radioactive waste, to lead poisoning, biological pathogens emanating from rodents, insects, or microbes that cause diseases and result in air, water, and soil quality contamination, and so on.

In the more global model of Indigenous healing and medical ecology, however, environmental health concerns are recognized as alterations in the socioeconomic, ecological, and cultural environment occur with resulting health effects for humans as demonstrated by a host of indices: substance abuse, teen suicide, spousal abuse, work-related injuries, automobile accidents, violence in the home and workplace, and so on. Although not directly related to air, water, and soil quality, many Indigenous people feel these social, economic, and cultural health problems emanate directly from a compromised environment that disrupts traditional cultures, ecological practices, and family member roles.

In this work, I view health in its broadest perspective through the medical ecology model and in the paradigm of Indigenous people: healthy environment, healthy culture, healthy people. In this broad concept of environmental health, the cultural health of the people is paramount. In this work, then, I will attempt to honor such vision by clarifying the connections between complex issues in environmental health, ecological theory, and justice as they affect Indigenous people. It is my hope that the expanded view of environmental health, as discussed here, could provoke and contribute to the current dialogue for curriculum and educational change within the healthcare professions.

In the historical study of the West's relationships to the natural environment, certain themes have a constant formative influence: the influence of the environment on the development of civilizations; the human attitude toward the natural environment; and the impact of civilizations on the natural environment (Hughes, 1975). Hippocrates, the Greek father of Western medicine, was one of the first to notice the effects of climate on human health. He is believed to be the author of a book titled *Airs, Waters and Places,* which highlights the importance of environment in cause, diagnosis, and treatment of disease (Hughes).

Women's contributions to environmental health hold the greatest impact. As a nurse and medical ecologist, I begin this discussion with nursing as the senior profession that includes the environment as a basic element of health knowledge.

As many health professionals know, Florence Nightingale, founder of American nursing education in the late 1800s, proposed that a clean environment was central to patients' survival and recovery from disease. Modern nursing scholars refer to her ideas as the Environmental Adaptation theory, the core of Nightingale's model of nursing. In Nightingale's perception, the environment could be altered to improve the patient's well-being. Especially crucial to her theory was the need to monitor clean air and provide for waste management. Ecological theory is congruent with Nightingale's Environmental Adaptation theory. Species Adaptation theory argues that when species' environment is altered—by pollution, climate change, or whatever—and limiting factors change,[3] that species must move, adapt, or die. Medical ecologists view health as the adaptation of a species to its environment (McElroy & Townsend, 1996). Kleffel's (1994) discussion of priorities is significant in this regard: "Modern nursing scholars still regard the environment as a major construct in nursing science, but they have not addressed it with the same depth and conviction as did Nightingale. Nor have nurse researchers addressed the broad environmental concerns" (p. 4). Most nursing theorists also view the environment in its immediate sense, as that which affects client care, and have not encompassed the global environment of the natural world. Kleffel continues: "Although nurses care for persons whose conditions are connected with environmental degradation, they have not addressed the larger physical, social, cultural, political, elements relating to the health and welfare of people" (p. 5). Nonetheless, since the theories of Florence Nightingale, the work of other women pioneers and theorists have contributed to the body of knowledge which documents the relationship between health and the environment.

Ecologist Rachel Carson's writing of *Silent Spring* (1962) gave birth to the modern environmental movement and the founding of the Environmental Protection Agency (EPA). In investigating the population decline in birds of prey, Carson discovered that the pesticide DDT[4] was the cause. Long touted as a "safe for humans," Carson's research discovered that

---

[3] Limiting factors: Abiotic factors such as optimal temperature, rainfall, sunlight, and nesting spaces as they affect species survival.

[4] DDT: One of the organochlorine pesticides used in South America and in other fruit-producing countries. DDT returns to the United States as residue in fruits and vegetables.

DDT created reproductive problems in birds of prey. When female raptors attempted to incubate their eggs, the eggs cracked and the embryo died.

Further investigations by Colburn, Dumanoski, and Myers (1997) have lead other researchers to acknowledge that DDT is an estrogen mimic and does not readily break down in the environment. Exposure to estrogen over time has been proven to cause some breast cancers. Additionally, as an estrogen mimic, DDT and other organochlorine pesticides, the xenoestrogens, unlock the estrogen receptor,[5] and create a situation in which breeding pairs of birds of prey are exposed to a plethora of environmental xenoestrogens that play significant roles in developmental changes in embryos (Colburn et al.). DDT was finally banned in the United States in the 1970s, but is still manufactured in the United States for use elsewhere. DDT returns to the United States on fruits and vegetables, such as canteloupe, strawberries, and green peppers grown in tropical countries for U.S. import. The world has become permeated with hormone disrupting chemicals such as PCBs,[6] DDT, and dioxin. To date, 51 synthetic chemicals including the PCB group have been identified as endochrine disrupters in one way or another (Colburn et al.).

An American Indian pioneer, Suzy Walking Bear Yellowtail, member of the Crow Reservation in Montana, was one of the first American Indian RNs. Ms. Yellowtail graduated from Boston City Hospital School of Nursing, Boston, Massachusetts, in 1923 and returned to Montana to become an advocate for a clean, healthy environment. As Weatherly (1995) describes her:

> She was a very direct, outspoken person and didn't sweeten the hard realities of reservation life. And that got her attention from the Surgeon General and ultimately from President Nixon.

---

[5] Estrogen receptor: Each hormone and its chemical receptor fit together like a lock and key. Once they are joined, they move into the cell's nucleus to "turn on" the biological activity associated with the hormone. The estrogen receptor is found in many parts of the body, including uterus, breasts, brain, and liver. Originally thought that each hormone would bind only with its specific receptor, new theories are emerging that document the fact that chemicals like DDT and other estrogen mimics can bond with the estrogen receptors.

[6] PCBs: A family of 209 chemicals, polychlorinated biphenyls were created by researchers who added chlorine atoms to biphenyl. PCBs are banned from production in the United States, but used by industries for lubricants, oils, and transformers and used as preservatives in lumber, paints, and plastics. PCBs are found today in the bodies of every mammal on earth, including polar bears in Svalbard and in the breast milk of Inuit women.

In the early 1950s, Suzy Yellowtail and her husband, Tom, promoted native cultures on a goodwill tour sponsored by the State Department to Europe and the Middle East (Cohen, 1995):

> She liked to wear a six-inch-wide leather belt that was almost a symbol for her life—strong, enduring, and imposing. She was a woman to take seriously, and people did.

As an activist, Suzy Yellowtail acted in a traditional role for Crow women, looking out for the well-being of women and children. She accomplished her work in a nontraditional white male world. In addition to being appointed to the Montana Advisory Committee on Vocational Education in 1959, Suzy Yellowtail was appointed to President Nixon's Council on Indian Health Education and Welfare in 1960, which helped to implement change on the Crow Reservation and on other reservations throughout the West. In 1987, she was inducted into the Montana Hall of Fame. She left behind a legacy of reform for the Crow Reservation and the image of a role model for women who follow her. She is known as the first environmental health activist on the Crow Reservation (Cohen, 1995). Although there may be other pioneers whose names are more widely known than Suzy Yellowtail's, their work is no more inspiring for American Indian women.

CONTEMPORARY NURSING THEORISTS AND ECOLOGICAL THEORIES OF ENVIRONMENTAL HEALTH

In the following section, I will briefly discuss similarities between selected nursing theories as they relate to ecological theory. Koithan (1996) and others at the University of Nevada, Las Vegas have expanded this discussion by beginning to examine the theoretical construct linking the philosophical tenets of the two interrelated disciplines, environmental science and nursing. As I do not presume to possess expertise in nursing theories per se, the reader is invited to dispute and contrast the minutiae of differences regarding these theories, which are presented for further discussion by nursing theory scholars.

Initially of significance here is Martha Rogers legacy but with this addition via Koithan: merging the *Unitary Human Being Theory,* in which

Rogers suggests that the human and environmental fields are integral, with the conservation theories[7] of Muir and others. Koithan's work seeks to define and describe implications for futuristic global health and ecological policy.

According to McQuisition and Webb (1997), Rogers supports the notion that nurses must promote health and well being for all persons and groups wherever they are. As her theory identifies two interactive energy fields, the human and the environmental, she suggests further that these energy fields are in continuous process as open systems *continually exchanging energy with one another* (Dailey, Maupin, Satterly, Schnell, & Wallace, 1989). Ecologists, of course, can only agree with Rogers' assessment and point to the most obvious related example in ecological theory: energy flow. Energy photons from sunlight are captured by chloroplasts in green plants and converted by photosynthesis into ATP, carbohydrate food energy for humans and animals. Energy is returned to the earth when humans and animals die. Through the process of decay via detrital trophic level,[8] the energy of organisms returns to the earth. Ecologists, however, do take issue with Rogers' statement that human beings *do not adapt* to their environment but are *integral* to their environment (Rogers, 1988). The difference, while surprising at first, is also decisive. In ecological theory, species are seen to adapt to their environments or die. When environmental changes occur over time, all species, including humans, exhibit survival adaptations by moving, adapting, or, if unsuccessful, then dying.

Building on Roger's theory, Rosemarie Parse's theory of *man-living-health* suggests that "man and the environment are inseparable. Man and the environment . . . interchange energy to create what is in the world, and *man chooses the meaning given to the situation he creates*" (Lee & Schumaker, 1989). In this regard, Parse's theory coincides with theories of deep ecology coined by Arne Naess in 1973. Questioning the fundamental views and attitudes of nature held by Western civilization, Naess' deep ecology promotes two norms: self-realization and biocentric equality. The more salient of the two for Parse's theory is biocentric equality, which holds that all natural things and ecosystems have an intrinsic right to exist.

---

[7] Conservation theory: Humans must work to conserve natural resources for the future of human beings.

[8] Detrital trophic level: In food webs, the detrital food web comprises bacteria, fungi, and other elements contributing to decomposition.

As Regan (1991) has put it: "The presence of inherent *value in a natural object is independent of any awareness, interest, or appreciation of it by a conscious being.*" Self-realization holds that humans are connected to the universe and to one another in myriad ways; for example, through societies, species, and life forms. In an examination of the ecological theory of interrelationships, ecologists again can relate to Parse's theory. Every living thing, which includes humans, interacts with all nonliving and living things within the environment. In this sense, Parse's theory is congruent with the American Indian worldviews indicating that humans are part of the environment and not separate from it.

Although widely criticized, Madeline Leininger's transcultural nursing theory is uniquely derived from anthropology. By comparison of world cultures with respect to their caring behavior; nursing care; health-illness values, beliefs, and patterns of behavior, Leininger has developed a methodology for the founders of a scientific and humanistic body of knowledge to provide culture-specific care practices (Alexander, 1989). In examining environmental health among Indigenous people, Leininger's provisions for culture-specific care do seem to support medical ecology theory and medical anthropology research into collisions of cultures as affecting environmental health. Within Leininger's Transcultural Nursing Theory, examinations of the cultural and ecological environments to assess communities, clients, and aggregates become a necessity.

Implications for Nursing Curriculum

> With influences of the environment on health so widespread, an understanding of environmental health is important in all areas of nursing practice including assessment, diagnosis, planning, intervention, and evaluation. The more we understand how we connect with our environments, the better able to preserve or change them. (Pope, Snyder, & Mood, 1995, p. 4)

The American Association of Colleges of Nursing (AAOCN) recommends that content related to environmental and occupational health be incorporated into every program that prepares professional nurses (Bellack et al., 1996). Recently the National Institutes of Health (NIH) issued a request for proposals for predoctoral and postdoctoral fellowships for nurses to gain additional training in the environmental sciences. For those involved in developing environmental health curricula for nursing students, the Institute of Medicine (IOM) provides guidance on the definition of environmental health curricula by defining essential content, competencies, and learning objectives in environmental health. The IOM curriculum development committee perceives that, although environmental health encompasses occupational health, the two areas are not treated as parallel in their discussion of curriculum content and objectives. Essential content includes four areas: (1) Nursing and the Environment, (2) Legislation and Regulation, (3) Exposure Assessment, and (4) Health Consequences. Specific recommendations for curriculum content can be found in Appendix D.

The importance of including environmental health in curricula for nurses cannot be over emphasized. However, in her review of community health texts, Neufer identified no text as having all of the factors necessary to address the concepts of environmental health in nursing (Neufer, 1994). She also found that community health nurses have not applied their skills in assessing and diagnosing community environmental health problems:

> The earth is facing ecological disaster, yet the environmental domain of nursing is currently understood as the immediate surroundings or circumstances of the individual or family. Such a definition keeps nurses from addressing the larger societal, political, economic, and global issues that affect health. . . . Nursing, essentially a woman's profession, and the environment with its female Mother Earth image share a long history of domination and oppression . . . an ecofeminist perspective offers a conceptual foundation for developing a new consciousness of the environment with the potential of liberation. (Kleffel, 1991, p. 5)

CONCLUSION

The evidence is mounting all around us that we have a crisis in survival of the planet. Persons in all academic disciplines and professional groups have a responsibility to use their expertise to do all they can to give future generations a viable planet home (Cinebell, 1996). The brokenness and toxicity of the planet affects our clients, patients, and students as well as ourselves and our children.

The required paradigm shift in nursing and health science regarding the environment is now in its embryonic stages. Nursing and health science educators are beginning to come to grips with the fact that we need to care for and understand the planet as we do our clients—in a wholistic manner. In addition, the question is *not* whether healthcare should include caring for the environment, but *how*. Nurses and other health professionals can be a force in shaping global health and well-being (Pope, Snyder, & Mood, 1995).

Chapter 2

RELATIONSHIP WITH THE LAND: ENVIRONMENTAL HEALTH IN FIRST NATIONS COMMUNITIES

My grandfather led us to the land. He taught us to fish for catfish, to thread the worms on the hook and not be a sissy, to thank the worm for giving its life to catch the fish. He taught us to be wary of the barbels on the catfish, to rub the cuts on the fish's belly if we got stuck. He taught my brother and me to find the blueberries. He honored us with the sound of his voice, with his touch. My grandmother, a Micmac Indian from New Brunswick, married a French Canadian, a white man, and lost her status in Canada as an Indian. She taught us the healing properties of plants and other earth medicines. We grew up in Boston far from the cultural influences of the land in Canada, but in my grandparents' home we always had plants, a garden. We lived close to the Charles River and every summer we camped at Lake Attitash. (Journal, 1996)

*I*n this chapter, I will explore First Nations' relationship with the land in several contexts: the history of how the land is integral with Native People's health and the experience of European contact and values as a struggle with First Nations' philosophies regarding health, balance, and the environment. It is important to remember that each First Nations' culture is unique, with specific differences in language, culture, and law. Each tribe also owns its own creation myths, stories, and ceremonies. In addition, I will examine how collisions in culture affect the environment and health of the nondominant culture, including Healthy Indian People 2000 Objectives as set by the U.S. Department of Health and Human Services. Targeted for environmental health content here are Objectives for Healthy Indian People 2000, as developed with the Indian Health Service but not necessarily with Indian people. I will introduce the Medicine Wheel-Medical Ecology model (Figure 2.1) as a viable

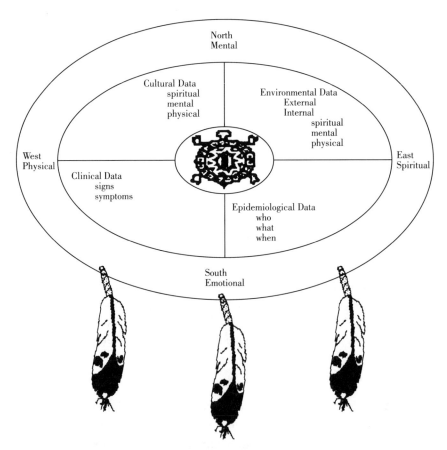

Figure 2.1 Medicine Wheel-Medical Ecology Model

means for comprehending environmental health in First Nations' cultures. Although not all First Nations' societies embrace this model, concepts of spirituality, mental balance, physical balance, and cultural competency are ever present in First Nations' cultures.

THE SACRED SOIL OF OUR GRANDMOTHERS: A BRIEF OVERVIEW OF EUROPEAN CONTACT

We walked a long way that day. Along the river. When it was evening we stopped in the shadow of the mountains. The clouds glowed pink from the radiant sunset. We set our feet in the water. It was black, smooth, and running fast. Here and there in little pools dragonflies hunted the first mosquitoes of the evening. Frogs "Harumphed." The grasses were brown, parched from the hot summer sun. Along the trail, goldenrods were beginning to bloom signaling late summer and heralding Autumn. Across the river, yellow wild iris, blooming late in the season, and forget-me-nots gave color to the brown grass. Old grandmother cyprus, ponderosa, and lodge post pines lined the trail with dark shadows of greens. I thought of the medicine in the plants, ancient healing secrets now lost to time because of cultural collisions. (Journal, 1996)

The collision of cultures in North America between First Nations' tribes and the invading Europeans caused societal dislocation and dietary changes of varying but increasing degrees. Begun in the 1400s, the after-effects of such changes remain problematic, even now affecting the health, culture, and economies of First Nations' communities. Almost a century ago, in 1906, the grandchild of Chitto Harjo, a Creek fullblood, asked him to describe what he knew about the coming of the Europeans to his land:

Away back in that time, in 1492, there was a man by the name of Columbus [who] came from across the great ocean, and he discovered this country for the white man. . . . What did he find when he first arrived here? (Debo, 1983, p. 19)

The *Conquest of Paradise* (Sale, 1991) is an exceptionally meaningful book by which to explore answers to the boy's question. With considerable documentation and clarity, Sale exposes the early effects of contact by Europeans on Indigenous people. Sale's work is especially helpful in understanding the ecological destruction wrought by Christopher Columbus and his expeditions on Hispaniola and other parts of the Caribbean.

When Columbus first returned to Spain with his exploration story, the rush started. Using the West Indies as a base, Spanish explorers set out in all directions. Columbus himself founded the first true colony on the island of Hispaniola (Espanola) in 1494 during his second expedition (Debo, 1983). Creating a lifestyle on Hispaniola as it had been in Spain required that Columbus import livestock, chickpeas, wheat, grapes, and olives. He did so with dispatch without considering the fragility of the local ecosystem or that these life forms from Spain might not thrive. Attempts to change the environment to suit the Castilian diet were never completely successful and, as a result, Columbus was forced to rely on imports from Spain (Sale, 1991):

> It hardly mattered whether the new species were malign or malignant, the more they adapted themselves to their new environment, the more they displaced native species, the more they altered and eventually transformed the stable ecosystem of the islands. (p. 163)

Cattle and horses were let loose to roam all over an island where the largest mammal was the size of a dog. Eventually, the herd numbered more than 8,000 and a ranchero mentality system was installed with cowboys on horseback complete with Spanish lassos to round them up. The Europeans developed a red-meat dependent culture in a tropical rain forest that ensured environmental destruction of the islands (Sale, 1991).

In his reports on the tropical rain forest to Queen Isabella, Columbus was at a loss for words. His description of the magnificent tropical forests with colorful, abundant species of birds, unusual flowering plants, multi-shades of greens, and delightful mammals devolved to little more than vague passing references, ". . . green, very green, big lakes, big trees not like ours" (Sale, 1991). His inability to describe the natural beauty of the Islands, however, did not prevent him from determining the usefulness and potential value of selling it in Spain. In his journal of 1492, October 19th, he writes:

Such handsome verdure and so different from ours, and I believe in it there are many plants and many trees which are most valued in Spain for their dyes and for medicinal spices. (Sale, 1991)

Plants such as daisies, dandelions, and nettles, brought by the Spanish grew in such prolific numbers in the lush rain forests that they soon crowded out Indigenous plants and invaded any open space. In just two decades, the agricultural practices of the Spanish led to deforestation of the islands. Rivers silted up and the general climate of the area was altered:

In just two decades, the islands were laid waste, inhabited only by wild animals and birds and useless for the service of God . . . It was the first to be made into a desert, but not the last. (1518 correspondence by Alonso de Zuaso to a friend in the Spanish Court in *The Conquest of Paradise;* Sale, 1991, p. 165)

The English at their Jamestown Colony in Virginia heralded the second invasion of Europeans in the Americas. Much like the Spanish, the English sought to impose their culture, exploit the land, and subjugate the people they found there. John Smith is quoted as saying Jamestown is "a verie fit place for erecting a citie." Nonetheless, for the first twenty years, hundreds of people died of starvation-related illnesses because the English did not know how to feed themselves in their new environment. In true Columbian (Christopher) tradition, the Jamestown colonists refused to adopt the ways of the Native People, refused to learn "foreign" farming techniques despite how successful they were, and became idle, lazy "gentlemen" (Sale, 1991). The commonality and continuity of such behavior rose, at least in part, from the simple fact that the Spanish and the English considered American natives as less than human. Contemporary 17th-century thought commonly involved ideas such as, "I cannot call them men; in order to Christianize them, they must be made into men." The historian Gary Nash also rightly notes that to call the natives "beasts" or "brutes" prepared a future for Native People as beings to be domesticated, controlled, or confined to parks and reservations (Sale).

Circumpolar people such as the Inuit, Inupiat, Sami, Lapps, Yakut, Aleuts, and Chukchi have a profound respect for the fruits of the Earth and the oceans. The sea is a sacred entity and life giving (Shephard & Rode, 1996). Such a worldview is in direct contrast to White doctrine that generally promotes subjugation of the environment rather than cooperation with it. Historians feel that European contact with circumpolar people in North America began when Viking explorers sailed north from Greenland and encountered Dorset settlements. More than 1,000 years later, British Whalers plying the waters off the coast of Baffin Island, Pond Inlet, and Cumberland Sound received gifts of Viking armor from Inuit people in return for needles, awls, and knives. By 1832, after several years of commerce with the Inuit, whole villages died of smallpox or diphtheria and the population of Bowhead whales was gutted. Today, 200 Bowhead (Greenland Right) whales are all that remain of that prodigious eastern Arctic population. Missionaries, French fishermen, and explorers soon followed the whalers. All brought with them cultural philosophies and diseases from Europe that impacted the health and culture of Northern Indigenous people. A Yup'ik hunter on St. Lawrence Island once described White people as, "The people who change nature" (Lopez, 1986, p. 39). The Upper Skaget Tribe in Washington call the Europeans, "The changers" (conversation with Vi Hilbert, 1997).

Europeans never really understood the culture they were trying to subjugate nor did they wish to until almost too late. What eluded and continues to elude Europeans was a sensibility, common to Native People, of intimate abiding interconnectedness with nature. Labeling it, also pejoratively, a religion of animism (from the Latin *anima*—soul) which sees life in all natural things, Europeans also failed to comprehend the complexities of the relationship between Native People and the diverse presences that comprised their world: mountains, lakes, rivers, trees, birds, animals, and so on. For Native People, the presences inhabiting nature comprise the very center of existence, a great unifying Life Force or spirit. Kinship with all creatures is very real. As Luther Standing Bear, a Lakota Sioux, put it in 1993, "The Earth is our nurturing Mother and we are equal, not superior, to the Web of Life that connects us all. We are totally dependent on the natural world for our survival."

Many so-called "educated people," whether university faculty or not, still don't understand that relationship even today. One questions the philosophies prevalent in the minds of professors who teach in our southern universities and who perpetuate the stereotypes of American Indians. Before coming to teach in Montana, a fellow faculty member was harassed by another member of her department, "HOW! So you are going out to teach the *Injuns,* do you have-um your-um bags-um packed-um?" (Journal, October 1996)

Healthy Indian societies made their Earth-relationship further apparent in how they lived on the land. Different environments fostered different approaches, but what is striking is the recurrent evidence that, as hunters or fishers or planters or pickers, Native People were ritualistically conscious and concerned about the effects of their actions on their surroundings and careful to see certain limits and constraints were observed (Sale, 1991). Identification with a specific territory was rooted in the spirits of the ancestors who were buried within the soils. The land was and *is* the culture.

We can examine the two basic contemporary approaches to nature and the environment by comparing the differences in environmental ethics between the European and First Nations' worldviews—the anthropocentric and the nonanthropocentric. Anthropocentric ethicists would argue that nature has value for human beings. It must be respected as a means to human ends (Chessworth, 1996). It is a vision that allows for technology and technological developments to solve immediate problems. It is a vision that exalts one species, Homo sapiens, as masters over the Earth.

In contrast, the nonanthropocentric ethic embraces many current variations from animal liberation, ecofeminism, and deep ecology. Here, human beings eschew their self-conceits and embrace a moral obligation of relationship; human beings are only part of a larger reality and need on occasion to sacrifice individual interest to those of the whole (Chessworth, 1996).

During the Dark Ages in Europe, the Christian Church was an entity powerful enough to suppress popular inquiry into the workings of the natural world. It was enough to know that "God" had created all. Forests were dark, evil places. Mountains fared no better. And what lived in all such forbidden places was a creature, part human, part beast, the Wild Hairy Man with exposed genitals who would carry off young maidens into the wilderness (Sale, 1991). Wilderness itself was a place to be feared.

European ecological heritage is born from such fear, dominance over nature, and hostility toward things unknown. Today, evidence of such ecological disaster in Europe is found in the form of deforestation, erosion, siltation, pollution, and extermination of species; all done in the name of providing for the betterment of society; all accomplished in ignorance of the natural systems and the human connection to them (Sale). Is it any wonder then that the Europeans called the Native People savages and beasts inhabiting a wilderness to be tamed?

> Europeans came to the Americas with their beliefs that not only were the women and children to be owned, but that the church and the education system were best for the "savages." They removed the Indigenous children from their native communities and placed them in residential schools. These children were then "parented" by nuns, priests, and often single female teachers who were inexperienced in child rearing. (Hill, 1996, p. 36)

During the American Revolution, both the British and the Americans labored to win over the Indians as active participants in the war. When England signed the second Treaty of Paris in 1783,[1] their philosophies regarding the land and Native People as things to be tamed were carried forward by the new Americans "for the good of society." To the diplomats in Paris, the Indians went along with the land. When the new United States began to establish peaceful relations with the Indian people, it did so with a hidden agenda—to acquire Indian lands (Debo, 1983).

> With European contact came a new set of beliefs and worldview. These beliefs conflicted with the Indigenous beliefs. . . . Natives struggled to retain both a cultural identity and a system of beliefs unique to themselves. The once open, honest teachings were forced underground along with their medicines, songs, and ceremonies. (Hill, 1996)

---

[1] Treaty of Paris: The Treaty of Paris ended the Revolutionary War and gave the newly independent United States jurisdiction over American lands formerly held by Britain. One of the most pressing tasks the new government faced was development of a policy toward Indians who inhabited that territory (Debo, 1983).

As the anthropocentric/Christian view dominated the westward expansion of European Americans, environmental destruction for the ecosystems of North America and the First Nations who depended on these ecosystems for survival soon followed:

> Missionaries and government agents applied pressure to the American Indians to change their culture soon after they were restricted to reservations. Among other changes, it was now impossible for the Plateau [Plains] people to depend on fishing and hunting, which had previously supported them well. Sufficient land was no longer accessible for these activities. (Ackerman, 1995)

By the mid-1800s, in the Plains cultures, the bison were decimated, the prairie grasses were over run with monocultures, Christian boarding schools were erected, languages and cultural ceremonies were lost, and much of what was known about a healthy Indian lifestyle fell victim to the "progress" of individual interests.

> Parents lost hope when their children left for the boarding schools. They turned to alcohol to lessen the pain of loneliness and sense of failure. Children returned for holidays and summer breaks and found their parents either intoxicated or gone. (Hill, 1996)

The experiences in the boarding schools continue to impact Native traditions and cultures. Grandparents have low self-esteem, with high suicide rates, substance abuse rates, spousal abuse rates, and child abuse rates:

> Because of the abuses suffered in boarding school, sexual as well as mental and physical, and the lack of nurturing from the natural mother, both men and women lost respect for the women and the role of women in the community. All of these . . . effects are the result of oppression, church domination, and the patrilineal government. (Hill, 1996)

Many Native People believe that such social/environmental health problems were not seen in First Nations' communities until European contact destroyed the healthy ecosystems and tribal cultures that people depended on (Hill, 1996).

The Effects of the Fur Trade

In 1605, the French established a trading post at Port Royal, Acadia. When winter came, the "savages" of the country assembled from far and near to barter . . . some bringing beaver and other skins . . . also moose skins . . . others bringing fresh meat. (Debo, 1983, p. 38)

With the establishment of trading posts, commerce between Europeans and Native People was systematized. Native People brought their furs to trade for European goods and supplies. In time, native families moved permanently to trading posts taking advantage of the available abundance of food, alcohol, and entertainment. Because families moved away from their tribes and communities, culture was soon lost or forgotten. In addition, as a result of over hunting the fur-bearing animals, dramatic changes in the environment prompted changes in Native People's life-styles with concomitant negative impacts on health.

Activities encircling the fur trade in North America provide a clear example of how Native People succumbed to the "delights" of civilization. The solitary fur trader entered the territory of a First Nations' community bringing trinkets, beads, kettles, and iron knives to trade for fur. The Native People recognized that through technology, in the form of iron knives, cooking kettles, and the like, their lives would be made easier— so they traded. Unfortunately, with the European appetite for furs never satisfied, fur-bearing animals were largely eliminated, changing a territory's ecology and forcing trappers farther and farther away from their home ground.

Today, Indian people are relearning and reclaiming the Old Ways from the oral histories of the elders. The return to cultural pursuits, spiritual healing, celebrations of sobriety, and Indigenous ceremonies have impacted in a positive, healing way. Nonetheless, collisions with the dominant culture in North America continue to affect Native Peoples in conflicts over land and sovereignty:

The ever-expanding consumer economy pays little heed to the amount of pollution that it may create, the disruption of traditional Indigenous economy that it may create, the need for ultimate renewal of the natural resources that are being exploited, or the cumulative costs that the raping of an environment may impose on future generations. (Shephard & Rode, 1996, p. 254)

Indigenous Healing and European Medicine

The knowledge that Indigenous people have about their environment is a testimonial to the ingenuity, creativity, resourcefulness, and ability of a people to learn and to teach a harmonious way of existence with nature. From methods of navigation, to the application of medicinal properties of plants and animals, to techniques of agriculture . . . is knowledge based over thousands of years and hundreds of generations. (Cajete, 1994, p. 102)

Indigenous people of the Americas long knew the healing properties of plant roots, leaves, and flowers which they formulated into tonics, teas, salves, and poultices. Plants were viewed as hairs of Mother Earth with their own spirit, their own communal life; they were providers of food, fibers, colors, and beauty. Plants were the basis of life. They held particular power and medicine and, as such, were bridges to the spiritual world. The herbalists, shamans, and other healers became keepers of cultural understanding and developed extraordinary skills in memory and observation called wisdom (Cajete, 1994, p. 102).

In North America, Indian people used witch hazel leaves as an astringent to soothe tired muscles. The fragrant balsam poplar, made into a salve, healed flesh wounds. Trillium eased the pain of childbirth and was given to the settlers for their women. Arnica flowers were prepared into a tincture used to treat the pain and swelling of sprains and bruises (Weatherford, 1988).

In the Andes of South America, Indian people learned the art of trephining performed by surgeons drilling a hole into the skull to release pressure built up after a blow to the head. Fractures were treated with casts made from hair, feathers, and rubber. Bathing, the sweat lodge, or the steam bath were integral components of healing rituals by Indigenous Americans, but frowned upon by Europeans as activities that contributed to disease. The whole realm of healing, the application of plants, and the understanding of the role played by the healer revolves around establishing and maintaining relationship to one's own natural healing process as well as spiritual, communal, and environmental healing processes. "Healing traditions provide a benchmark expression of the intimate relationship that Indigenous People established with their environments" (Cajete, 1994, p. 112).

As Indigenous medicine in the Americas flourished, European medicine evolved from good and evil spirits and the Humoral[2] theory of medicine. Blood-letting, cupping, and leaches were all part of the Humoral theory. In their fear of evil spirits, and fear of their own teachings, Europeans attempted to tame the "children of the devil" by conquering and civilizing them. Today, such methods carry the contemporary euphemisms of assimilation, genocide, integration, acculturation, and racism (Hill, 1996). But Europeans failed to recognize and understand established healing practices of the Indigenous people. In its place, Indian people of America were given the Indian Health Service as custodian for their healthcare needs:

> Today, American Indian people are faced with a number of health-related problems. Many of the old ways of diagnosing and treating illnesses have not survived the migration and the changing ways of life of the people . . . skills have been lost . . . modern healthcare facilities are not always available . . . social and economic factors are suspected contributors. (Spector, 1991, p. 243)

YEAR 2000 OBJECTIVES FOR HEALTHY INDIAN PEOPLE

Since 1955, the U.S. Public Health Service, through its Indian Health Service (IHS) component, has had the responsibility of providing comprehensive health services to American Indians and Alaska Native People in order to elevate their health status to the highest possible level. The mission of the IHS is to provide a comprehensive health services delivery system for America Indians and Alaska Natives with the opportunity for maximum tribal involvement in developing and managing programs to meet their needs. (Trujillo, p. i, 1995, Assistant Surgeon General)

---

[2] Humoral theory of medicine: There are four humors, which must be kept in balance for good health: blood, phlegm, black bile, and yellow bile.

Healthy People 2000 Objectives[3] contains 700 pages of health data collected, compiled, and developed by the U.S. Department of Health and Human Services. It demonstrates areas of health success and health deficits. Although targeting American Indians and Alaska Natives as a special minority in its assessment of health among American people, Healthy People 2000 Objectives notably does not examine environmental health problems for any group of Americans including those chiefly related to reservations. These include health effects resulting from ecological pollution and collisions of culture, and emissions of toxic waste dumps, mining, and air pollution. In addressing health problems arising from collisions of cultures, loss of identity, and economics, Young's study (1994) presents further in-depth, detailed statistics through the process of biocultural epidemiology. "Diabetes, alcohol abuse, suicide, and spousal abuse are the direct result of culture loss and that includes loss of tribal lands" (conversation with Ron Therriault, 1996, member of the Salish Tribe, Montana). Young indicates that acts of violence are intimately related to the mental health of individuals and the social health of the community.

Healthy People 2000 Objectives record leading causes of death for American Indians as heart disease and cancer, although injuries involving motor vehicle accidents and alcohol account for one-fifth the total number of deaths. Alcohol is also a known factor in suicide and homicide rates. Alcohol abuse, diabetes, and obesity are other risk factor problems for American Indians (U.S. DHHS), but are not addressed as environmental health issues.

> Suicide and homicide are extreme (and lethal) outcomes of violent behavior, whether inflicted on oneself or directed at others. The excessive mortality and morbidity associated with these conditions among Native Americans, in comparison to non-Native populations in North America, are almost universal across tribes and regions. (Young, 1994, p. 189)

---

[3] Healthy People 2000 is the product of national effort involving 22 expert working groups, a consortium that has grown to include almost 300 national organizations and all the state health departments and the Institute of Medicine at the National Academy of Sciences (U.S. Department of Health and Human Services, 1992).

Just as there are cultural differences among tribes, researchers emphasize the diversity and cultural specificity of suicide rates (Shore, 1975). For example, in Alaska during the oil boom of the 1960s and 1970s, the suicide rate increased dramatically among the Inupiat of the North Slope and among the Athabascan Indians of the interior, both of whom were affected culturally and socially. In Canada, Garro (1988) found that the more isolated and more northerly the tribe, the lower the suicide rate. However, this was the reverse for Alberta and Manitoba tribes where the suicide rates for northern reserves were 2.3 times higher in Alberta (Bagley, Wood, & Khumar, 1990) and 2.6 times higher in Manitoba (Garro, 1988) than for the southern reserves. Suicide rate was also correlated with distance from an urban center as well as per capita income (Bagley et al., 1990).

Billson (1995) indicated that substance abuse, spousal abuse, and child abuse were not present in Inuit Arctic communities until Inuit were brought by the government into settlements. In settlements, a male-female role reversal ensued. Women worked outside the home for the cash economy and men no longer hunted, but tended the home and the children.

Infectious diseases were problematic for American Indians throughout the period of contact. Today, immunizations have reduced the epidemiological significance of measles, rubella, mumps, poliomyelitis, tetanus, and diphtheria in Native communities (Young, 1994). For infectious diseases generally, Native People are at higher risk than non-natives, reflecting both the distribution and frequency of specific infections and related local ecological, socioeconomic, and cultural factors (Young, 1994). In this context, it is interesting to note the effect of more recent technological interventions. As Young (1994) reports, "The building of the Alaska Highway during World War II by the U.S. Military resulted in a series of epidemics among Natives in the Yukon." On other reserves, examples of infectious disease epidemics include the poliomyelities epidemic in Chesterfield Inlet, Northwest Territories, contacted from White workers stationed in Churchill, Manitoba, resulting in a 2 percent mortality of the total population (Adamson, Moody, & Peart, 1949). In 1952, a measles epidemic swept through the Ungava peninsula of Northern Quebec, infecting 99 percent of the population, resulting in a 2 to 9 percent mortality of the total population. This epidemic was traced to Goose Bay Labrador, where a large Air Force base has been in operation for years (Peart & Nagler, 1954).

An Interdisciplinary Team: Medical Ecology and Health Professionals

Medical ecology emphasizes the study of health and disease in an environmental context and answers the question, "How do these people survive in this environment?" (McElroy & Townsend, 1996). As a functioning member of the healthcare team—alongside nurses, clinicians, and epidemiologists—medical ecologists examine health within the parameters of culture, clinical data, epidemiological data, and environmental data. Although medical ecologists do not provide direct care for individual clients in groups or in aggregates, their holistic research aids in the development of theories that can be applied by healthcare providers. In contrast to physicians who examine one health problem at a time, medical ecologists mesh three established disciplines—anthropology, ecology, and medicine—within one focus. In medical ecology, health and the environment are linked in an equilibrium model, which holds that a population with the resources to respond to the challenges and constraints of the environment has a high potential for health (McElroy & Townsend, 1996). Understanding the health of Native North Americans also requires recognition of issues linked with Native spirituality. Thus, I incorporate within the medical ecology model the concept of the medicine wheel (p. 16), which is especially useful in examining health problems in First Nations' communities.

The Medicine Wheel-Medical Ecology Model

North American Indians used the turtle shell as their first calendar (Figure 2.2). They noticed a relationship between the thirteen scales on the rounded hump of the Eastern Box turtle and the thirteen moons (months) that passed before the same season returned. They used the moon as a guide and called her Grandmother. Grandmother moon appeared and disappeared. Through her, women knew when they would be fertile or when their menstrual cycle or moon time would begin. The turtle shell bore thirteen moons of the year inside a frame called the sacred hoop, or medicine wheel (Sams, 1994). The sacred hoop, or unifying circle, represents the circle of life and the path that the Earth takes around Grandfather Sun.

The medicine wheel (p. 16) is used to guide the people on their pathways. It is recognized as an ancient, powerful symbol of the universe.

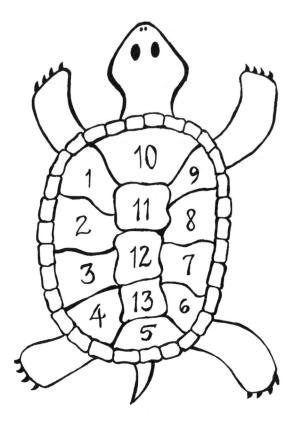

Figure 2.2 Turtle Shell Calendar
by Emily Colomeda Fyant

Linked to many Indigenous cultures, the medicine wheel comprises an interconnected system of teachings. It relates the inseparability of the physical, emotional, mental, and spiritual needs of an individual's life. It speaks of the need for balance, harmony, and respect as bringers of happiness (Coyhis, 1996).

Using the model of the medicine wheel or sacred hoop, I have superimposed the medical ecology model (Figure 2.1) first demonstrated in researching health among the Yanomamo people in the Andes of South America and by Ann McElroy in her work with Inuit people of Canada's Arctic (McElroy & Townsend, 1996). In this model, healing and health are represented by the turtle. Similarly, in applying the medicine wheel-medical ecology model to issues of environmental health and justice among First Nations' people, informational balance is sought in four aspects: culture, environment, clinical, and epidemiological as well as in the four directions of North/Mental, South/Emotional, West/Physical, and East/Spiritual. The aspect of culture also shares components of the four directions of the medicine wheel mentioned above: spiritual, mental, emotional, and physical. Environmental components arise from the internal and external environment. Care of Mother Earth and the natural world, a significant component of the spirituality of Indigenous cultures, is also expressed by certain ritual actions, including fasting and seeking solace in the mountains or the forests, burning of sacred herbs, revering special animals, and so on. The land is everything; it is the reason for life. For a Native Person, it is abhorrent to contaminate the Earth or to do injustice to the animals, the four leggeds, the winged ones, and those that crawl. First Nations' people, connected to the land mentally, spiritually and physically, are well aware of the danger that contamination causes. Many have spoken about the destruction to the land and the illness that it causes them, not only physical illness, but also mental and spiritual anguish. Some elders have spoken out against the youths of their own tribes, "They go up into the woods reserved for tribal members, where they leave cans, litter, and other debris. It is disheartening and we have to do a better job of educating them." These elders feel powerless against their own youth who seem to have succumbed to Western culture and traditions.

Application of the Medicine Wheel-Medical Ecology Model

Within the framework of the medicine wheel-medical ecology model, and under the paradigm of feminist theory and qualitative research, this work seeks to answer the following questions: How do Indigenous people define health? What are the relationships of Indigenous people to environment and health? How has spirituality and culture been compromised in cultural transformation by the dominant culture? How have Native People as nations and as individuals dealt with issues of environmental justice? What is their vision for the future?

Since this work is grounded in feminist methodologies and qualitative research, a review of these methodologies follows.

Review of Feminist Methodologies

As we discussed in Chapter 1, ecofeminism embraces a nonanthropocentric model of ethics in which humans are part of nature. It is a theory that has evolved from various fields of feminine inquiry and activism such as the peace movement, women's healthcare, the antinuclear movement, and the environmental movement, among others. Calling for an end to all aggressions and rejecting oppression within the natural world and among human beings, ecofeminism focuses on life's interconnectedness (Gaard, 1993). Many ecofeminists also believe that the modern technological assault against the earth derives from a history of European patriarchal attitudes, a Europe that was man-centered rather than human-centered (Zimmerman, 1990).

Because many women, especially Native women, are poor, single parents surviving in trailers or substandard housing that borders landfills or toxic chemical dumps, environmentalism is more germane to their lives; they are primary victims of industrial pollution. Their children demonstrate the effects of mental retardation from lead poisoning and birth defects and leukemia from toxic chemicals. They are the caretakers of their families and take care of the Earth. In the last few years of this century, more women have gathered to council and to conference to heal the Earth and to change old attitudes.

"We are called to a politics and set of actions that come from compassion, from the ability to feel with all living things on the Earth and to take action and find direction" (Starhawk, 1990). Ecofeminist ethics portends to dovetail with the ethical theories of many First Nations and, in that respect, it is not unique to apply ecofeminist theory when addressing environmental health and injustice among First Nations' people.

Feminist methods include *reflexivity* on and in the research process itself, as documented in journals that express the researchers' responses which then become part of the process of inquiry. Another aspect of feminist inquiry concerns the emotional interactions between researcher and interviewer, and a recognition of their importance. Expressed emotions become a vital component of the journal writings and are incorporated into the whole. Finally, feminist research is directed toward an actual response to the given condition; in other words, a plan of action (Fonow & Cook, 1991).

The Paradigm of Qualitative Research

Qualitative research is often called the art of listening, hearing, and sharing social experiences (Rubin & Rubin, 1995). Intense listening, respect for person and culture, and a systematic effort to really hear and understand what people say are foundational. In the worldview of Indigenous people, qualitative research theories and methods support the values, respect for person and culture, oral histories, relationships to one another and to the land, and tribal traditions and ceremonies. With interviewees describing experiences in their own words, I listened intently, respectful of the words, the relationship of the teller, and formulated meaning for myself, for healthcare professionals, and for other readers of this work. Through qualitative interviewing, I set out to learn about the world of Indigenous people while recognizing that real meaning may be elusive. Even when we speak the same language, words may have different cultural meanings (Rubin & Rubin, 1995).

Successful qualitative interviews require an understanding of the culture, which affects what is said and how the interview is heard. Emotions and cultural understanding impact the interview both ways. As a result, to improve communication, the participant must teach the interviewer about the meanings of the words they use (Rubin & Rubin, 1995).

In this book, I used topical and cultural interview strategies. Within the American Indian community, cultural data is communicated through stories, which convey values and themes. Topical interviews deal with defined subject matter (Rubin & Rubin, 1995). Emphasis here was placed on cultural values, and themes of environmental health and justice.

In this work, we hear the concerned voices of First Nations' men and women living on reserves across Canada and reservations in the United States; words and concerns from people who sacrificed much in the name of "progress." They have forfeited their land, their culture, and their health. It is a process that continues today as cultures collide in the interest of resource development, economic and social development, and tribal "initiatives" on reservations by waste management companies and the like.

Many readers find it difficult to imagine that airborne pathogenic disease results from the building of a dam or the laying of a highway in a remote area, but these new arteries create conduits on which pathogens affecting humans travel freely. When mining companies develop environmental impact statements, generally they do not address the cultural component and the value of the land to traditional peoples. The resulting collision of cultures can prompt negative changes for affected tribes. In addition to issues of air, water, and soil quality, environmental health among First Nations' indigenous people also embraces issues of teen suicide, work injuries, drunk driving, highway safety, spousal abuse, substance abuse, housing, radiation risks, and violence—all issues I will address further.

CONCLUSION

In this chapter I discussed aspects of colliding cultures between First Nations and invading Europeans. I addressed the divergent paths and the meaning of nature for Europeans and First Nations. I highlighted changes in environment and lifestyles resulting from activities such as the fur trade and linked deficiencies in the area of environmental health with Healthy Indian People 2000 Objectives. Finally, I introduced the medicine wheel-medical ecology model as a significant aspect of feminist and qualitative research methods.

Chapter 3

RELATIONSHIP WITH THE LAND: MONTANA

What are the rights of the natural world? Where is the seat for the Buffalo or the Eagle? Who is representing them . . . ? Who is speaking for the Trees or the Forests? Who is speaking for the Fish, for the Beavers, the Whales, our children? We are the indigenous people of this land . . . we are the landkeepers . . . our brothers are all the natural world. It is a time to be strong . . . to think of the future . . . to think of the destruction of your grandchildren. (Oren Lyons, 1984)

I begin this chapter on Montana with its unique bond between Indigenous peoples, their spirituality, and the land. Montana is home to more than 60,000 Indian people living on seven different reservations. Environmental health and justice issues are affecting these tribes as a result of disruptions in air, water, and soil quality. I conclude the chapter with a definition of environmental injustice by American Indians themselves.

MONTANA: HER PAST

The land is rich with the lives of our kin. Grandmother and grandfather ashes blend with the soils to share new life with plants and animals.

Women's curves contour the surrounding hills like a brown-skinned girl lying on her side. In contrast, hills like brown buffalo, rippled and muscular, run alongside her. Long prairie grasses playing in the wind give a sense of shadow and movement. Effortlessly, red-tailed hawks and harriers soar over the fertile fields in search of meadow mice or voles.

Winter snows blow down from Canada, staining the brown-skinned girl and buffalo hills milky brown. Coyote and family announce their hunting presence with a chorus of yips and barks that blend with the soft moans of cattle.

Time to a mountain is but a whisper. During the Ice Ages, enormous glaciers filled the Rocky Mountain trench of British Columbia and slowly moved southward through the Flathead Valley (Alt & Hyndman, 1986). Evolutionary theories and fossil evidence suggest that this broad, fertile valley at the foot of the Mission Mountains developed 70,000 to 130,000 years ago when the glaciers melted forming Lake Missoula. Glacial pond kettles near the Ninpipes Reservoir are also evidence of large masses of ice that were buried in the moraine, then melted.

In an alternate worldview, however, Indigenous people of North America share a disparate vision of origins than that theorized by archaeology and anthropology. After Coyote formed the Earth, the ancestors of First Nations' people migrated *west*, not *east*, across the land bridge of Beringia and populated the rest of the Earth in Europe and Asia (conversation with Floyd Nikolai, member Salish Tribe, 1997).

In spring, on their way to the Arctic, migrating waterfowl find abundant food and water in the Ninpipes Reservoir. In spring, snow-capped mountains dominate the ponds where blue winged teal, Canada geese, ruddy ducks, canvas backs, western greebs, and cormorant can be found nesting in the kettles. If one listens closely, the melodies of red-winged blackbirds and meadowlarks fill the air. Plants such as fringed gentian, lupine, dog-tooth violets, and common buttercups add color to the rich green grasses.

Perhaps 8,000 years ago, from across jagged mountains to the east, the first people trekked to this valley in Montana, before it was known as the Flathead Nation. With the glaciers melted, they moved freely and easily. Nomadic people, hunters and gatherers, they observed the curving hills and the running buffalo. In the oral histories of elders, their descendants came to gather bitterroot and Camas, the first sacred plants of spring given to a starving people by the Creator. They came to hunt the buffalo, to honor it, and give thanks to the Creator for its flesh. The buffalo clothed and fed them: women created sewing needles and awls and men crafted weapons from the bones. Nothing was wasted. These are the First Nations' people of Montana whose women are keepers of the earth's fire. Their cultural values include the Earth as our Mother.

MONTANA, 1996: THE BUTTERCUP MONTH

Spring creeps up the mountains from this valley and carries with her newly born fawns, awakening bears, glacier lilies, buttercups, and migrating birds. The hills turn green. Another circle of life begins. Days loiter late into evenings. The setting sun whirls orange and purple over the hills and buffalo. Farmers plow their fields, long plumes of dust swelling behind their tractors. Swallows, hungry and greedy, chase a feast of mosquitoes and flies. They dip and swoop behind the tractor.

High in the Mission Mountain wilderness, tribal foresters plant seedlings of ponderosa pine, tamarack, and lodge pole, replacing grandmother trees that were harvested for timber. Stubborn snowfields blanket the tops of the mountains where newly awakened grizzly bears wander about lethargically in search of grubs, bulbs, and delicacies.

In the Ninpipes Reservoir and along the southern shore of Flathead Lake, tribal aquatic biologists examine the waters determining water quality and stream health. It is the cleanest in the world. Nesting osprey migrating here from southern climes replace the niche of wintering eagles:

> One of the natural laws is that you've got to keep things pure. Especially the water. Keeping the water pure is one of the first laws of life. If you destroy the water, you destroy life. (The Wisdom Keepers, 1994, p. 66)

In American Indian culture, everything is understood as living, as being alive. Each living thing has a specific role as a teacher and family member. Everything on Earth, whether stone, tree, creature, cloud, moon, sun, or human being, is one of our relatives (Jaime Sams, 1994, p. vii).

The relationship between health and the environment is not a new concept. Native People long ago recognized that humans are part of the environment, not masters over it. Although there are over 5,000 Indigenous cultures worldwide, most subscribe to Mother Earth as the central being in the universe, the living Mother who nourishes us and gives us life:

> I fasted when I went up into the mountains for four days . . . no water and no food. I brought with me only my Pendleton blanket to keep me warm. I hadn't been up to those mountains in four years and I really missed going up. The trails were grown over, they looked so different from the last time I went up and I lost my way a couple of times. I was charged up knowing I would come home feeling peaceful. (conversation with a Native American spiritual leader)

Flathead Reservation: Description and History

The Flathead Reservation is the only reservation in Montana located west of the great Continental Divide. Flathead Reservation land is not land that was *given* to tribes by the United States; it is sovereign territory that was *retained* by the Flathead Nation (the Confederated Salish and Kootenai Tribes) when they ceded over 22 million acres to the United States in the 1855 Hell Gate Treaty.[1] The Flathead Nation retained possession and control of the land as a way to preserve, within a very small portion of their original territories, the right to follow, establish, and protect their own ways of life—not just in a political sense, but in the broadest cultural sense (language, spirituality, social organization, land use, mode of subsistence, etc.). In 1982, the courts ruled that Indian tribes still possess those aspects of sovereignty not withdrawn by treaty or statute (*Merrion v. Jicarilla Apache Tribe*, 455 U.S., at 149, n. 14).

---

[1] In the Hell Gate Treaty of 1855, the federal government ordered three tribes, the Salish, Kootenai, and Pend Oreilles, to settle on what is now known as the Flathead Reservation and become the Confederated Salish-Kootenai Tribe. In return, the tribe ceded 22 million acres of traditional land to the government. The Treaty was broken with the Daws Allotment Act which opened the reservation to White Homesteading in 1910.

Roy Big Crane: The Kerr Dam, Land Rights, Conflict and Loss of Cultural Health

Roy Big Crane, member of the Flathead Nation, is my friend. Although I have only known him for eight years, I know his spirituality, his goodness, his respect for life, the rituals, and the old ways. His prayers and ceremonies guide his life. When he stands, he towers above my 5'3" frame. Roy's brother Art teasingly calls me, "Micmac Paddi Wack."[2] Although kind and gentle, Roy can be a coyote, a trickster and prankster. He folds his brown arms across his chest, brown eyes sparkle and his smile lights up the room. His hair carries the faint scent of juniper berries and willow and is braided in the style of his great grandfather.

I come to ask a serious favor of him: to speak of the Kerr Dam. Although we both know I should ask an Elder from the Culture Committee, I ask Roy because of his filmmaker role and recent award winner as American Indian Filmmaker of the Year at the International Anthropological Film Festival in Parnu, Estonia. Roy's film, *Place of Falling Waters,* documents the history, economics, and change wrought by the building of the Kerr Dam on the Flathead Nation.

Roy is 40 years old, wise beyond his age; he speaks to me in his rich baritone voice, thick with the accent of the reservation.

> I didn't grow up here all of my life. I guess when you're little, a kid, you're just playing . . . it seems like there were less people here. [There was] a lot of fishing and hunting. I remember the older people, but I didn't hang around them much except maybe my grandparents, my dad's parents, mostly because they lived here all of the time.
>
> I come from a big family; my parents didn't want to pack up seven or eight kids and go anywhere. Many times we stayed home [at Dixon

---

[2] Micmac: Originally, the French Canadian bastardization of the word "nechemac" which means *friend* or *blood kin.* From the first trade meetings between the French and the First Nations of New Brunswick, a First Nation's man of this particular Algonquin language group would raise his hand and say, "nechemac." It was misinterpreted to mean, "I am Micmac." and the name stuck. Even today this particular group calls themselves Micmac. My grandmother was a member of the New Brunswick Micmac. She married a French Canadian and became a non-status Indian in the eyes of the Canadian government. Five years ago, the Canadian government changed the law in which Indian women lost their tribal identity if they married a White person. My grandmother died before the law went into effect.

Agency] left with a babysitter. I did go to some pow wows when I was with my grandparents. Not all of the time. . . . Who wants to go anyplace with a car full of screaming, sniveling kids?

I never say I am a spokesman for anyone else, but there are people who think like me, [who share] my relationship with the land. I think I am losing [a] lot of my relationship with the land because of the language I don't have. I don't have the Native Language down very well and I know there is a lot of interpretation from Native Language to English that is lost. Our description of the land and nature is more of a relationship. It ties you in closer, but with the English I think I lose some of the close relationship of the language to the land. But I feel I have a close relationship with the land that goes beyond words. When I am out in nature, even just walking from building to building [at the college] or spending a little time outside with my kids, I am conscious of feeling the sun or the wind, or the cold, or whatever, and most of the time I am pretty happy in being alive. That comes from my heart, my gratitude to feel these things and to hear my kids playing . . . so I feel that connectedness without the words; but I know that words [for example], if someone like an Elder is trying to give me a lesson or explain something to me about nature or describe it to me, I can't [understand] good enough. Then I miss out on the knowledge they want to tell me about, especially with the wind and water.

We lost a lot of the language through Christianity and the Catholic boarding schools. The language was beaten out of the kids. There's a lot of stories from the people, not just this tribe, but different tribes who got abused for speakin' their language. The people were pretty much shamed into not bein' who they are, American Indian or Indian, or however you want to say it, being ashamed to talk the language, but it [the language] is still there. I don't know how I am going to pick it up and get the true understanding of the language cuz I think now when they teach you the language, they don't tell what the meaning is. They just say [for example] this word is for car, but they don't tell you that the word for car means "wrinkled feet" which is a description of the tires or that means "salt" or "pepper" or this means "tree." Many times I wish they would say, or I should ask them [the Elders] to say what is the real [descriptive] meaning. I am sure it is more descriptive than the English language. Like the word "tree" in the English language has a root where it comes from. Maybe it is a deeper meaning than "tree" cuz that word doesn't tell you a lot of things.

I'm a young person. I don't have a lot of the knowledge that somebody older than me has, and I wasn't lucky enough to hang around a lot
of really older people. From what I understand, my dad was one of those
people who hung out with the older people. I don't know a lot of the
specifics about this tribe. I should learn it. Hopefully, I will learn more,
but from what I understand from common knowledge is that the women
took care of the house and the children and the men hunted and de-
fended their people; they sought spiritual power. I think a lot of the men
and women knew the plants, the medicines. They participated in ceremonies together as far as I know. I feel deprived [of my culture] all right
because of the changes here [on the reservation]. When you're a young
person, you don't recognize the importance of asking questions and
maybe I still don't ask a lot of questions. It's just my nature. I assume
somebody will tell me somethin' some day that they want me to know or
I'm ready to know. I wish I would've asked my gramma. My grampa died
in 1971 or 1972 when I was 16. I was pretty foolish at that age, a lot of
drinkin' and drugs and I didn't think of askin' about the old ways. They
are pretty strong Catholics, too, so I don't know if they wanted to share
the old ways with me. They knew a lot because they were really around
older people at that time. Dad's dad was born in 1897 and dad's mom
was born in 1900, so they would've been around a lot of older people
who were alive and well before the Treaty was signed. Even after the
Treaty, the land was pretty much our land, so there would have been a
lot of knowledge they would've had. I feel gypped. Probably I'm gyp-
ping myself now . . . I could go [right] down to the Culture Committee
and request some old stories and listen to some things that I am interested in.

My kids may go to immersion schools [for the language]. I know baby
talk, that's all. I hope they teach the real meanings of the words for
"sky," for the "land."

The land for Kerr Dam was taken away to benefit the corporations,
Montana Power Company and Rocky Mountain Power. They were two
corporations with the same mission. One was a subsidiary for the other.
I wasn't the main researcher for the film [Place of Falling Waters], but I
learned that the BIA [Bureau of Indian Affairs], which at that time
wasn't always lookin' out for our best interests, and Montana Power
wanted this certain piece of the river [Flathead River]. It was a nice
rapids area. I've seen some 1930s newsreel footage, how and what that

area looked like; it was pretty awesome. The power that the area had! [You could tell] by listening to the sound of the water. So that is how the dam people looked at it and they could see money. They see somethin' that isn't bein' used. They don't consider that we go there and pray and talk to the water spirits. They don't consider that as being "used." It has to have somethin' on it that's going to make money. Whether its farming where you put cattle on a piece of land as opposed to hunting on it or diggin' roots and berries out of there. At the time, the thought was that it wasn't really bein' used; it was bein' wasted. They thought the rapids was like that and they could see the money that could be made. I don't know how much they cared about electricity for the local people, but [they did care about] electricity to power their mining plants over in Butte. There was a big mining industry over there at the time and they tried to wave a few carrots in front of the people and promise them some things. I think some people thought it was a good idea and some didn't. I don't think it was a unanimous vote one way or the other. It must have been pretty hard on the chiefs at that time who had the final say. Or maybe they didn't have a real voice in it on whether they agreed or not; or maybe the leaders didn't think it was going to be done, or that it was a good idea.

The people who had a real connection to that area [the Rapids] knew what was going on. They didn't want it at all, of course. It was a place where they could go and commune with nature. They didn't want to see it destroyed. I think both tribes [Salish and Kootenai] used it. I've heard more stories from the Kootenais about their spiritual relationship to the area; but not much from the Salish about strong communication that was going on there. Maybe I just talked to the wrong people. It was a fishin' place, a place where people could commune with nature and the spirits. It was an environmental injustice that really hurt our people [when it was taken from us]. . . . A place where we could go to recharge our batteries . . . its not there any more. It's going to hurt us and it's going to make our people sick. I think some people tried to stop it and it has hurt us. We're getting money from it but I don't know in the long run if it was better or not. It's like tearing down Bear Butte in South Dakota, a spiritual place, or all over this country, all the spiritual places where the spirits like to gather and where our people like to go cuz we know where they [the spirits] like to be and that's where we go to commune. People still like to go there [The Rapids where they built Kerr Dam], but I don't know if they go to look at the scenic view or they go to make some prayers. If people are doing that [praying], they don't tell anyone what they're doing.

As of November 1996, Montana Power is trying to sell out earlier on the lease we [the tribes] negotiated ten years ago. In the agreement, they had a 30-year lease that would expire in 2015, but now as of a month or two ago, Montana Power said that they could sell it to us early. I think almost right away. Our people are weighing the options. They won't tear it down; it is a big money maker. It was generating for Montana Power Company as of ten years ago $50 million a year. At that time it was a lot of money. But I don't know; our people may say we don't need it. It is hard to imagine them tearing it down. They are talking about a steady flow out of the dam instead of off and on. It's the off and on that's destroying the fish habitat. Steady flow would be more consistent for the fish.

I would tell other tribes to be wary about what the corporations say. There are many promises no better kept than the treaties [were]. I don't know how people can get away with it these days, even if it is signed on paper. I'd be leery especially about get rich quick types of things; like build a dam and get $50 million, or whatever. There is a price to pay for that, I'm not sure it is worth it in dollars. Money can cause trouble. I'd be leery about it. I think it still would be a hard decision for a leader to make. A real leader would weigh the options and think about the future generations; what would be good for them. Putting somethin' in on that would be an insult to the land, the natural way of the land. It might be good for the people in the long run, but it might be detrimental. I think it would require a lot of prayer and help with the spirits to make the right decision on it.

Tribes are stronger [today]. They know the system. It's good our people are educated to these ways. Governments and big corporations won't pull any wool over our eyes. Our lawyers are just as smart as the best of them. A lot of times our people are being told to sacrifice land for a dam or mine or highway. We could talk and talk to these bureaucrats about our relationship to the land and how, when we see bulldozers diggin' in and taking minerals out and destroying habitat, they don't see how much it hurts us and nature. We know it hurts the land. Our communication with these things is like communicating with another person. These bureaucrats don't hear that. To them it is just Indians' mumbo jumbo and talking about Mother Earth. I can hear my Brother the Eagle talking to me and to them and telling me not to do it [hurt the land]. Their communion with nature is a walk from their business office to their car. It's funny how that's not been changed since the time of Isaac Stevens[3] when he was negotiating the treaties. There was a Nez Pierce or may be a Yakima was tellin' him about the relationship with the land and this Isaac Stevens, a 35-year-old punk kid talkin' to these warriors, very elderly spiritual leaders, who were religious people, told them: "I don't want to hear such talk, will you sign the treaty or not." He didn't want to hear that about communing with the land. I think the bureaucrats and the big corporations and these people like that [spiritual people] don't mean nothin' to them. We have our own people now who know how to use the system, the law, how to talk the talk. Hopefully, we are communing with the traditional people [elders], telling them why we don't want this highway or dam here or that clear cut over there. That's so our people can put the brakes on. Contemporary history has shown a lot of times are ruled in our favor because of that [our legal people]. We have our own legal beagles doin' that type of work and another group who is praying and sweating[4] and doin' things in the old way to help ensure the land doesn't get hurt any more, that we have a good home for the future generations and these animals.

It is an awful thing that's goin' on in South America to have those people hunted like dogs down there. Boy it would be hard to stop trying through prayers to stop it [the decimation of the rain forest and traditional lands]. So-called "civilized" countries should put a stop to it themselves. I'm sure American corporations have a hand in it one way or another. It is in the best interest of the United States government to get what they want out of there too. They don't care anymore about the land than they have before [the time of Indian–White conflict]. [Like] McDonald's buying cattle from them down there and these poor people trying to make a living clear cutting the rain forest to raise cattle for two or three years before the land is dead. It's all about money. I think our people who are living here on this continent, they still pray, and pray hard. That's why we're [the Indian people] still here. They [the U.S. government] were doin' the same thing to us, killing our people like dogs and killing off the land. They knew it would kill us if they killed the land. That's what they tried, but someone was still praying and

---

[3] Isaac Stevens: The army agent for the U.S. government who negotiated the reservation treaties in Montana.
[4] Sweating: Ceremonial prayers and chants and songs taking place inside the sweat lodge.

doing the ceremonies; that's why we're still here. The South American governments aren't going to listen. I don't think they have any conscience. I don't know, I think they [the United States] has more of a [conscience] since the beginning of this country. The Canadian government steps on native rights. Besides our people being lawyers and helping you through the courts, people are still prayin' hard, besides pickin' up a gun!

For my kids: the more I learn through sweating and prayer brings me more understanding—the big picture, the whole thing. Because Nature is part of the Creator like we are. I think when I'm doin' these things I have them [my kids] with me. They are still young kids and all the world is still magical and mysterious and beautiful, and its that way to me now because I got over my foolishness [of drinking and substance abuse]. I had to reprogram myself from what the public school did to me . . . that the land is more important than just a science. Hopefully, I can keep my kids involved in a ceremonial way, and that door [through which] they have to see the world will never be closed. They will always see the world as a magical, mysterious, beautiful place because for all kids that is a door that is open; they can see things that adults can't see. Their senses are sharp and their logical mind hasn't taken over. They are dreamers, still. As time goes by they will always have that connection and love, to know our ancestors are still here with us, that they [our ancestors] are part of this land still and that they are here. Sometimes we don't know that they are standing right beside us or behind us or in front of us, but they are still here. They are the water, the wind, the mountains, the trees. Nature is like your relation, and our ancestors love to visit us whether at pow wows or wherever the people are happy, they like to be around all the time.

I hope that my kids will feel, when I'm gone, my love for this life and for this land. When they're out walking and communing with the spirits, their love will bring me to help them out—like my love for the land that my ancestors had and how I try to understand things; my feeling and my love will bring them back to me. I hope it is that way for my kids and my grandkids. I'll always be around because of them and their love and concern for the land. If I just live right, they will pick it up. If the public school tries to teach them the wind is not the breath of the creator, but hot and cold air masses bumping into each another or this or that, it might be good to learn that view, but it is much more than that. I want to be able to tell them "Ya, what your teacher said is right, but this [way of seeing] is also right."

The Kerr Dam: Collision of Cultures

Coyote made the world safe for Indian people and everything on the land was alive with Indian power. (Big Crane & Smith, 1991)

Before Kerr Dam was built, the people of the Salish, Kootenai and Pend Oreilles Tribes lived in the traditional ways in vast areas of Montana. The land held sacred power. Indian life *was* the air, birds, water, and animals (Big Crane & Smith, 1991). The Dam was constructed on the sacred falls of KwaTaqNuk [Place of Falling Waters], a place sacred to the water spirits of the people. People used the area for prayer, to honor and commune with the water spirits. Such prayer and communing was part of the culture, and helped maintain mental health and balance. The destruction of this sacred place for a dam expanded the collision of cultures on the reservation. With the expansion of the dominant culture, the people of the Flathead Nation grew increasingly dependent on a cash economy, and the dietary and health changes that resulted from an increase of carbohydrates in the diet. Today, diabetes, cardiac problems, hypertension, and the plethora of disease caused by obesity plague many members of the Flathead Nation (Personal conversation with Roy Big Crane).

In the 1850s, the industrial market economy lead to a conflict in life ways between the government of the United States and the Native People of Montana. When the Hell Gate Treaty of 1855 was signed, 22 million acres of Indian lands were ceded to the government in return for the Flathead Reservation. It was the first step to the construction of Kerr Dam.

After the treaty, the people tried to maintain the cycles of the traditional way of life. The people picked berries, hunted, searched for Camas, bitterroot, game, and waterfowl. Agnes Vanderburg, Salish Elder, shares about how game meat was passed around to the members of her family who lived in nine tipis. She reveals that everyone helped one another in a way of life free from hunger (Big Crane & Smith, 1991). People lived in harmony and they continued to practice their conservative methods. Larry Parker, Salish Elder, speaks about the abundance of fish and how the Indian people worked to conserve them for the future (Big Crane & Smith, 1991). The life ways of the people were far from the world of wages and the technology of Kerr Dam.

In the old days, the Blackfeet, enemy of the Flathead Nation, traveled across the northern plains over the Great Rocky Mountains of the Continental Divide, through what is today called "Glacier Park," to the lands of the Flathead. Here they counted coup,[5] raided horses, and took women. In retaliation, in 1841, the Flathead Nation invited the Black-Robed Jesuits to bring their "power" to the people. With plea in hand, two runners were sent to St. Louis to request the Jesuits establish their power on the Flathead Nation. On their way to St. Louis, both emissaries were killed. The following year, the tribe sent two more runners to St. Louis.

Within two years, the Jesuits and Urseline sisters established a church and boarding school in St. Ignatius and *demanded* that all Indian children be brought there for instruction. The federal policy of assimilating Indian people into White culture was exacerbated by religious sects. In their predilection for annihilation and incorporation, religious denominations were invited by the government to set up their churches and schools on the reservations. Generally, each religious sect took a different reservation, but in the case of the Flathead Nation, the Jesuits were invited. However, to the Flathead People the results of the Jesuit presence were unexpected. With the children conscripted to "religious" school, the boys' braids were cut[6] and their traditional clothing burned. They were forced to wear White man's clothing, eat strange foods, and pray to a new and punishing god:

These children, removed from their families, communities, and nations were emotionally [and physically] abused. They were forbidden to speak their language, and some totally blocked their language to adopt English or French [in Canada] as a survival mechanism. . . . when they returned home to their communities, their grandparents, the only people who could give them support, could not understand them. They were isolated in their own communities. (Hill, 1996, p. 70)

The only way we could get them to learn English was to get them away from their families. Then, they would stop talking Indian. After six months in the boarding schools, they were oriented to the White ways. Each one would help the other learn. . . . We were educating them in our faith, we made no effort to learn their faith. (Big Crane & Smith, 1991)

---

[5] Counting coup: The most daring act for a warrior is to "count coup" or touch his enemy with a coup stick and not kill him.
[6] Cutting braids was only done in the case of a death in the family.

Tribal member and history professor, Ron Therriault, tells that regardless of the presence and philosophies of the Jesuits, the people attempted to maintain their own culture, ceremonies, and traditions which were and are so much a part of their mental health. "Many embraced Catholicism, but many also maintained their own culture," he said (Big Crane & Smith, 1991).

Instead of relying on store-bought foods with its increased sugars and carbohydrates, the Indians hunted at Libby. Joe Aniste, Kootenai Elder explains, "They killed 100 deer, dried them, brought the meat home, and lived on it. It was good a long time ago. To have meat tied on your horse going home, it is a good feeling. In the old days there was no occasion to be hungry. There was a lot of food."

According to Betty White, tribal historian, tribal members and Jesuits still hold conflicting points of view concerning that time of shared history with the tribes. The ethnocentricism of the Jesuit religion lead to conflict. Jesuits arrived with a simple mission: to eradicate a culture they thought inferior to theirs. The Jesuits also were convinced that the only way to convert the Salish was to have them settle in one spot, learn Catholicism, and acquiesce to agriculture in place of hunting.

Known for rekindling interest in the culture of the Flathead Nation, Agnes Vandenberg (quoted in Big Crane & Smith, 1991), a revered Salish Elder and participant in the boarding school culture of the Jesuits and Urseline sisters, remembers how children growing up in the boarding schools quit speaking Indian. She indicates that there are a lot of those Jesuits down there [in Hell]. "If the children spoke Indian, the Jesuits would spank them," she added.

A bill introduced in Congress by Indian Agent Dixon, the Flathead Reservation Allotment Act, changed the reservation forever. The bill would end communal ownership of land on the reservation and open it to homesteading. Each Indian was given 80 acres. The rest was open to White homesteading. Soon after the bill became law, in April 1910, Whites flooded the reservation for homesteading eventually to outnumber the reservation Indians themselves.

Homesteaders, calling themselves farmers or ranchers, plowed up the land in the valley of the reservation. Some Indian people began raising gardens then as well. Mary Small Salmon, Salish Elder, remembers how her father had a big garden up at Crow Creek, where he raised potatoes, carrots, corn, watermelon, squash, cantaloupe, and beans. She says that they were not poor because they had deer, dry meat, and the garden (Big Crane & Smith, 1991).

The Indians called it "makin' checkers" [cutting up the reservation]. But "80 acres, that was nothin'," explained Joe Aniste, Kootenai Elder, who remembers that his allotment was all rocks. He had no plow and wondered how he was going to care for his kids. All the land where the wild foods grew was given to the Whites (Big Crane & Smith, 1991), who then plowed up the wild foods, the Camas, bitterroot, and berries. The Indians were soon made to feel as if they were visitors, as if they didn't belong in certain parts of the reservation. Before the government intervened, Indian people could camp anyplace, but after the implementation of the Allotment Act an 80-acre restriction was placed on their holdings. The rest of the land was put up for homesteading as private property. The Indian people also believed that the president of the United States understood their traditions and history. Thus, the president knew that they did not know how to farm. They had no plows, but more importantly, they were and had always been hunters and gatherers.

In 1908, the Flathead Irrigation Project, which promised Indian people local water for their gardens, was begun. Many tribal members resented the project and some even attempted to sabotage it by removing survey markers, but it was constructed despite local protests. The project changed the water table and helped to destroy the fisheries. A grocery store opened on the reservation and Native People, now more dependent on the cash economy, lived in poverty.

Joe Aniste, Kootenai Tribal member, remembers the government doling out beans, bacon, "all kinds of stuff." Some people went to pick it up for Kootenai Chief Koostatah, but he couldn't eat it because of the high salt content. Many other Indians responded similarly, using the bacon finally for firewood (Big Crane & Smith, 1991).

Two big corporations joined the push into the reservation. Needing more electricity for their operations, Montana Power Company and Anaconda Mining set their sights on the construction of a dam on the sacred waters of the tribes. Ignoring tribal sovereignty, the corporations attempted to purchase the area needed for Kerr Dam for $5 million. They held a pow wow for the people, so the people would sign away the land in a petition for the dam. Frank Kerr, president of Montana Power, bought all of the groceries for the pow wow.

The Secretary of the Interior refused to pay a lawyer to help the Indian people oppose the dam. No one stepped forward to protect the tribes' interest. Before the dam was built, however, something told the Indian people not to let it go, that it was important to them; that it was where the spirits were (Big Crane & Smith, 1991).

Somehow a lawyer was found who supported the tribe's position with Montana Power and a paltry deal was made which gave tribal preference for construction workers and an annual payment of $140,000 to the tribes as rental. But the Indian men who worked on the dam received the lowest paying jobs and some of them were killed in rock slides.

Joe Eneas, who worked cleaning rocks, remembers one incident when five tribal members were killed. Joe was cleaning all the rocks from the cliffs when a landslide occurred. Two died from a rock slide and three from a cave in. It had been raining all night and they were working under the cliffs. Joe lived because he was not with them. Pay for such dangerous work topped at 45 cents an hour although most of the Elders thought it good money then. As Mary Small Salmon recalls, "It was good money at the time. My brother worked there. He got a wagon with real tires" (Big Crane & Smith, 1991).

Opening Day, 1938

In their coverage of a similar story regarding the opening of a dam in Washington State, Movietone Newsreel headlined the story, "Once More the Red Man Bows to White Man's Progress."

President of Montana Power, Frank Kerr, in his opening day speech promised free electricity for the tribes. "We will make use of this idle water for you," he explained. But the water was not idle, the water had never been idle to Indian people.

Eighty-four years after the Hell Gate Treaty was signed, the dam was completed. It is a symbol of domination of tribal sovereignty. During all those years, the people got lost, a whole generation of people who, in their own way, paid for the rest of us to be here today. It is a culmination of 80 years of assault which "increased cultural deterioration of the tribe" (Germain Dumontier, Big Crane & Smith, 1991).

As the Tribal Council became stronger, it challenged Montana Power Company for control of the dam. The confederated Salish and Kootenai tribes then brought suit for the license which would bring with it control of all revenues and water use. Non-Indians feared the takeover of the dam by the tribes. Today, the tribes receive several million dollars yearly from the power company and hold the license. In the year 2000, the tribes will purchase the dam from Montana Power Company outright, with dam ownership reverting back to them.

People are questioning whether the present and future revenues received from the dam will help regenerate cultural life for the people of the Flathead Nation or help to destroy it.

Other Environmental Issues Concerning the Flathhead Nation

In 1984, the Tribal Council of the Flathead Nation declared the reservation a nuclear free zone, the only reservation in the country to do so (Bryan, 1985). In addition, in 1982, the tribes set aside 89,500 acres of wilderness in the Mission Mountains as a unique environmental resource. For many years, the tribes sought air quality redesignation from the federal government. In May 1982, Class I air status was granted to the reservation. Only one other reservation in the United States has this designation. Despite these environmental control measures, agricultural chemicals are suspected of flowing in from agricultural lands and contaminating one of the tribes' best fisheries at Crow Creek. Currently, the tribes are seeking remedial and preventive measures regarding the use of toxic chemicals on the reservation (Bryan, 1985).

Summary

A collision of cultures most affects the health of the nondominant culture, including in this case the mental health and well-being of the Flathead Nation. The development of the Kerr Dam brought about exploitation of resources, foods, and sacred sites. It resulted in the mental depression of the people and, in the dissolution of a healthy culture, the decimation of traditional food sources. It is an issue that continues to inflict pain, suffering, and heartache on the Elders. In many ways, it will continue to affect the youth of the Next Seven Generations.

THE MOON OF THE HUCKLEBERRIES: MONTANA

To heal ourselves, we must heal the Earth _____

The acre of forest was clear cut. Every tree a victim of the chain saw. Every blade of grass, every wildflower scraped clean by the bulldozer. The trees were carried off by trucks screaming down the highway to the lumber mill to make wood chips for paper. The trees, homes for western flickers to raise young in standing dead wood, resting places for Clark's Nutcrackers feeding on the lodge post pine seeds, and hunting places for great horned owls, are forgotten in rolls of computer paper, toilet paper, and all other breeds of paper we need to operate a "progressive lifestyle." I wonder if any people behold pieces of paper as living trees and habitats for native species? When the forest was denuded, it changed an entire ecosystem. Sun no longer filtered through layers of forest, instead it burned through an open cut in the canopy with an intensity never felt before by gentle forest lilies. Humans hauled their old trailer onto the raw, bare sandy earth and called this place "home." (Journal, July 1996)

Across the great prairies and towering mountains that are Montana, crisscrossed with skeletons of trailers, remnants of old homesteads, ranches, farms, the development dreams of modern people, Indian tribes and ecologists are targeted by corporations for natural resources exploitation and waste disposal.

Fort Belknap Reservation: Description and History

Late winter in Fort Belknap fades harshly into the promise of spring. Snow patches still cover the brown Earth. Slate grey clouds, pregnant with unborn snow hover on the prairie landscape. Dry, bitter winds blow down from the Canadian Arctic chilling the very marrow of the bone. In winter, it can be the coldest spot in the nation as arctic winds bite down from the fertile plains of Saskatchewan, Canada. People huddle around wood stoves in their drafty trailers or government houses, sharing coffee and the latest stories about their community. Winter food supplies, fish, and game are stored away in freezers or have been smoked. To hunt, people have to travel far from the reservation these days as cyanide leach pads from gold mining have contaminated the waters on the southern end of the reservation. In spring, some tribal members farm the land in spite of traditional beliefs that it is wrong to tear up the land because the Earth is a living creature.

Home to the Assiniboine and Gros Ventre tribes and bordered by the Little Rocky Mountains in the south and the Milk River in the north, Fort Belknap is named for William W. Belknap, secretary of war in 1855. In 1855, the governor of the Washington Territory concluded a treaty to provide peace between the Blackfeet, Flathead, Nez Pierce Tribes, and the United States. The Gros Ventre signed the treaty as part of the Blackfeet Nation whose territory became common hunting grounds for all tribes signing the treaty. In 1888, these tribes ceded 17.5 million acres of their joint reservation and agreed to live on three smaller reservations. These are now known as the Blackfeet, Fort Peck, and Fort Belknap Reservations.

Arriving in Fort Belknap, I have the feeling of traveling a century back in time, when brick was the building material of choice for the Indian Health Service hospital and the tribal college. Fort Belknap Tribal College is a focal point of the town located near Harlem, Montana:

Fort Belknap College was started as a tool to fight the effects of economic plunder of a century, and to fit people left behind by the modern world with the skills to meet its challenges. It is the sole post-secondary school in an expanse of 282 miles east and west and 215 miles to the south, and hundreds of miles of Saskatchewan prairies to the north. (Fort Belknap College Catalog, 1995)

The college offers two-year degrees, pre-nursing, and certificate programs for the residents of Fort Belknap reservation. With many residents seeking better employment skills, the student body at the college is expanding. In response to the growing student body, Fort Belknap has recently added more buildings. "The leaders within Fort Belknap have an unwritten policy of seeking the best education possible for tribal members so they can obtain jobs elsewhere" (Bryan, 1985, p. 33).

Like most Montana reservations, Fort Belknap residents are economically poor, living in depressed ranching country with over 10 years of drought. Unemployment is at an all-time high at 70 to 80 percent. Non-Indians living near the reservation are descendents of trappers, smugglers, and homesteaders.

In 1895, gold was discovered on reservation land. In the words of the residents of Fort Belknap, "The United States government threatened to starve us residents of Fort Belknap until we signed a treaty giving away the land so the gold could be mined" (personal communication, Grandmother Little Shell).

> In the late 1880s and early 1890s, prospectors roaming the hills of the Little Rockies found gold, and they paid little attention that their strike was within the boundaries of the Fort Belknap Reservation.... In 1895, President Cleveland appointed three commissioners to negotiate with the Fort Belknap tribes for the gold mining country. (Bryan, 1985, p. 36)

The Indians were told, ". . . if you don't make any agreement with the government, you will have to kill your cattle and then you will starve. If you sell some of this land and get money enough to keep going for some years. . . . after that, you will be just like White people and be able to take care of yourselves" (Bryan, 1985, p. 36). Eventually the tribe was convinced to sell a strip of land to the government seven miles long and four miles wide for $350,000. It was bought by Pegasus Mining and today is the largest low-grade heap mining operation in the western world (Bryan, 1985). Today the mine still produces $80 million dollars a year for others. In 1985, the mine paid taxes to the federal government, the county, and the state in excess of $1 million. "This is hard to take when the per capita income of the Fort Belknap Reservation is $1,000" (Bryan, 1985, p. 37). Although the mine employs 100 people, some seasonal, some tribal members, with an annual payroll of $5 million, the tribe is furious at the environmental contamination effects from heap leach mining procedures.

Erin's Words: The Month of the Huckleberries

Erin Lewis, a young student and new mother attending Salish Kootenai College, questions the health of her reservation and wonders about a future for her child. She is small of stature with long, straight black hair. Her big brown eyes wide with inquisitiveness as she ponders the future of her people.

I grew up on the Fort Belknap Reservation. I am an enrolled tribal[7] member. I come from the tribe called the Gros Ventre. The other tribe [on the reservation] is called the Assiniboine. On my reservation, or just a few miles off the reservation but on the boundary of the reservation, we have a mining industry called Pegasus Gold Corporation and another called the Landusky Mining. Cyanide heap leach mining is how it affects our land, animals, and community. The mining is degrading the environment close to my reservation. The tailings from the mine are going into our fresh water streams and our fresh water. This happens when the spring thaw comes, when all the snow comes off the mountains. The tailings[8] get there by the blasting that goes on day and night. I have seen how the water looks from this pollution. It has an ugly yellowish brown look to it; it isn't very pleasant to look at. Comparing some of the water that looks contaminated to the streams that haven't been damaged by the pollution, you can tell there is something wrong with this whole mining thing. This mining first started when I was 3 years old in 1979. I have seen what the mountains looked like before they started mining and they were really beautiful. I can remember one time I went hiking in this area called the South Fork to go look at some beavers and beaver dams that were up in the canyon. When I got to the place where the beaver's homes were supposed to be, I wasn't amused by what I saw. I saw a dead beaver and there was nothing alive near those beaver dams. It had an ugly look to it, like something just came through and took its pride away from it. So I figure when the spring thaw came off the mountains, it brought death from the mines. I know everything used to look beautiful up there on that side of the reservation line before the mining. I am afraid that sooner or later our side of the mountains is going to end up looking like that if we don't start doing something about it now instead of waiting till it's too late.

I have learned that the people are so greedy that they don't take people or animals into consideration. They just keep on working and polluting. They don't stop to think that migrating birds die from drinking

---

[7] Enrolled tribal member: Having enough blood quantum to qualify as a "real Indian."
[8] Tailings: Left over debris from mining.

contaminated pools that they put their tailings in. Animals don't know if the water is good or bad. 'Cause to them, everything is good and nothin' used to be polluted. I will tell you a little about these pools they use. These pools are supposed to be lined with a special liner that is supposed to prevent seepage. These pools [liners] have a tendency to tear and rip and the workers seem not even to care.

There are abandoned mine pits which slowly refill with water to become massive pit lakes, and rocks unexposed to air can leach into the water forming a toxic brew. There's another thing hurting the land by mining industries. It's called "dewatering." That is when the mining companies pump water not only from the mining pits that run deeper than the water table, but from surrounding areas creating enormous tracts of arid land. People really can't do anything to prevent this because they [the mining company] just ignore you like you never even talked to them or tried to explain the problem.

On our reservation a doctor from some city came to do some tests on the children for lead. After the tests were taken, he discovered that out of 70 children, 20 had high counts of lead in their blood. When they tried to tell the environmental health workers off the reservation, they said the blood was probably tampered with before it reached the lab. So again, they put this important issue aside. Another thing, on our reservation a lot of the men and women have gotten cancer: women get breast cancer and men get prostate cancer. When you try to tell somebody about this, somebody that you think might help, it turns out that they ain't going to give you the time of day.

My grandmother had breast cancer and it hurts me to think that it could have been caused by the mines in the canyon. My grandmother lives next to the mouth of the canyon that leads to the mine. The way things are going on now, it seems like there's never going to be a day when it will end.

We have a lot of sacred things in the canyon, sacred things that deserve respect. Respect was all we wanted when we asked them to quit mining for a few days while the Sun Dance in the canyon was going on. But they just ignored the request and went on blasting during the ceremony. During the pow wow, you can always hear the workers that work nights and the workers that work days come off the mountains and pass through the pow wow grounds. So actually, we people who are here never really get peace from all this.

I figure the reservation was given to us, not the mining industry. I think sooner or later the government is going to try and take our side of the mountains to make their greedy little hearts happy and to fill up their pockets with the gold that they find. It hurts me to see the Elders of our reservation have to worry themselves about this when all they should be worrying about is their health. They probably want the memory of a beautiful mountain range. Instead they are going to get the ugly run down mountains—if we don't do something now about the mountains.

Sometimes, I am told that I live here because of how beautiful it is. Fort Belknap is my home and I should try to make a difference in the environment here. I can't do very much now except to learn about the mining and I hope that later in my life all this [knowledge] will pay off in the long run. I think later on there is going to be some political war or an environmental issue war if somebody doesn't make some kind of progress. I hope it don't come to that cause that would put the people of Fort Belknap in a predicament they won't want to be in. We might even end up losing everything we have now, even though [what we have] is just a little. We still love our piece of land even though it ain't much. Maybe later on down the line, the people who are mining will realize they are destroying lives and the environment. But it ain't the mining workers that are going to make change. It's going to be the proud American Indians of Fort Belknap.

Grandmother Little Shell Speaks about the Gold Mine

"Too young to be a grandmother," she tells me, but her daughter honored her as a grandmother by giving birth quite young. Today, she is a revered tribal member, one of the few who graduated from college. Her mother and several of her relatives are suffering from cancer. Grandmother Little Shell looks out at me from behind the frames of her glasses. Her black eyes glint with anger as she speaks the words:

Not only has the mine caused a great deal of surface destruction in the form of denuding the mountains of rocks, soils, trees, it has contaminated everything around us. Pegasus Gold Mining Company has created cyanide leach fields which for years have been leaking and contaminating the water. There are no native fish living in the streams. The game animals that people depend on for food are contaminated with tumors—no one would eat them. Although some of the tribal members work for Pegasus, many feel that Pegasus is guilty of

environmental racism.[9] It has destroyed a way of life for the people of
the Fort Belknap Reservation.

What the mining company does is pile up a huge heap of soil, rocks
and material taken as they tear down the mountains. This material is
piled together in huge areas the size of several football fields. Cyanide
is sprayed on the soil then water . . . to saturate; as the liquid seeps out,
the gold leaches out. The water and the cyanide trickle down into the
sub soils and runs off into holding ponds. When the linings in the holding ponds leak, the cyanide leak out and contaminates the water supply,
streams, everything in its path.

We went up the canyon, out to the creeks one summer to look for
beavers, but they were all dead from the mining.

Rose Main: Natural Resource Officer, Fort Belknap[10]

Rose Main, a presenter at the Haskell University Environmental Resource
seminar, is the Natural Resource Officer for the Gros Ventre/Assiniboine
Tribes of the Fort Belknap Reservation. A graduate of Haskell Indian Nations University in Kansas, Rose earned a master's degree in public admin-
istration from Montana State University. Her department, just three years
old, was funded with a grant from the EPA to examine water quality on the
reservation—where there is 75 to 80 percent unemployment adjacent to the
Pegasus gold mining operation. The Natural Resources Department works
as a cooperative site for students in the natural resources program at Fort
Belknap College. She speaks to the audience in the melodious accent of the
Fort Belknap Reservation (her lecture has been edited and abridged in the
following segment):

Cyanide contamination of the water on Fort Belknap Reservation,
Central Montana, is the classic struggle between Indian people and
the mining companies. Mining began in the Little Rocky Mountains in
1979 just south of the Fort Belknap Reservation. Those mountains
are traditionally called, by the people of Fort Belknap, The Island

---

[9] Environmental racism: "Racial discrimination in environmental policy making, the enforcement of regulations and laws, the deliberate targeting of communities of color for toxic waste facilities, the official sanctioning of life threatening poisons and pollutants in communities of
color, excluding people of color from the environmental movement" (Bullard, 1994, p. 278).
[10] Adapted from a seminar at Haskell Indian Nations University, 1996.

Mountains, since all around them is prairie and the Mountains just pop up out of nowhere. The land was taken away from the tribes under the Grinnel Agreement.[11] The reservation is bounded on the south by the Missouri River. There are two mines, the Zortman Mine and the Landusky Mine, but both are owned by the same Canadian company. Tailings from Zortman mine contaminated the town of Zortman. Some of the area was reclaimed in 1985, but very little of it. There has been devastation of the vegetation, and the blasting causes air pollution on the reservation. In Hays, located on the border of the reservation, is Mission Canyon Road and our Sun Dance Grounds. There are creek drainages located in the mining areas and tailings in King's Creek travel to the People's Creek, through the reservation and on into the Milk River which is the northern boundary of the reservation. There are abandoned sites with mine tailings and some of them are in sacred areas. The contamination is pretty bad. Deer come to the contaminated ponds for water sites. Some beaver areas have been contaminated by tailings. Although we requested the mining companies not to blast during our sacred Sun Dance, the requests go unheeded and they continue to blast.

Up in Montana Gulch, the old people used to camp there, but no one does now. The water isn't fit for human consumption. The soi is the color of yellow diarrhea leaching into the water. During the flood last year, some of the earthen walls of the water impoundments were destroyed and the contaminated water poured out into the streams.

The mining companies are proposing an expansion. They want to do it in 11 stages, so they nibble away at the reservation lands little by little. Children have been tested by an independent physician and were found to have heavy levels of lead in their blood. The BIA[12] said it was because the vials were contaminated on the way to the labs. The BIA is supposed to protect the interest of the tribes, but it doesn't.

We are seeing an increase in breast cancer in our women and prostate cancer in our men. The blasting goes on 24 hours a day. It causes spiritual and emotional upset to our people. Where are they getting the water to put on the leach pads? Fort Belknap has water

[11] Grinnel Agreement: Proceeding of the appointed commission to negotiate with the Fort Belknap Indians, from the records of Bureau of Indian Affairs, file number 25450-1922-051.
[12] BIA: Bureau of Indian Affairs: The government agency responsible for the welfare of Indian people in the United States.

rights which aren't being observed. A new waste water treatment plant was built in the south, but that doesn't help the people of the reservation because the water from the mines flows south. They need one in the north as well.

Mine tailings were used by the BIA to pave the highway on the reservation. There is a lot of lead in those tailings. The BIA is negligent. There are supposed to be nets over the ponds that are contaminated so wildlife and birds won't use them as drinking water sites. A mine in South Dakota was fined for not using them. We need them here, too.

All of the wildlife is poisoned and the people have to live on subsidized diets. This thing threatens our health and our lives.

Health Effects of Cyanide

Cyanide releases into the water from cyanidation processes in the extraction of ores such as gold. Cyanide solutions are sprayed onto heaps of low-grade ore to extract the gold. The cyanide trickles down through the crushed ore, dissolving the ore and releasing the gold. The processing solutions are collected from the base of the heap leach pile, and the gold is chemically extracted from the solutions.

The cyanide and water are contained under the leach pad, generally. Environmental problems developed soon after the initiation of open-pit mining. Acidic, metal rich drainage into King's Creek on Fort Belknap increased significantly from numerous leak sites. Processing solutions contaminated with cyanide began leaking into an underground drainage system beneath the heap leach pad where they mixed with ground waters.

Mine wastes have poisoned over 10,000 miles of rivers, according to the U.S. Bureau of Mines.[13] The release of mine wastes into the environment has resulted in many cases of fish kills, such as the dramatic trout kill on Montana's Clark Fork River and the cyanide spill from a gold mine in Guyana, South America, which resulted in dead fish and hogs floating down Guyana's biggest river. About 60 Super Fund sites are abandoned

---

[13] U.S. Bureau of Mines: The federal government agency under the Department of the Interior which regulates mining in the United States (Department of the Interior also includes the Bureau of Indian Affairs [BIA] and the Bureau of Land Management [BLM].

mines. More than a dozen of these are currently active and pose both human health and environmental problems.

Generally, humans are exposed to cyanides from breathing contaminated air and water, coming into contact with contaminated soils, or eating cyanide contaminated foods (U.S. Department of Health and Human Services, 1993). At high levels such as in mining, cyanide becomes toxic to soil microorganisms. Because the soil organisms are no longer able to transform cyanides into other chemical forms, they pass through the soils into underground water. Even in minute amounts, cyanide can kill many life forms. In addition, heavy metals such as arsenic, lead, mercury, and cadmium are often found in the waste products of the tailings. Such waste products accumulate over time in fish and fish eaters, such as migrating herons, egrets, and pelicans. In Nevada alone over 5,000 migrating birds have died from ingesting fish or water from ponds contaminated with cyanide:

> Cyanide poisoning results from inhaling hydrogen cyanide or more commonly from the ingestion of cyanide salts [in water]. Cyanide inhibits cellular respiration (inhibits the cell's ability to burn oxygen and sugars to produce energy) especially in tissues requiring high amounts of oxygen, like the brain and heart. When cyanide is inhaled, rapid absorption can quickly lead to death. When cyanide is ingested, it may take weeks before death occurs. (Ostler, 1996, p. 99)

Health Effects of Lead Poisoning

Mine tailings containing lead were used to pave one of the roads on the Fort Belknap Reservation. The U.S. government banned lead from paint and from gasoline in the 1970s, but the BIA decided that mine tailings would be fine to use on Indian reservations for the roads. High levels of lead affect the mental development of children and cross the placental barrier to the developing fetus in pregnant women. Severe exposure in children (blood levels of above 80ug/dL) can cause coma, convulsions, even death. Low levels affect the intelligence and impair neurobiological development. Investigators report reading disabilities, attention deficit problems, low IQ, fine motor coordination, and lower class ranking (U.S. Department of Health and Human Services, 1991).

Exposure to lead usually occurs in the first few years of life. With treatment, some of the immediate effects on the brain, other parts of the central nervous system, kidneys, and heart are reversible. Still, some 90 percent of lead settles in the bones and is handled much as calcium is. This means that during pregnancy, lactation, and menopause, lead—with the calcium—is released from the bone back into the blood.

Ellen Silbergeld (1991), epidemiologist and toxicologist for the Environmental Defense Fund, explains that lead levels in the blood of pregnant women "change over pregnancy, and lead is rapidly transferred across the placenta to the fetus." She notes that women whose diets are low in calcium and Vitamin D will have "substantial bone demineralization" during pregnancy and lactation during which lead as well as calcium subsequently migrate into the hearts, brains, and kidneys of both mother and fetus or infant. During menopause, Silbergeld notes, remobilization of lead reoccurs. "In postmenopausal women compared to premenopausal women, there is about a 22 percent increase in blood lead levels." This again puts such women at risk.

Grey Wolf's Words: The Month of the Buttercups

Grey Wolf is not his real name, but is a name I gave him to maintain his anonymity. To me he is an Elder, but if I told him, he would laugh and say, "I don't know enough to be an Elder." Like the grey wolf of the Canadian forest, he is a survivor in his own Indian lifeways and in his tribal culture. Once dark and thick, his hair has greyed over the years. His life has been long, rich, and interesting. Remembering the culture from his grandmother "who lived in the horse days," his spirituality and experiences shine out from behind his soft brown eyes. I am honored to know him and privileged to share his wisdom:

> I'm from Fort Belknap, but my father was brought up over there in Saskatchewan, Canada. My mother is a Sioux Assinoboine. I grew up speaking Lakota Sioux and Cree. So I am a Cree and Assiniboine, but my grandkids are Blackfeet—my daughter married a Blackfeet man. In the old days, the Cree used to go over there and "borrow the horses of the Blackfeet, maybe borrow their women too." [He laughs at the thought of this.] My grandfather talked about many things that influence

my life in this day and age: things such as respect, kindness, culture and tradition, generosity, extended family, and religion as a way of life. Pollution in our early life was uncommon. Everything was green, and by seein' this you had a happy feeling. Today, everything is drab and gray and the respect for nature is gone. Alcoholism is a big thing that affected our family, my father and my mother and I remember the old folks talkin' about them boarding schools and how they molested the young boys and girls. That generation is lost and they can't pass anything down to the young because they lost everythin', even the language. Those old people up there in Canada, I love to go talk to them about the old days. I remember one man in particular who was there. He always wore short moccasins and a breech clout. When he went to sleep, he would strip down to his breech clout. I remember them teasing one another. Even now it makes me laugh to think of those old men teasing and playing with each other. When I went to school up there we used to go in a caboose, they called it. It was a long box on a sled pulled by horses. It had a glass window in the front and the driver used to hold onto the reins through that window. Inside there was a wood stove and a floor filled with hay. All the students used to sit on the hay and keep warm with the wood stove. That's how we would go to school in those days. Imagine how cold it was 50 degrees below zero.

My grandfather used to take us up into the mountains there and we prayed, had visions, and stuff like that. Today my tribe [is] in Canada, we do the Sun Dance, we go to the sweat lodge, belong to the Native American Church. When we have food celebrations, the old [holy] man or woman smudges the food with sweet grass smoke, then prays for blessings to the Creator. Everything we do is done in a circle. See the arbor that the pow wow dancer dances under? It is in the shape of a circle. The circle is the drum. It is the shape of the sun and moon. It is the way we lead our life . . . in a circle.

Alcoholism is up there on my reserve. It is something that the people didn't invite but it is there, so they drink. They drink because they forgot the old ways and the culture. My kids . . . I feel like I didn't do right by them in teaching them about our language and the culture. I wish I taught them more, but I was an alcoholic then and didn't know the culture myself. It's hard. See, I speak to you in your language because that is respect. When I go home, I speak my own language because I respect those old people too. I take care of my grandkids, though; I am bringing them up in the traditional way. It is a way that will keep them healthy and drug free. It is a way to help the next generation stay healthy because I am a role model for them. They see me goin' to school, an old guy like me, and I have turned my life around and they say, "See if uncle _____ can do it, I can do it!"

But I worry too. My doctor told me if I don't lose weight and bring my blood pressure down, I will die soon. It scares me. I might not be able to bring up my grandkids in the traditional way—so they can be safe.

My grandson is a dancer.[14] He has a bustle[15] with over 100 eagle feathers on it. I made it. He is going with me to Canada this summer to dance in the pow wows. He is a good boy because I am teaching him the traditions and the culture. My grandfather was a medicine man. He would pray with anyone. One time I remember the medicine man was praying and they tied this guy down with a rope . . . arms and legs tied in rope with little knots . . . and put little sticks with pieces of cloth tied on the sticks all around him. Then the medicine man called in the spirits. I could feel the room shake and there was a big noise like the wind, and it was dark in there, you know, but when it was over the man was still tied and all those pieces of cloth were braided into a hoop.

But that alcoholism is a big problem on my reserve. My nephew was killed in a car accident; he was 18. A big semi hit the car he was driving. There was no alcohol involved. But I promised to make him a bustle of eagle feathers because he wanted to dance . . . so when he died, my brother reminded me of that vow. I am bringing it to Canada this summer and the boys will do an honor dance at the pow wow around that bustle. One of the boys will be touched, my brother will know who to touch during the honor dance, and that boy will become my brother's new son.

[Recently], they found oil up there on the reserve in Saskatchewan and the oil companies are going to be taking out the resources there. Some oil company from Calgary, I guess. They tried to take the oil out from off the reserve, but it wasn't possible. I guess they didn't want to pay the Indians for the oil; so I guess there will be a lot of rich Indians up there. Imagine, they gave the Indians the worst land when they made the reserves—land that was all brushy and poor, but now we have the best land . . . everyone wants it because of the oil. But what happens when there is no more oil to rape and disfigure in this land of ours. It

---

[14] Dancer: Traditional pow wow dancer; men's fancy dancer, men's traditional, grass dancer.
[15] Bustle: A circle of eagle feathers decorated with longer tail feathers and worn over the lower back of the body. The eagle is sacred; a powerful messinger spirit. In this way, the dancers honor the eagle.

makes me sick emotionally to think of the mining companies and the oil companies drilling for the sake of money.

Rocky Boy Reservation: Month of the Chokecherries

Rocky Boy Reservation is the smallest of the reservations in Montana, located on the north central plains. "Unlike other reservations, Rocky Boy was not established by treaty, but rather by an Executive Order in 1916" (Stone Child College, 1992). The land is accessible from the Highline or Highway 2 which crosses the northern tier of Montana. After passing the Bear Paw Mountains, the highway leading through Rocky Boy Reservation winds through the treeless plains, rocky foothills and prairies of north central Montana to the heart of the Agency[16] proper. Named for a Chippewa leader and translated from the Chippewa language, it was the last Indian Reservation to be established in Montana.

Teresa Standing Bear, a student at Salish Kootenai College, and a descendent of Chief Luther Standing Bear, told me the story from her grandmother of how the Bear Paw Mountains, which border the Rocky Boy Reservation, were named.

> The Great Bear, Ursa Major, came out of the sky and stepped on the North Central Plains of Montana. Now called the Bear Paw Mountains the Great Bear left its footprint at the entrance of the Rocky Boy Reservation.

On a relief map of Montana, the bear paw is easily discernible, but in ancient times it is a mystery how the ancestors knew the mountains were in the shape of the bear's paw.

The original bands of people who comprise the members of the Rocky Boy Reservation severed ties with tribes from the Great Lakes region and migrated to the northern plains. Composed of Chippewa and Cree peoples, they moved freely from Montana to Canada. Montanan's considered them to be Canadian Indian. In 1896, Congress appropriated monies to deport them back to Canada, but they returned to Montana (Stone Child College, 1992). Weary of a hand-to-mouth existence both leaders, Little

---

[16] Agency: The area of the reservation where the Indian Agent lived; today it is the site of government buildings on any reservation.

Bear and Rocky Boy, agreed to relocate on the land now known as Rocky Boy. Today, the members of this reservation are ranchers and dry land farmers and run small family-owned businesses. Keeping their traditional games and rich heritage is paramount to the members of this tribe.

For a community project in an Environmental Health course, Teresa Standing Bear incorporated the medical ecology model with the nursing process as an investigative technique on human health effects of open burning at the reservation dump. Applying content from the class regarding the health effects of dioxins and cancer incidence, Teresa began her work through a community assessment of cancer incidence [epidemiological data], clinical symptoms, ecological effects, and interviewing families who live adjacent to the dump [cultural data]. In her inventory of burnables in the dump, Teresa discovered that the municipality openly burns household refuse including plastics, newspapers, and other recyclables. The burning of plastics releases dioxin, a known carcinogen. Teresa documented more than 80 cases of cancers in families adjacent to the dump. By applying critical thinking skills and good assessment techniques, Teresa came to her diagnosis that open burning at the dump may be causal in cancer incidence. Teresa plans to expand and continue her research for an advanced degree in nursing.

Dioxin: Description and Effects

Dioxin, "the most toxic chemical on earth and an inadvertent by-product of twentieth-century life" (Colborn, 1996, p. 113), is a chemical contaminant formed during the synthesis of any product using chlorine, for example, in manufacturing pesticides or herbicides such as 2-4-D, wood preservatives, as well as bleaching paper. Dioxin is released in the burning of trash containing plastics and paper. Dioxin is generated by the chlorine content in the waste stream (smoke emissions) burned in medical and garbage incinerators.

Agent Orange of Vietnam fame contained dioxin and is carried with the herbicide wherever it is applied. Agent Orange was sprayed by the U.S. Air Force over thousands of acres in Vietnam to destroy crops and expose enemy lines. Power companies sprayed Agent Orange over power lines to inhibit the growth of vegetation. Native People who gathered wild berries under power lines became ill over time.

Another major source of dioxin emissions is the pulp and paper mills. Dioxin is formed when chlorine is used to bleach pulp or paper. Naturally occurring phenols in wood pulp react with chlorine to form dioxin. It does not readily break down in the environment but bioaccumulates in the food chain. This means that the human body accumulates dioxin.

Dioxin is a highly toxic estrogen mimic causing skin rash, liver cancer, shrinking of the thymus gland, and birth defects such as cleft palate or malformed limbs. Mutagenic to bacteria, dioxin also can damage the immune system, decrease the size of testes, and reduce sperm counts. It is felt that dioxin is one of the leading players among chemicals causing environmental cancers and causal in many breast and prostate cancers. The cancer rate was 50 percent higher for farm workers in the United States exposed to dioxin over two years, for instance, than in the general population (G. Lee, 1994).

Experiments with adult male rats confirmed that dioxin could have interfered with hormone levels in utero causing their testosterone levels to drop and their testes to shrink. As they matured, male rats born to mothers who were exposed to high levels of dioxin showed sperm counts reduced by as much as 40 percent. The male rats also demonstrated feminized sexual behavior in mating encounters. It was then concluded that dioxin interferes with the developing fetus' reproductive system (Colborn, 1996).

According to the EPA, 90 percent of human exposure to dioxin occurs through diet, with foods from animals being the predominant pathway. Animals are exposed to dioxin that settles on the soil, water, and plant surfaces. When ranchers use herbicides and graze cattle in the treated areas, cattle carry dioxin in their bodies. Soil deposits enter the animal when the animal eats plants or drinks the water. Humans take in dioxin from beef, other meats, fish, dairy, and eggs. Dioxin also enters the body through the lungs in areas of open burning dumps (Lester, 1995).

How Dioxin Affects Cells

When dioxin enters the cell, it binds to a protein called the Ah receptor, which is present in human liver, lung, lymph, and placental tissue. With another protein called ARNT, dioxin binds to the DNA in the cell nucleus activating the production of various proteins. The cluster of dioxin and the two proteins may cause genetic changes or DNA transcription errors that can result in cancer or proliferation of tissues. The proteins created through the dioxin-activated genes are believed to influence hormone metabolism and growth factors affecting reproduction and the immune system (G. Lee, 1994).

Continuing studies of humans exposed to synthetic chemicals mimicking estrogen point to increasing rates of testicular cancer, male genital defects, and suppressed sperm counts in humans (Colburn, et. al., 1997). Among animal species exposure to xenoestrogen (foreign estrogen) seems to be the cause of crossed bills in birds such as cormorants, loss of libido in male bald eagles, and clubbed feet, missing eyes or twisted bills in gull chicks. In male alligators, extremely small penises are attributed to exposure to synthetic chemicals mimicking estrogen (Colburn et al., 1997).

Marine mammals such as polar bears, seals, and whales seem to be the most affected. Persistant chemicals accumulate in top of the food chain predators and in the marine food web. Marine mammals carry heavy layers of fat and blubber, specific adaptions for warmth and reserve fuels. Chemicals such as dioxin and PCBs accumulate in their body fat. Researchers feel there is a strong correlation between the accumulation of chemicals in the fat of marine mammals and their decreased reproduction, high incidence of tumors, uterine dysfunction, and depressed immune systems.

Native People, such as the northern Inuit, Inupiaq, and Yupi'k, who depend on marine animals as a food source are at great risk. At the top of the marine food web, Native Peoples are ingesting the highest doses of contaminants ultimately affecting their health and the health of their children. PCBs have been found in the breast milk of Inuit women in northern Quebec at a level of 14.7 ppm (Colomeda, 1996; Lowell, 1990). Tolerable levels, according to the federal standards in Canada and in the United States, is 2 ppm. However, PCB levels have been found at 800 ppm in animals that live in the waters near the Mohawk Reservation in New York and in the fat of polar bears and whales worldwide.

Many Toxins Target Women Specifically. Women, rather than men, seem to be uniquely susceptible to toxins in the environment, including pesticides and lead which leads to seemingly unrelated medical problems from cancer to chronic fatigue as Rovner (1993) explains:

Although there are many principles of health research that are the same for males and females, there are special susceptibilities experienced by women (and children).

For the most part, these differences are attributed to the presence of estrogen and the physiological changes brought on by menstruation and menopause. Interaction of these factors with environmental toxins can lead to a range of disorders. For example, chemicals like polychlorinated biphenyls (PCBs), organochlorines (DDT), dioxin, and other industrial byproducts are xenoestrogens and all have estrogen-like activity. These toxins can replace natural estrogen in cells, stimulating the production of various hormones or blocking such hormones. The toxins often lodge in fatty tissue—such as the breast—where, over time, they can influence cellular function.

Estrogen targets specific sites in the female body including bones, brain, cardiovascular system, liver, skin, uterus, and vagina. Diseases related to estrogen exposure include breast and uterine disease, cancer, as well as endometriosis, fibroid tumors, premenstrual syndrome, and reproductive dysfunctions such as infertility or lactation suppression.

More than likely, open burning on Rocky Boy Reservation is not the only source of dioxin or organochlorines for the people who live there, but it is a significant factor contributing to poor environmental health.

NORTHERN CHEYENNE: DESCRIPTION AND HISTORY

Located in southeastern Montana, the Northern Cheyenne Reservation is 500,000 acres of beautiful Ponderosa Pine lands. After defeating Custer in the Battle of Little Big Horn, the Northern Cheyenne were taken as prisoners of war and marched off to Indian territory in what is now Oklahoma. Unused to the heat and humidity, while in Oklahoma many died of malaria and other diseases. Little Wolf, acting as spokesman for the tribe, approached the Indian agent: "We have come to ask the agent to send us home to our own country in the mountains. My people were raised there, in a land of pines and clear, cold rivers. There, we were always healthy, for there was enough meat for all. . . . This is not a good place for us . . . there is too much heat and not enough food" (Weist, 1977, p. 80).

Because the Indian agency refused to let the Cheyenne people leave, the Cheyenne sneaked out of the fort in Oklahoma to make their journey back north in the dark of an early September 1878. They would rather die fighting for their homeland than die of White man's disease as his prisoner. Leaving most of their belongings behind including horses, they had to march many hundreds of miles weakened by illness and hunger. Nevertheless they fled through snowstorms, through White ranches, and marauding army troops. Only a few hundred Cheyenne survived the walk north to Montana to Dull Knife's territory.

Little is known about the very early days of the Cheyenne people. The language is linked linguistically with the Algonquin groups of the Eastern Woodland tribes that stretched from Newfoundland to Hudson's Bay and North Carolina. When the Elders speak of these times, they begin by saying, "Before the Cheyenne had bows and arrows . . ." The people were fish eaters, using seines to trap a variety of species of fish living in the lakes of the Eastern Woodlands of North America. Nothing was wasted, even the bones were pounded into oil. Children and women gathered nuts, berries, roots, and wild fruits.

In the oral histories of the Cheyenne, the Elders tell of the tribe's population expansion and the southwest migration from the Great Lakes through the marshes of what is now Minnesota and southern Ontario. Here in the marshy areas, eggs were gathered in spring and water fowl composed much of the diet. It was here that they were able to tame young wolves and dogs to carry supplies. In the 1600s, changes came to the tribes. The Cheyenne learned to plant corn and settled down to become an agricultural people. Also by this time the people learned to make bows and arrows which helped the men to hunt animals as food sources.

Because of the fur trade and expansion by the Dakota Sioux tribes, the Cheyenne were pushed farther west and by the 1700s they were trading with the French fur traders for guns and ammunition. War-like tribes, Assiniboine and Cree, drove the Cheyenne westward once more and they settled in North Dakota where they lived for over a century hunting buffalo and deer and planting gardens of corn and squash. By 1750, the Cheyenne people tamed the horse and were transformed into legendary buffalo hunters and horsemen of the plains (Weist, 1977).

The Cheyenne demonstrated that they are a people possessing a strong will with the ability to adapt to countless changes, both in society

and with the land. When the Whites began expanding into the West, however, it was turmoil. Many tribes became war-like and aggressive. The
Cheyenne ability to adapt helped them to survive. In the north, Cheyenne
and Sioux became like one. Many Cheyenne spoke Sioux, adopted the
Sioux buckskin style of dress, and fought side-by-side with Sioux, Arapahoe, Oglalas, and Brules to preserve their way of life and the land. Even
today, many Cheyenne men and women live on Sioux Reservations and
have married Sioux people.

Under the Fort Laramie Treaty of 1868, the Great Sioux Reservation
was formed which ceded original lands, claimed by the Sioux, to the U.S.
government. Red Cloud of the Oglalas and Spotted Tail of the Brules
signed the treaty, but Crazy Horse of the Oglalas and Sitting Bull of the
Hunkpapas did not sign. Some Cheyenne people aligned with Crazy Horse
who did not sign the treaty, but other Cheyenne people, the Brules and
Arapahoe, lived on the Great Sioux Reservation. The Sacred Black Hills,
included in the reservation, was a place of religious significance where
people would go to pray, to fast, and hunt. Around 1872, White miners illegally went into the Black Hills and found gold. The government bought
the Black Hills under Indian protest, but the Northern Cheyenne never
took any money and are still fighting the government to give back those
sacred hills:

> Because of the narrow escape from Oklahoma and the long march
> northward to be with the Sioux in Red Cloud's territory, the Northern
> Cheyenne Reservation in eastern Montana represents the blood, sweat,
> and tears of our grandparents and the legacy of today's Northern
> Cheyenne. (Small, 1994)

*Coal Mining and the Northern Cheyenne: The Month of
the Chockcherries*

Gordon Fyant (Salish tribal member) is an avid motorcyclist. Everyone on
the reservation recognizes Gordon when he cruises up and down Highway
93 on the Flathead Reservation on his Honda motorcycle with 187,000
miles logged in. For years, Gordon worked for Montana Power Company
near the mine in Colestrip and raised his family on the Flathead Reservation, 500 miles away. During the week, he maintained a trailer in Colestrip

and on weekends he visited his wife and family on the Flathead Reservation. Like his brothers, he served in the U.S. Navy and traveled all over the globe only to be drawn home to his beloved Mission Mountains. Although not a member of the Northern Cheyenne, he knows much about the effects of coal mining near their reservation. Many of his friends from Colestrip worked in the mine. I interviewed him at the Arlee pow wow where he links to his culture through men's traditional dancing. His outfit is rich with the spirits of animals, eagles, and the history of the people. His unique breastplate is crafted of polished bones, adorned with red, gold, and black beads, the team colors of the San Francisco Forty-Niners, his primary sports passion.

Gordon Fyant, Salish Tribal Member, in Men's Traditional Dance Outfit. Arlee Pow Wow, Arlee, Montana 1997. Photo by the author.

This is a good story [of how I got to Colestrip, Montana, on the border of the Northern Cheyenne Reservation]. When we lived in Helena, I used to run back and forth to Arlee [Montana, on the Flathead Reservation] to get drunk, you know. This friend of mine was on the Tribal Council,[17] he owned a cafe down there in Arlee right across from the bowling ally. I came in early one morning about 8 AM because I needed a beer. So I bought one and I said, "John, I need a beer." And we was just standin' there talkin' cuz we were the only ones in there. And he says, how would you like to go to work? And being the smart ass that I am, I said, "Are you talkin' to me?" He says, "Ya, you're the only one in here." And I says to him, "Where am I goin' to work?" And he says, "Colestrip." I asked him, "Where in the hell is Colestrip?" So he got the map out and looked under the index. He said, "Here it is, clear on the other side of Billings."

While I was working in Helena, I was the maintenance guy for a 16-unit apartment. I was the janitor, I was the cop, I mowed lawns. I was making $500 a month, but $200 went back to rent. And she [my wife] was working at Colonial Inn.

So I went down to Colestrip to interview for the job and the guy kept asking me if I was an electrician and I kept telling him I wasn't. I wish I was because they were lookin' for electricians. I told him that I could only, well, I knew some things, but I wasn't an electrician, I was only an operator, but if I have questions, I'll surely go ask. So we visited for an hour about this job and a place to live. About six weeks later, I get this letter in the mail that I have to go see Dr. so 'n so in Helena for a physical. So I went over there for the job. Talk about a long ride; I didn't even know where I was goin'. In them days the road was like someone was followin' a cow trail. That was 1977. There was the interstate through, but not to Lame Deer or Colestrip. The highway was a beaten path; [it] looked like you could be followin' a cow or chasin' a snake.

So I go to work down there [for Montana Power]. I start out in somethin' they call a waste water concentrator. All the water that goes through the condenser is recycled to cool the condenser. And it goes through a cooling tower and all the acid that is mixed in there goes into the atmosphere with the steam. I ran that for about the first month I was there and they decided to put me somewhere else.

---

[17] Tribal Council: The governing body for the tribe. Led by the Council Chair. Similar to the U.S. Senate.

Then we had a three-year apprentice program, [with] 36 jobs . . . to learn about. Every night after work we had to study. We had a handbook, go to classes, take tests to work our way up in the three-year apprentice program. Talk about long and drawn out! Everybody worked together. Then I worked with water treatment, water quality. That consisted of doing the regen [regeneration] you know with two different kinds of resin that cleaned the water. The mine was a separate area. I had nothing to do with the mine. But before Three and Four [Generating plants from Montana Power that use coal from Colestrip to generate power] was built, everything that was hauled in [to the mine] was on a belly dumper. It all came in by belt. Everything was brought in by belt . . . into Western Energy Mines. But it was five miles from our department. During the construction of Three and Four, there was at least another 2,000 people there [in Colestrip]. They had trailer parks for everyone. Gail [my wife] was over there with me, too. We didn't move home [to the Flathead Reservation] until I went on 12-hour shifts. I began to commute after 5 years. I was over there for 18 years and 4½ months. We used to use Lame Deer IHS [on the Northern Cheyenne Reservation] for our medical. If it was out of their office like an operation or something, it came out of my pocket.

There's three mines over there along the highway and [when] you take the back road to Hardin you can see more mines. Them buckets [used to take the ore out of the mine shaft] could hold four cars. They were huge. It was an experience. The mine was jobs for the people in Lame Deer. When Power Plant One and Two were built, the Indians got priority over hiring. Same thing for mines Three and Four. The Northern Cheyenne have their own coal reserves over there on their reservation, but it is up to the Tribal Council if they are going to use it. The people don't want it.

I didn't see any health effects from the mine. The people work around coal and they are breathing it all the time. You have to wear a face mask and gloves, safety glasses. When I first went down there we didn't have all that—ear plugs or glasses—but after awhile people started to complain about it and things started happening right away. My father-in law, he's passed on now, but he worked for the mines [in Butte, Montana]. He died of a heart attack. He worked too hard.

The coal dust cloud . . . when you left Colestrip going north if you kept going on the back roads of the forest service to Round-Up, you could see that black cloud a mile up in the air . . . all black streak. It wasn't . . . well, it isn't coal dust, but smoke from the smoke stacks.

They had scrubbers. Which I'm not allowed to talk about because I signed an agreement paper about it. We lived a mile away [from the mine], but you could see the dust on your car. And if you parked right there it was worse. I didn't know of any kids with asthma, but Gail had skin allergies the whole time we lived there. She took Benedryl for years while we were there [18 years]. I never heard anyone complain about it. That cloud was never there all the time. It doesn't smell like the [effluent] cloud in Missoula at Stone Container. Over there everyone had their own cleaning areas that they tried to maintain the best they could, but there were days you couldn't keep anything clean because of the coal dust and with the wind blowing all the time and storms coming through. They had nozzles to spray the belts while the coal was coming through. But it is a pretty useless sytem. There is nothing they can do in the winter time [when the water freezes]. There were times it got bad, but I don't think it was all that bad as far as anybody's health. The mines border the reservation east, west, north, and I think there are mines, not big mines over near Broadus. I miss my friends over there. It is a strip mine, but they have to reclaim it. It is Western Energy, Peabody Coal. The traditional people in Lame Deer don't want the mining.

The coal company wants to build a railroad track right through the Reservation along the river. That is a big problem for the people on the Reservation. I know that everybody over there is fighting them. They were fighting ever since Colestrip existed. But the future is the future. We need the development. Montana has some of the best coal in the country. If they can take it out using safe mining practice, they are not hurting the people on the reservation.

Strip-mining coal companies surround the Northern Cheyenne Reservation. In the 1970s, the Bureau of Indian Affairs leased over half the Reservation to the coal companies. The Northern Cheyenne, who were poor to begin with, spent the last 15 years trying to reverse the decision. The Northern Cheyenne have refused extravagant offers from the coal companies while investing every penny they have in fighting legal battles against the coal companies. Tribal members have sacrificed their infrastructure to pay the legal fees (Small, 1994). In contrast, the Crow Reservation just adjacent to the Northern Cheyenne Reservation is turning a profit from coal mining and development.

As with other regions of the country, the environmental devastation reaped by the coal industry is varied. The mines have so thoroughly contaminated the air quality for the residents that respiratory disease and complications are extensive, especially among the elderly and the young. The second leading cause of ambulatory visits to IHS clinics for the people in Lame Deer and on the Crow Reservation, served by Billings Area IHS, is respiratory ailments, 11.1 percent in 1990–1992 (Trujillo, 1995, p. 86).

THE CROW RESERVATION: THE COLDEST MONTH

In the beginning, two ducks made the human race out of mud. . . . The only creatures on the Earth were the ducks and "the Old Man" (the Sun). The Old Man was the same as Old Man Coyote. The Old Man told the ducks to go to the middle of the water and dive for some mud. The Old Man Coyote, who is also the Sun, took the mud and began in the East. He proceeded to build the Earth, making it as large as he could. He made the buffalo, horses, and the rest of the animals. He made te-pees and people out of mud. He made a wife out of mud and Old Man Coyote and his wife made all the bows and arrows for the people. (Lowie, 1918)

Much like their Northern Cheyenne neighbors that share the Reservation boundary in Montana, the Crow tribe has its roots in the Eastern Wood-lands. In the middle of the 16th century, their ancestral tribe lived in a land called "land of the lakes." Anthropologists currently place the area in southern Manitoba. Originally called Apsaalooke, or "children of the large beaked bird," the Crow people were forced out of this land perhaps by hostile tribes or by the lure of better hunting grounds. When the Crow people moved to live among the Mandans of North Dakota, they planted tobacco, celebrated the Sun Dance, participated in sweats, and hunted buffalo. Theirs is a matriarchal culture where women are teachers, artists, and especially celebrated as caretakers of medicine bundles (Frey, 1987). It is from the women that we seek stories of environmental health and jus-tice concerning the coal mine on the Crow Reservation.

Several people from Crow Nation contributed to this section: Thanks to anonymous nurses, Lanette Walker, and others. The following excerpts are typical reactions to my inquiries:

The mining company has been here since I was in Junior High, maybe in the 1970s. I can see that the health effects are not that bad. The company has to reclaim the land when all the coal is gone. It is in the agreement. But everyone is worried that they won't plant the trees [when they're done]. The people really want the mine. I don't think there has been any water pollution, but I am not sure. Half of the tribe works in the mine. The tribe gets some money for leasing the land, but I don't know how much that is. There is a dispute with the state on taking state taxes out of the lease money.

The state of Montana has been taxing the Crows without authority for the sale of coal mined from the Crow Reservation. The Crow tribe has sued the state, and may be winning. If they win, over $58 million in principle and $250 million in interest is owed to the Crows. A considerable amount (60 percent) of the coal being mined in the state is on Crow land.

We haven't seen a lot of health effects in the people [general Reservation population] from the mining operations, but there has been an increase in upper respiratory diseases this year, especially among the old and the young. One of the miners came into the clinic and he was really having a hard time breathing.

I am working at Dull Knife College, but not in the environmental field, so I can't say anything about the mine, but I don't think the people see it as a bad thing.

Conclusion

In this chapter we have seen *Earth as Mother Principles* guiding the actions and behaviors of First Nations' people in Montana. To reiterate what was written in the previous chapters, I outline the following principles:

- The Earth is a living organism.
- Treat the human body with respect, just as the Earth should be treated with respect.
- The Earth is the giver of all life, food, shelter, and medicine.
- Land belongs to life and life belongs to the land.

- In order to maintain health, one must maintain the relationship with the Earth (Spector, 1991).

- In our religion, we look at Earth as a woman.

- She is the most important female to us because she keeps us alive.

- We are nursing off her (Mary Gopher, Ojibeway, 1993).

- We are all people of the Earth, the Mother Earth.

- We are made from Mother Earth and we go back to Mother Earth.

- We can't own Mother Earth.

- We're just visiting her. We're the Creator's guests (Leon Shenandoah, 1993).

Similar ideals guide other Indigenous and First Nations' people across North America and around the world from the Maori in New Zealand to the Yanomamo in Brazil. Only when non-Indigenous people subscribe to these values will environmental health be a reality and the Earth as Mother be safe. Apart from the obvious ethical implications involved, culture consumption of industrial societies is a direct result of Social Darwinism.[18] Old attitudes embedded in the culture of the Europeans were passed on to new descendents, now Americans, after the Treaty of Paris in 1783. Although resource exploitation and conflict over land rights are causes of destruction of tribal peoples and cultures affecting the health and well being of a people, it is the *attitude of ethnocentrism or believing that one's culture is superior to another's* which becomes the basis for forcing irrelevant standards upon tribal peoples (Brody, 1987).

Environmental Injustice: A Foundation

Why are environmental regulations vigorously enforced in some communities and not in others? Why are some workers protected from environmental threats while others, such as migrant farm workers, are allowed to be poisoned? The developmental effects of environmental contamination

---

[18] In Social Darwinism, the dominant culture considers the resources of another culture to be under-exploited and uses this philosophy as justification for appropriating them (Brody, 1990).

can be demonstrated in newborns or in the developing fetus; reproductive effects including low sperm counts in males or breast cancer in women can also be the result of environmental contamination. Other effects of environmental contamination include an increased incidence of asthma in children and neurotoxically derived psychological problems or developmental delay in children. But risk, which is usually defined as an "emphasis on . . . the probability of fatality," addresses only part of the health threats (Bullard, 1994).

Public and community health workers receive very little information regarding the magnitude of some of the problems related to pollution. Little has been done to eradicate lead poisoning in children, a preventable disease and primary environmental health threat (Agency for Toxic Substances and Disease Registry). Although phased out of gasoline in the 1970s, lead was removed initially to prevent damage to the catalytic converter in automobiles (Bullard, 1994). Many communities are still affected by unhealthy air, unsafe drinking water, dangerous chemicals, lead, pesticides and toxic wastes. People of color and especially American Indian people are strengthening their efforts against actions by government and private industry that compromise the quality of life in their communities.

First used by Reverend Benjamin Chavis, executive director of the Commission for Racial Justice at the people of color environmental summit held in Washington, DC, in October 1991, the term "environmental racism" now defines racial discrimination in environmental policymaking as "the enforcement of laws and regulations, the deliberate targeting of communities of color for toxic waste facilities, the official sanctioning of the life-threatening presence of poisons and pollutants in communities and the history of excluding people of color from leadership in the environmental movement" (Bullard, 1994, p. 278).

Reservations are Sovereign Nations. In their unique position, Reservations are not subject to state and local environmental restrictions. As a result, more and more Reservations are being seen and used as dump sites for toxic chemicals and nuclear waste by corporations and the federal government. Under the guise of "jobs" and economic development projects, Native People are being asked to choose between economic development and the preservation of the sacred soil.

Trends in Indian Health (Trujillo, 1995) demonstrates a rising cancer incidence among Native People. For men and women, the leading cause of death is heart related; women die more often than males from cancers while for men the second leading cause of death is motor vehicle accidents. Although higher among Indian people and Alaska Natives, homicide and suicide rates are declining. Chronic liver disease, said to be alcohol related, but in some instances the result of environmental contamination, and pneumonia and influenza are also leading causes of death among American Indians and Alaska Natives. Many of these leading causes of death could be the result of a compromised environment.

Beyond the borders of Montana, where tribal identity is strong, other First Nations are affected by environmental health issues leading toward environmental injustice. In the following chapters, I will address a selected number of problems in North America and globally. But make no mistake, the list is hardly exhaustive, there are hundreds more.

Chapter 4

RELATIONSHIP WITH THE LAND: NORTH AMERICA

When we show our respect for other living things, they respond
with respect for us.

Arapaho

*A*cross North America's reservations and reserves (Canada)
waste companies have targeted tribal lands for mining, dumping, and other activities affecting the health of First Nations'
people. This section reviews literature, case studies, and interviews from
First Nations' reservations and lands outside Montana which are compromised in issues of environmental health and justice.

I include in this section as well situations involving Indian people
from South Dakota and Oklahoma whose health is compromised by mining
and toxic wastes. I also discuss the environmental health issues of First
Nations' people in Northern Canada. Special focus is given to the Cree of
Northern Quebec, tribes in Northern Wisconsin, Michigan, and Minnesota
whose cultural identity is being eroded as this work is written. It begins
with the Lakota in South Dakota.

South Dakota: The Month of
the Huckleberries: Lakota

During the month of the huckleberries, I travel across the great divide to the plains of eastern South Dakota to meet with Indigenous Maori women from New Zealand who are guests of the Lakota. Sioux Falls is so green and humid compared with western Montana. Here on the High Plains are the sounds of summer, katydids chirping as they have since before people came. The evening sun a golden glow, we travel back one hundred years in time to an open field shielded from the rest of the world by low-growing scrub. The Drum greets us, the heartbeat of The People. Six drummers with open mouths sing songs to the Creator in their language. The friendship circle . . . we greet our hosts, the Lakota community of Vermilion, members of the Standing Rock Sioux. The Elders tell us of the history of their sweat lodge . . . "made of bent willow bark . . . the pit is set in the center of the womb . . . seven ancestor rocks heated from the sacred fire . . . we are in tears as we send prayers to the spirits . . . to our ancient ancestors . . . to all our relations . . ." The Maori are intrigued. We pray together to our grandfathers and cry when we think of all of the environmental injustices around the earth. (Journal entry, July 1996)

The Lakota, sometimes known as the Oglala Sioux or Dakota, once members of the Woodlands tribes around the Great Lakes area, were pushed westward for over 200 years by the militant Iroquois, the French fur trade, and other hostile Whites. By moving to the High Plains ecosystem from the Eastern Woodlands, each generation of Lakota made new adaptations for survival that impacted on their traditional woodlands culture (Steltenkamp, 1993). With the abundance of guns and horses, the Lakota fanned out over the High Plains in search of buffalo. In the perception of some historians, especially Viola (1994) and Hoxie and Josephy (1992), the culture of the High Plains tribes extended back to primordial eras; however, the Oglala Lakota only crossed the Missouri in 1775.

At the heart of tribal society for the Lakota is their kinship with everyone and their relatedness to the universe (Steltenkamp, 1993). The Lakota feel it is dreadful to be without relatives. The phrase *mitaku oyasin* (all my relations) is used throughout all gatherings. Hence, both the Maori and we were unofficially "adopted" as part of the Lakota concept of "all our relations." According to DeMaille (1979), the complexity of kinship relatedness is the heart of Lakota lifeways. One can be made a relative through a ceremony known as *hunkpapi,* a rite that conferres family status for an individual who is subsequently treated as a father, mother, son, daughter, sister, or brother (Steltenkamp, 1993).

The Lakota are the most poverty-stricken people in America with a per capita income about $300 per year (conversation with JoEllen Koerner). Issues of environmental health among the three Lakota Reservations—including Brule Sioux, Rosebud, and Pine Ridge—involve economic recovery, hunger, and substance abuse.

The Pine Ridge Reservation has a deep and rich history, but is probably most remembered for the massacre at Wounded Knee. Here, Chief Big Foot and 350 Lakota Sioux followers were massacred over a century ago. In the middle of winter, mostly women, children, and old men were set upon by the Seventh Cavalry in retaliation, some Whites say, for the Custer massacre at the Battle of the Greasy Grass [Little Big Horn]. Eighty miles from the graveyard of Wounded Knee, a Connecticut waste company has proposed exhuming the 90-year-old Good Road Cemetery on the Pine Ridge Reservation in South Dakota, then placing a 5,700-acre landfill underneath it and the surrounding lands and then returning the bodies and the tombstones (Ruben, 1991).

Russel Means, currently the director of the Colorado chapter of the American Indian Movement (AIM), is touted as the most famous American Indian leader since Sitting Bull or Crazy Horse. Means joined AIM in 1969. His name is familiar with the Walk in Freedom and 1973 seige on Wounded Knee. He speaks about one of many environmental issues affecting Lakota people:

> Right now today, we who live on the Pine Ridge Reservation are living on a lot of uranium deposits. White culture, not us, needs this uranium as energy production material. To get at the material, the cheapest way is to dump the waste products at the digging sites . . . The waste is radioactive and will make the entire region uninhabitable forever. . . . Along the way they plan to drain the water table under this part of South Dakota so that makes it doubly uninhabitable. (Means, 1988)

The Black Hills as an Issue of Environmental Health

The name Black Hills comes from the Lakota Sioux Indian words, *Paha Sapa,* which mean "hills that are black." Located in western South Dakota and eastern Wyoming, the Black Hills encompass rugged rock formations, canyons, gulches, open grassland parks, tumbling streams, deep blue lakes, and unique caves. Archeological evidence suggests the area was in use nearly 10,000 years ago. Known as a sacred place, Arapaho, Cheyenne, Kiowa, and Sioux Indian People sought visions and purification in the stillness of its many canyons. The Black Hills were also a sanctuary where tribes at war could meet in peace.

Forever guaranteed to be in the hands of the Lakota under the Fort Laramie Treaty, the Black Hills have never been ceded by treaty to the U.S. government. Mount Rushmore and the many tourist traps that surround it stand illegally on Lakota land. Although the U.S. government offered the Lakota $17.5 million plus $330 million interest, the Lakota people never formally accepted the offer.

Historically, fur traders explored the Black Hills and settlement of the area ensued rapidly. In 1874, George A. Custer wandered into the sacred Black Hills of the Lakota on a geological survey and found gold. Miners and prospectors soon followed, ignoring the treaty. "Custer's Last Stand," the Battle of the Little Big Horn, or the Battle of the Greasy Grass as it is known among the Lakota soon followed:

> In the words of Black Elk, the Lakotas and Cheyenne "painted their faces black"—went to war—to regain the Black Hills. The result was Custer's Last Stand, one of the best remembered debacles in U.S. history. (Grinde & Johansen, 1995, p. 204)

The U.S. government has always believed, however falsely, that they "bought" the Black Hills from the Lakota people. In American Indian lifeways, one cannot *buy* the Earth. The Native People thought that the government was paying to "use" the land, much as Indian people use the land. The fight for the return of Black Hills continues today.

Gold mining in the Black Hills, an ancient ceremonial site for many tribes including the Lakota,[1] has caused cyanide leaching and environmental problems similar to those seen in Montana on the Fort Belknap

---

[1] Lakota is the preferred term used today and is linguistically more precise although Sioux is still used. For years, anthropologists have lumped all of the people under the label Dakota. This term applies only to most eastern groups, further west were the Nakota; the Lakota were from the high plains. Sioux was actually an Iroquois word meaning "big serpents."

Reservation. Issues of cyanide poisoning in a sacred site makes the environmental desecration doubly painful.

Recently, gold mining companies want changes implementing less restrictive standards in water quality affecting streams in mining areas. The standards would allow higher levels of toxic heavy metals in the water than currently allowed in the rest of South Dakota. If biologists find there are few amphipods[2] in the water, nine toxic heavy metals and chemicals—specifically cyanide, cadmium, chromium, copper, zinc, lead, mercury, silver, and selenium—would be allowed to reach higher levels than in the rest of South Dakota (Mercer, 1997).

In 1977, uranium was discovered in the Black Hills. Ignoring the treaty rights of the Lakota Sioux, companies such as the Tennessee Valley Authority (TVA), Johns-Manville, American Copper, and others filed for certificates to mine the ore. Because the Black Hills is a watershed for much of western South Dakota, native people as well as local ranchers and farmers objected to slush mining[3] because it could contaminate the underground water on which farmers and ranchers rely.

Most AIM members suggest that mineral resources and especially uranium was a major factor in focused FBI attention on AIM activities in the late 1970s (Grinde & Johansen, 1995). Following the shooting deaths of two FBI agents during the occupation of Wounded Knee, the Pine Ridge Reservation became the focus of FBI activity. Whether coincidentally or not, FBI activities coincided with the uranium rush to the Black Hills and the activities of AIM. At the Fargo, North Dakota District Court, an AIM activist, Leonard Pelitier, was convicted, many believe unjustly, for the shooting just mentioned. Pelitier's view on environmental racism, however, has much truth to it:

In the late 19th century, land was stolen for economic reasons. . . .
Today, what was called worthless land suddenly became valuable as
the technology of White society advances. . . . [That society] would
like to push us off our reservations because beneath the barren land lie

---

[2] Amphipods: Crustaceans commonly found in streams. Amphipods provide food sources for newly hatched fish and are sensitive to heavy metals.
[3] Slush mining: Strip mining and underground mining in which a solution is injected into the ground to dissolve the uranium. The uranium-rich slush is then drawn to the surface.

valuable mineral resources. (Leonard Pelitier, 1976, statement at extradition hearing, Vancouver, BC, May 13)

Louise Schmidt: The Month of the Celebration Dances

Louise Schmidt, a member of the Rose Bud Sioux Tribe is 62 years old. From her outward appearance, she seems 10 years younger. Her hair is still dark and worn in a short bubble cut, her face unlined. Louise is the curator of a museum near the Reservation. She speaks of her early life on the Reservation in the well-articulated voice of a high school teacher.

I'm Louise Schmidt of the Rose Bud Sioux Reservation in South Dakota. When I was a young child, life was fun. It was hard times and good times And I remember all the good times. For some reason, I don't remember the bad times. I grew up north of Martinsville, South Dakota. There's a little place by the name of Hisel and I went to school at Holy Rosary Mission. I lived in Rapid City after that. The good memories are the times when I went to day school and would come home to my mom in the house, making bread and cooking bean soup. I just love bean soup and she would always have a kettle of bean soup and I remember my grandmother and my granddad. My granddad would put all the grandchildren around the potbellied stove after supper and read us the bible, tell us about the bible; every evening he would tell us about that devotion. We had rations during that time to get stockings and shoes. Some days they would give us prunes and raisins . . . they [also] gave us new shoes and socks. I went home that day and that night we all sat around the potbellied stove after supper for our family devotion. I kept putting my foot on the stove and granddad kept on reading, and he would say, "Louise, take your foot off the stove. You're going to burn your shoes." And I would take it away until he started reading again. [Then] I would put my shoe again up there, and the third time it burst into flames. Granddad put the book down and untied my shoe. They were high laced shoes and he untied it and threw the shoe outside and my shoe, my new shoe, was all curled up in a ball. I remember him telling me, "Experience is the best teacher." I never did forget that. I always remember that time. So that was one of the bad things, but I remember it.

My granddad loved his land, he took care of it. He had a few milk cows and he had a sod house, a barn, built into the hillside. He would

garden and plow up the garden. He took care of his place, . . . the place
we called home and he took care of it. He loved it. He leased part of it
to different people who lived around there, different farmers, you know.
But the part that he kept, he took care of it—and planted trees. It was
big land. Well, it seemed big to me. I was just a little kid though.

From what I see of my granddad and my grandmother, grandmother
always followed granddad. He was head of the family; We respected him
and did whatever he wanted us to do. We thought that everything he did
was right and good. She followed him. He was the leader. My grandmother, all of us, helped water it. They had a log house that my granddad built—we grew up in that area. I don't remember too much of my
mom and dad. I know when I was real little, but I remember she used to
cook and make us candy. But most of the time I was with my grandparents. I would be over there to their place. There were so many of us that
we kind of took over [the house]. There was 14 of us—6 of them died
real young, and now I only have one sister left.

I remember hunting. My dad bought my oldest brother a 22 [rifle] and
he would go hunting in the evenings. I don't know if you ever ate cottontail . . . they would bring [home] those small rabbits called cottontail and
my mother would clean them all up and put them in the roaster and roast
them, sometimes she made rabbit soup. They would go shoot pheasants,
bring them home and we ate fried pheasants. My mom saved the feathers
and made little crafts things out of them. I remember she glued pheasant
feathers onto a hat she always wore. She made a pretty design on it. Then
we had Prairie Chicken or grouse. Oh, we just thought that gun was the
best because he brought stuff home to eat with it, you know. So when
Christmas came, we would all save our money and buy him a box of 22
shells, so he could go get more pheasants and rabbits for us to eat. That
is one of the best memories. I enjoyed the guns that way. I don't recall
him bringing any deer home. He could have, later in the year, but I don't
remember it. We went fishing a lot. My grandfather used safety pins and
made hooks from safety pins, and we went fishing. We caught sunfish
mostly and granddad cooked them and made them good. I remember all
those times. I remember in the Fall after the garden was all ripe and
everything, we used a big stone, a big flat stone, and my grandmother
would pound the chokecherries that we picked and pound them into little
cakes and she would dry them. That is what we had to eat for the next
winter and fall. She did the same with corn—because they planted a lot
of sweet corn, and that's what we did. We took the corn off of the cob,

dried that corn, and the following winter they put the corn into the soup. They made *Wojapie* out of the chokecherries.

I remember having cattle and planting the garden. The neighbors came over and they cut hay and piled it up with a dump rake, and they had horses tied up to it. They used one horse to pull the plow and they had one person to push the plow. I remember that. We used to sit on the harrow so they could level the ground to plant potatoes. That's the only thing I remember about the land.

I remember the sprayers coming to spray the wheat [with pesticides]—you had to cover all the house plants and the tomatoes. It would kill the tomatoes . . . so we used to cover all the outdoor plants before the sprayers came. And they fertilized the places where the plants grew. That wasn't way back though.

There is one corporation that is a big farmer and from what I hear eventually the people say that all the little farmers will be gone and the big corporations will take over.

I am not too familiar with the term *environmental justice*. I think most people around here own some land somewhere and they care for the land. They lease some land. I think everybody around here is cautious about what they do with the land. I don't know anything about mining. I have no idea about mining. I have never been into the Black Hills to look at the mining.

One of the environmental injustices affecting the tribe is the guy [a tribal member] who has the trash dumps. We have a landfill and people don't use it properly and the trash blows around the whole area here, especially toward the Mission along the fence. There has to be better ways to deal with the trash around here. We had someone from the outside trying to dump their trash . . . out toward the west here. Someone from the outside from Chicago—had land that he dug up and he let all these people dump their trash there from the city. They found a lot of syringes and rubber gloves. It was on the reservation. He got fined. They made money in using the land to bury waste. I don't like that. It brings in pollution and sicknesses; they need to get rid of that the right way [but] it comes out in the ground water. But I don't know too much about that. I wouldn't want a big hole dug in my land and have people come and dump in it! If they keep doing the landfill, things will get worse and people will come in from the cities and get rid of their waste.

The tribe is trying to clean up and keep people out, but in a lot of places people will go through the dump to see if there is anything they can use. I think whatever is thrown away should stay there. Because we might get some kind of sickness or disease from it. I can't tell people not to do it, because they have their own ideas—I can't tell people what to do. I think our land should be like our own bodies—we should take care of the land like we take care of ourselves.

I don't think the very young generation has any respect for anything. They go out and shoot at road signs and stop signs and they go running over the stop signs and all that. I don't think they have any respect, but maybe it is only some of them. They should have been taught more re-spect growing up. That is what is so hard to believe. I see some of the kids running around until after midnight like they don't have any par-ents. I blame the kids and the parents for this. Parents are supposed to teach their children; the children [should] have respect for the parents, [children] are supposed to learn from them. It is hard to say now-a-days. It is scary. I think it is too much freedom; the kids don't finish school and they go on to do what they want. Maybe they don't care. When I was growing up, I cared about things. And my kids—the same way. I think it should come from the parents to tell them to take care of what they have.

The culture years ago was good. The older people, they have more respect because we were taught to respect our Elders and obey our par-ents and if parents involve their kids in things . . . I think it was all lost somewhere down the line. The older people took care of their land, fam-ily, relatives, and everything. They took care of each other. I think kids stayed out of trouble because the kids were with the family . . . not with everyone going in all different directions.

Yankton Sioux Tribe

All over the world, among Indigenous and non-Indigenous people, cancer rates are soaring. We are seeing an increase in immune supression diseases such as diabetes, non-Hodgkins lymphoma, and breast cancer. Scientists and researchers believe that such diseases are the result of increased use of agricultural pesticides and biocides coupled with increased toxic contami-nation (Abzug, 1997). Charon Asteyor, a member of the Comanche Tribe liv-ing in south Dakota on the Yankton Sioux Reservation, is also executive director of the Native American Woman's Health Resource Center and a delegate to the United Nations in Geneva for Indigenous nations. The following are highlights from her presentation at the World Breast Cancer Conference:

- The Yankton Sioux have the largest concentration of Intercontinental Ballistic Missiles (ICBMs) in the United States.
- The Reservation has been the target of toxic wastes from multinational corporations that promised the people jobs and economic development. The case is up before the Supreme Court in Washington, DC, to return 848,000 acres back to the tribe. We want the 1848 Treaty upheld. The EPA [also] is partnering with the tribe to govern toxic waste into reservations.
- We are seeing an increase in cancers.
- The IHS in the Aberdeen Area, which is in the service unit for the tribe, has reported the highest mortality rates for cervical and breast cancer: 18.3 percent for breast cancer and 15.3 percent for cervical cancer (Trujillo, 1995).
- We have open burning in the landfills on the reservation. The stream passes through the landfill on its way to the Missouri River where our intake valve for drinking water is. The landfill contains acid and lead from batteries [among other things].
- In addition, all people are victims of spraying and crop dusting by air.
- The farmers who spray and wash out their pesticide containers near the wells that people use for drinking and the pesticides gets into the ground water increasing the contamination.

Oklahoma: Indian Territory: The Month of Popping Trees

To provide more arable land for settlers in a young United States, President Jackson initiated the Indian Removal Act of 1830. The new law ordered the five civilized tribes—Creeks, Chickasaws, Choctaws, Cherokees, and Seminoles—removed from their homelands in Georgia, Mississippi, Alabama, and Florida into an alien land now known as Oklahoma. It is a featureless, desolate land, dusty, arid, and unkind. The peaceable Choctaws were the first to move to the new Indian territory. Many died from hardships, but many also died of heartbreak:

One observer noticed that many of them reached out and touched the trunks of the trees before they turned away on their journey . . . the wailing of the women as they sat in groups with their children, their heads covered with blankets, their bodies swaying, and their cries rising and falling in unison. (Debo, 1983, p. 119)

The Creek Nation was the next to be removed. Many Creek escaped to their friends, the Cherokees, but in the end they were hunted down by the military and dragged off to Oklahoma:

Those who survived remember . . . . Many fell by the wayside, too faint or too weak to keep up . . . only a bowl of water was left within reach and these fragile ones, the Elders, were left to die alone. When they finally reached their destination, 45 percent of the tribe was lost. (Debo, 1983, p. 120)

Well educated in the ways of the Whites, the Cherokees under John Ross fought for their homelands with all the resources of their learning. But in the end, they, too, were removed like cattle to Oklahoma. Whites who were there note:

I saw the helpless Cherokees arrested and dragged from their homes, and driven by bayonet into the stockades. In the chill of a drizzling rain one October morning I saw them loaded like cattle or sheep into wagons and started toward the west. (Debo, 1983, p. 125)

Under the Indian Removal Act, other eastern tribes were targeted for removal to Oklahoma's Indian territory, among them Florida Seminoles. Guided by the wisdom of Chief Osceola, many hid out in the Everglades only to be hunted down with bloodhounds by the army and navy. Many Seminoles were found and brought home in chains. . . . Eventually, they too were shipped out to Oklahoma Territory. "(T)transported to a cold climate, naked, without game to hunt, fields to plants or huts to cover their little children" (Debo, 1983, p. 127).

Oklahoma Today

Once oil was discovered in Oklahoma, the government meant to seize the land from Native Peoples. Although only a tiny Reservation on the border of Arkansas remains in Oklahoma today, the state boasts the highest Indian population of any state in the United States.

Members of the Cherokee Nation in Oklahoma, where unemployment and poverty levels are two to three times higher than for non-Indians, were employed by Sequoyah Fuels until 1992. Ruben (1993) states that it is the most harmful employer in Vian and nearby Tahlequah. The company crushed uranium into a fine powder and processed uranium fuels for bombs and nuclear reactors. The plant also produced the prime ingredient for the dense and slightly radioactive uranium used to make armor-piercing bullets and shells. Receiving 50 percent of its uranium from Saskatchewan (Penna, 1992), the company was cited with over 21,000 violations during its 21-year history (Ruben, 1993), including the release of toxic gas causing 34 people to seek medical attention (Lord, 1992). Because of many years of sloppy operations, there are 21,000 pounds of uranium in the groundwater surrounding the plant (Penna, 1992). Mutant frogs have been discovered near the plant where the company disposed of thousands of tons of toxic and radioactive waste by calling it "fertilizers." The facility operated without proper licenses for the past several years (Penna, 1992). Lance Hughes from American Indians for a Clean Environment helped to shut down the operation in November 1992 (Ruben, 1993). A comprehensive report concerning the health of the workers at Sequoyah Falls is unavailable at this writing; however, data from the Indian Health Service Unit serving Oklahoma states will be noted. In addition, a health survey conducted in the community demonstrated that 50 percent of the people living near the facility has some form of cancer (Penna, 1992).

Health Effects of Uranium

An in-depth discussion concerning the health effects of uranium can be found in further chapters focusing on Navajo, Athabascan, and Sami people. As recently as the 1930s, scientists and healthcare workers linked the high incidence of lung cancer in European miners to uranium. After 1949, scientific evidence confirmed that link. A by-product of uranium decay into radium is highly carcinogenic radon gas. Depending on the length and levels of exposure to any radioactive materials, cancers, birth defects, and sterilization of the reproductive system can result. Data reported from the

Oklahoma IHS service unit list age-adjusted mortality rates from malignant neoplasms at 76.9 percent for the years 1990–1992 and the second
leading cause of infant death as congenital anomalies at 22.2 percent (Trujillo, 1995, pp. 65, 41):

> not only is cancer caused by radiation . . . also genetic mutations . . .
> are caused right down to the lowest levels. It is now confirmed . . . by
> the scientific community that mental retardation is caused by radiation
> in the womb, and this seems to be also linear, [or] proportional to dose,
> right down to the lowest levels. There doesn't seem to be any cut-off
> point. And so, we have now discovered yet a third category of docu-
> mented and scientifically accepted harmful effects of radiation and that
> is mental retardation in children who are irradiated while still in the
> womb. (Edwards, 1992, paper presented at the World Uranium Hear-
> ing, Salzburg)

The Kiowa Nation

> Sayday, the Kiowa culture hero, wandered alone on the sunless Earth
> until he discovered the Kiowas living underground. He enabled the
> people as ants to crawl upward through a hollow cottonwood tree and
> pulled them through a Saw-pole's (owl) hole upon the darkened face of
> the Earth. (Boyd, 1983)

If, as archeologists believe, the Kiowa are descended from Asians who
crossed the ice bridge from Siberia to Alaska, tribal memory, oral history,
and Kiowa myth contain huge gaps of knowledge about this event. For the
most part, Kiowa scholars suggest a link between the Athabascans of
Canada, the Canadian Rockies, and the relationships with tribal people
along the Saskatchewan River (Boyd, 1983). By the 1600s, when the tribe
settled in Montana near the headwaters of the Yellowstone and the Missouri Rivers, locations become more specific:

> There is a Kiowa legend that in the old days when the Kiowa lived in
> the North, they were a large tribe. A quarrel arose with the band chiefs,
> and the tribe separated, one group remaining in the north; the other, the
> group that called themselves the Kiowa, traveling south. The Old
> Kiowas think the other band may have been the Crows although they

recognize the difference between their own language and customs and that of the northern tribe. (Marriott, 1977, p. viii)

Originally calling themselves the "coming out" or the "pulling out" people, Kiowa creation myths begin at a time when their oral history depicts a great flood followed by a drying of the Earth, destruction of the spruce forests, climate changes, and migration to the Great Plains (Wunder, 1989).

Long ago the Spirit Powers unleashed a mighty deluge upon the Earth. The four winds blew, the rain fell in torrents for days, and the rivers and seas broke their bonds. All living things were swept away by the flood that engulfed the land. Only Grandmother Spider survived on top of the waters, for she was light and she could float. (Boyd, 1983)

When the Sioux pushed the Kiowa out of the Black Hills area, their migrating companions were the Kiowa-Apache, who were neither Kiowa nor Apache, but Athabascans from Canada. As they left the mountains of the Yellowstone Region, their Crow friends introduced them to the Sun Dance and to the nomadic horse-buffalo culture of the plains. Before the latter part of the 1600s, Kiowa history describes tipis made of buffalo hides and elk, buffalo, and antelopes as food and clothing animals, but they had since to evolve the traditions and ceremonies that combined the horse with the buffalo. Eventually, the territories of the Kiowa wanderings included the Great Plains south to the Rio Grande, Mexico, where they traded for horses.

In 1865 after the Civil War, the U.S. government developed a policy of removing Indians from their traditional lands. The Kiowa chief, Dohasan, along with Kicking Bird, Lone Wolf, Satanta, Heap-of-Bears, and Stumbling Bear, the chiefs of the plains tribes, signed the treaty agreeing to relinquish raids on New Mexico, Colorado, and Kansas and move to Oklahoma Territory where the U.S. government had set aside lands specifically for Indians. From Oklahoma, the tribes continued to hunt buffalo and carry out raids on Texas territories (Boyd, 1983).

By the summer of 1879, not a buffalo could be found on the southern plains to sacrifice for the Sun Dance Ceremony. The Kiowa ate their horses to prevent starvation. With the glory days of the horse and buffalo culture ended, the tribe became more dependent on the government for food. Denied access to their hunting grounds and barred from their religious ceremonies, the Kiowa lost their self-esteem. To make matters worse for the Kiowa, in 1892 the Jerome Agreement was reluctantly signed allowing them to sell their "surplus lands" to the government for $1.25 an acre and to accept allotments of 160 acres per person. Much like the plight of the Salish and Kootenai Tribes of the Flathead Reservation in Montana, the lands not taken up in allotments were opened to White settlement (Boyd, 1983).

In all treaty agreements with Indian people, the government agreed to provide rations of flour, beans, clothing material, bacon, coffee, and sugar. However, as among other tribes who signed treaties with the federal government, food was not always available and many Indian people died of starvation in a land of empty promises.

HEALTH EFFECTS FROM HYDROCARBONS

Millions of years ago, plants in the primeval forests capitalized on their chloroplasts[4] by capturing sunlight energy in the biological process known as photosynthesis. Over time, geological forces and volcanic action brought changes to these ancient forests, trees, and plants. During the orogenic[5] process, forces thrust forest plants underground, deep underground, where their rich energy sources from the sun were converted by geological pressures into coal, gas, and oil, the fossil fuels we recognize today.

Hydrocarbon molecules are released in the burning of fossil fuels. As hydrocarbon molecules are released into the surrounding air, they can be carried across the land, falling at last into the water to contaminate entire ecosystems. Hydrocarbons are also released into surrounding ecosystems by oil spills. The world has documented massive oil spills in recent times such as the Exxon Valdez off the coast of Prince William Sound in Alaska, in the North Sea, off the coast of New England, and recently off the coast of Japan. Today, the health effects from hydrocarbons leaking into the ground water from an abandoned APCO refinery are cause for

---

[4] Chloroplasts: Plant cells containing chlorophyll.
[5] Orogenic: Mountain building.

oppression among the Kiowa Nation in Oklahoma. William Hensley, environmental water specialist, states that the company has been in operation since 1920 and closed down in 1984 in bankruptcy. Presently, the refinery site is designated as a Super Fund[6] site by the EPA. Indian families living along Lady Creek near the refinery are drinking water from wells contaminated by hydrocarbons. The chemicals' spill off means the contamination is carried by these waters to fishermen and recreation swimmers in the creek. The hydrocarbon contamination is well-known and has been contaminating water over several years. But by April 1997, months after it was designated as a Super Fund site, nothing has been done to remedy the situation. Although there is a dearth of information concerning the documented health effects of hydrocarbon or petroleum ingestion on humans, ingestion of hydrocarbons released from the Exxon Valdez were causal in reproductive disorders such as decreased egg shell thickness and strength. Through external contact, pneumonia and respiratory distress in sea birds and sea otters off the coast of Alaska were also reported Stubblefield, Hancock, Ford, Prince, & Ringer, 1995). Oceanographers have estimated that 700,000 tons of petroleum tar are floating on the world's oceans, with their principal sources contaminating water from river run off (Scheffer, 1991).

Recently, illegal trash dumping has become problematic for the Kiowa. William Hensley, water quality specialist for the tribe, describes the situation, "Everything is in there. Paint cans, Clorox bottles, empty pesticide containers. And all this is sitting in the creek. Even the cattle are drinking it and being contaminated." Hensley is concerned that people will eat the contaminated cattle meat.

The Kiowa also fear a similar situation will occur on their land as it did at Love Canal, New York, in the 1970s. Mentally retarded children were being born to families living adjacent to the polluted canal, pregnant women miscarried at a rate far above normal, and newborns had a greater number of birth defects such as abnormal hearts and kidneys (Scheffer, 1991).

In 1976, *hazardous waste* was defined by federal law as solid waste that may contribute to serious illness or death or pose a threat when

---

[6] Super Fund site: Congress enacted legislation on hazardous waste sites in 1980 when it passed the Comprehensive Response, Compensation and Liability Act (CERCLA) known as Super Fund (Steingraber, 1997, p. 293).

improperly managed (Scheffer, 1991). In 1978, then-Congressman Al Gore noted that hazardous waste may be the most significant health issue of the decade (Scheffer, 1991). Seventy-one percent of hazardous waste is generated by chemical and petroleum industries, with metal industries generating 22 percent (Scheffer, 1991).

The tribes, however, are collaborating with Indians and non-Indians to develop a waste management plan that includes a recycling center and transfer station. The state of Oklahoma has tied up the process in red tape, but as a sovereign nation the Kiowa does not fall under state but only federal jurisdiction. It is through the efforts of the EPA that the contamination will hopefully and eventually get cleaned up.

GREAT LAKES, UNITED STATES, AND CANADA:
ANISHINABE NATION

The Ojibwe people of the Great Lakes region are known also as Ojibway, Chippewa, or Anishinabe, and are known to the Europeans as Eastern Woodlands Indians. Among the Ojibwe people, health is a most important aspect of spirituality. Health, to the Ojibwe people, is a gift from the spirits and dependent upon a personal relationship of harmony with the natural world. For this reason, humans must constantly ask the spirits for help. The Ojibwe people embrace the Medicine Wheel as a resource for health and balance. Health is promoted through balance in the Medicine Wheel and by living "The Indian Way"—by expressing respect for all living things, by participating in ceremonies, by sweating, fasting, and offerings of tobacco. By "Good Medicine," the Ojibwe maintain their spirituality, their relationship with the natural world and their health (Turton, 1997).

Morning mist shrouds the outlines of ghostly pines laced with hoarfrost. Pale pinks blush on a horizon where water meets sky. Wavelets lap at black smooth rocks. Loons cry their high pitched "woooowooooowooooowooo," claiming this portion of the lake for themselves. Farther on in the meadow, a pale dawn adds color to fall leaves laced with frost crystals. Autumn has embraced the land. Above the water, on the trestle of the railroad, Native People in traditional outfits gather around the drum for celebration. Dressed in the powerful spirits of animals, eagle feathers, and colors of the dawn, jingle dress dancers and the people give thanks to the Creator for this day, for this land.

In July of 1996, The Bad River Band in Odanah, Wisconsin, set up their drum (the heart beat of the people) on the tracks of an active railroad to stop the transportation of sulfuric acid across their reservation. Members of the Indian and non-Indian community questioned the safety of the tracks and the decision of the EPA and Michigan's Department of Environmental Quality to issue permits to Copper Range mining for a mining project. In their effort to leach out the remaining copper ore, the project plans included an injection of 11 billion gallons of sulfuric acid solution over a 20-year period into a 25-square mile underground copper mine five miles from Lake Superior. The process had never been used before (http://www.alphacdc.com/treaty).

Previous mining activity had ruptured a salt water aquifer, with the flowing water to fill the mine in 30 to 50 years. The toxic salt water will eventually flow out of the mine into the mineral river and into Lake Superior. Chief of the Band, Mr. Wilmer, states that it is environmental blackmail. The train tracks in question lie along wild rice beds that the Indian people depend on as a food substance. If one of the trestles collapses in the spring when the river is flowing fast, the rice beds in the 16,000 acre sloughs would be wiped out in 12 hours; fish in the spawning areas would be decimated. If a spill occurs when the river is flowing slowly, all life along the river would be destroyed (Morrison, 1996a).

The tracks, winding through some of the most pristine wetlands in Wisconsin, have been ruled unfit for passenger trains, but officials feel they are safe for transporting 550 million gallons of sulfuric acid. In 1996, a tribal attorney walking the tracks pulled one of the spikes out of the tracks by hand (Morrison, 1996a).

As a result of public and legal pressure, in October of 1996 the EPA announced that it would make a full environmental assessment of the mining project. The tribe continues to fight and seek support from Congress for the right to be involved in decisions concerning the shipment of hazardous wastes across its reservation (Morrison, 1996b).

Threats to American Indian cultures in Wisconsin, Michigan, and Minnesota are inseparable from environmental racism. The Chippewa, together with other Indian nations in northern Wisconsin, suffer from environmental risk of illness and other health problems from eating fish, deer, and other wildlife contaminated with industrial pollutants such as airborne polychlorinated biphenyls (PCBs), mercury, and other toxins deposited on land and water.

In ancient times, First Nations' people and animals spoke the same language and the stories shared by them were part of the natural fabric of life. Today, animals in the wild are accumulating high amounts of toxic chemicals posing substantial health, ecological, and cultural risks to American Indian populations who rely heavily on local fish, plants, and game for subsistence.

"We have had a lot of trouble with spraying," said Betty Riffel, Waubauskang Reserve, Ontario (Native Canadian Ojibwe). Aerial spraying of herbicides and pesticides in forest areas is a practice both in the United States and Canada. Defoliants and pesticides are used to increase the size of tree growth. Spraying occurs in the same areas as berry picking and plant gathering. Often there is no communication between pickers and sprayers (Mino-Bimadiziwin, 1993). "We went over to this spot where the government said they would not spray. We went to pick cranberries in an area and there was a big sign saying that they sprayed it already." Immediately after the spraying of herbicides, the berries appear normal, but they are not.

Chemicals used for spraying include 2-4-D or a variation that is mixed with diesel fuel as a propellant. Roundup and Vision herbicides are also used in Canada and in the U.S. (Mino-Bimadiziwin, 1993). 2-4-D and 2-4-5-T are the primary chemicals in Agent Orange, the military's name for the defoliant used to strip away the canopy of the rain forest in Vietnam. From 1962 to 1971, the U.S. military dumped more than 19 million gallons of Agent Orange over 3.6 million acres in Vietnam (Colburn, et. al., 1997). 2-4-5-T is easily contaminated with dioxin during its manufacture (Colburn, 1996). At the height of the Vietnam War, Agent Orange was sprayed from planes, helicopters, boats, jeeps, trucks, and on foot with backpack sprayers. Health effects include dizziness, skin rashes, genetic mutations of offspring, soft tissue carcinoma, and Hodgkins and non-Hodgkins [lymphoma] disease. Today, 2-4-D continues to be sprayed throughout our farms and on suburban lawns.

Vietnam veterans have a high incidence of non-Hodgkins lymphoma as do farmers in Canada, Nebraska, and Kansas who use 2-4-D as a weed killer, and which is marketed under names like Ded-Weed, Lawn Keep, Weedone, Miracle, Plantguard, or Demise (Steingraber, 1997). Dogs also acquire lymphoma from 2-4-D. As studies have shown, dogs living in households whose lawns were treated with 2-4-D were more often diagnosed with lymphoma than dogs whose owners did not use weed killers (Steingraber, 1997). "By 1960, 2-4-D accounted for half of all U.S. herbicide production. Current annual use of pesticides in the U.S. is estimated at 2.23 billion pounds" (Steingraber, 1997, p. 95).

As Reiffel, Williams, and Peliquan (1993) continues: "It is a constant race to keep ahead of the aerial spraying in order to pick berries only in areas that are not sprayed."

> Several studies have linked childhood cancers to . . . pesticide use. Childhood cancer in Los Angeles was found to be associated with parental exposure to pesticides during pregnancy or nursing. In a 1995 study in Denver, children whose yards were treated with pesticides were four times as likely to have soft tissue cancers than children living in households that did not use yard chemicals [pesticides]. (Steingraber, 1997, p. 96)

In the Bemidji IHS Service Unit, which is the service unit for the tribe, I also found that the age-adjusted mortality rate for malignant neoplasms is 164.3 per 100,000 (Trujillo, 1995).

Eighty-six percent of Sokaogon Chippewa families rely on hunting and fishing for food, and over 90 percent rely on gardening, ricing, and picking wild plants. For Indian people, natural resource harvest is more than a means to provide food; harvesting rice or other plants are cultural activities that renew the spirit, bringing Indians closer to ancient relatives and ways. The Wisconsin Department of Natural Resources has noted the centrality of wild rice to Chippewa culture in their analysis of Exxon's proposed mine: Rice Lake and the bounty of the lake's harvest lie at the center of their identity as a people . . . . The rice and the lake are the major link between themselves, Mother Earth, their ancestors, and future generations.

> The knowledge of the forest is still here. With the right approach it will come back through ceremonies, but when the forest is cut down even with ceremonies, it will be all gone. I think the lack of respect for the

environment must worry some of the people. (Tom Stillday, interview, 1993)

Threats are not new to the region. Just recently, the White Pine, Michigan, smelter, operated by the Copper Range Company, agreed to a multimillion dollar settlement in an air pollution lawsuit. The smelter was emitting mercury, lead, and arsenic over the waters of nearby Lake Superior at five times the legal limit. These emissions were seen by the Lake Superior Tribes as a direct threat to their treaty rights to enjoy consumption of uncontaminated fish.

Mining adjacent to all reservations or Indian homelands continues to have a disproportionately negative impact on tribal lands and cultures. For example, the Indian people of Mole Lake Reservation (formed in 1939) are the prime harvesters of wild rice in Wisconsin. The objective for development of Mole Lake Reservation is to guarantee forever the Sokaogon's control of the aquatic resources of Rice Lake, its clean water, fish, waterfowl, and, most important, its wild rice. The Exxon/Rio Algom proposed mine, immediately adjacent to the Mole Lake Reservation, is still in the permitting process; the pre-mining operation has already threatened important Reservation water resources: "As a result of ground water discharges by Exxon Minerals Company to Duck Lake in the early 1980s, the lake's water chemistry was altered. A state threatened species of pond weed, which was found in the lake before the discharges, has not been found there since."

Mole Lake Chippewa leaders fear that Exxon's extensive ground water pump tests in the area may have already affected the flow of water into Rice Lake and be partly to blame for the failure of the 1995 rice harvest.

Ojibwe Nation, Canada: Month of the Celebration Dances

She greets me in her native language, *"Ahnee Boozhoo. Geezheptot ndizhnikaaz. Wagasteiniga ndoonjbaa. Mulewa dodem."* We sit on the steps of the university. She is a modern Ojibwe woman, articulate in two cultures, dressed in shorts and Docksider shoes. We meet in Canada at the World Breast Cancer Conference. Her knowledge and openness are impressive. I look into her face and see my own face as a young graduate student. We share a similar name.

My name is Lorrilee McGregor. I'm from the White Fish River First Nation in Ontario. I am from the Bear Clan. I went to the University of Toronto for Environmental Studies and I am currently doing a master's degree with Antioch [at a distance] in Ohio. The program at Antioch allows me to do my work at home and to go down to the university a couple of times a year. I didn't really want to move away from home. I live in the Province of Ontario—there are about 130 First Nations' communities in Ontario. In the area [where] I live, there are seven First Nations' communities on Manitoulin Island with another fourteen in the area [as a whole]. Most of the Reserves are very small with a population from, say, 40 people living on the Reserve to a couple of hundred. There are several larger communities that have populations of a thousand or so. The Reserves generally have a fairly large land base depending on which Reserve, but people tend to be clustered in communities, just because it is easier to build sewage infrastructure that way. So clustered—we never lived like that before. There are unusual pressures [on us] because of that. We never lived in each other's backyard, so closely. In my area, the Treaties were signed to set up the Reserves in order to preserve the land and to ensure we had a home. The Robinson-Huron Treaty was signed in 1850. Prior to that, in 1836, the Lieutenant Governor of Upper Canada, Sir Francis Bond Head, had initially designated Manitoulin Island as a big Reserve. He wanted everybody to go there—basically to get everyone out of the way. Plus, he wanted all the lands people were living on, especially in Bruce Peninsula, which is rich agricultural land. He wanted people out of there so that White people could move in. His plan didn't work. Some people did move in there but people didn't go for his big idea. But as time went on and as settlers came in and were squatting everywhere, people realized they had to save their land. They tried to preserve it. They asked for treaties to be made, so they could set aside lands for people . . . [to] use our land like we always used our land. We had [the] Potawatami [tribe] who came up from the States [during the Indian removal in the States]. Actually, my grandmother is Potawatami.

People lived in fairly small groups generally through the winter. They lived in family units. In the summer time, when people got together for particular fishing sites, that's when larger groups of people would get together—people did have their specific roles. It wasn't an easy life. It was a hard life and there was nothing romantic about it, but it was a good life. I guess some of those roles still carry on. The men are the hunters and bring home the game and the women take care of the game and prepare it. The game is shared. That still goes on in my family. When my brother and father go hunting and we get a deer, they don't just keep it to themselves; it is shared in our family. I don't personally feel connected to the Ojibwe people in Wisconsin, but on another level I do because we are members of what the anthropologists call the Algonquin Language Group. Because of the artificial border between Canada and the U.S., there isn't as much visiting back and forth as there used to be. People who are on the pow-wow trail feel a lot more connected to the tribes in Wisconsin. My First Nation has connections to the tribes in Michigan state on other types of issues. But I don't think there is [as] much interaction as before.

I am working on the EAGLE Project. The acronym EAGLE stands for Effects on Aboriginal People from Great Lakes Environment. It was started in 1991 and I started working on the project in 1993. The purpose is to examine how the environmental contaminants affect the health and well-being of First Nations' people who are living in the Great Lakes basin. The project targeted 63 First Nations' communities living on the Canadian side of the Great Lakes Basin. The communities are mostly Ojibwe in the north, and Mohawk in the southern part of Ontario. I work with 21 of the First Nations' communities from Sioult Ste Marie to Wisoxin or Perry Sound and the communities on Manitoulin Island. I've been really successful in working with the communities. About 18 of the 21 communities have participated in at least one of the studies.

The first study we did was an eating pattern survey. We knew that First Nations' people eat a lot of freshwater fish and game—we did a survey to verify that. And our result showed that First Nations' people [in the study] ate 6–10 times more freshwater fish and game than nonnative people. . . . Then we wanted to . . . know what is in that meat. The Ministry of Environment and Energy does have a fish sampling program where they take samples of fish fillets and analyze them for different contaminants. We were able to access their database. Where there was information lacking in near-by First Nations' communities, we [personally] gathered samples of fillets from there. We also did a wild game sampling project in my area. The samples are under analysis at the moment. So we have samples from deer, moose, rabbit, beaver, muskrat, all kinds of stuff. The results that come out of that will be significant because there is very little data on contaminants in wild game. Then we wanted to figure out what is showing up in people's tissues, so we did a blood and hair sampling. . . . We will be doing it in six or seven more communities this fall. We want to know what people are eating, what contaminants are in the food, and what is showing up in people's blood and hair. People in the communities tell me we have terrible rates of diabetes; cancer rates are on the rise, respiratory problems, asthma, heart disease. [All caused from immunity depression.] We are a sick people; people keep telling me how sick they are.

The Reserve communities in my area are [also] adjacent to huge industrial pollutants. We've got a couple of huge paper and pulp mills and Sudbury is the nickel capital of the world . . . they mine nickel, copper, iron ore and there are smelters there. We really have a long-range transport of their pollutants and we have uranium mining—the community downstream really suffered from the effects of that. Initially a lot of the men were miners and they were directly exposed to the uranium. What people tell me, and what I see as well, is the change in water quality, the change in availability of fish, the change in the fish quality. The water quality is not as good [as before] and the numbers of fish are decreasing. You catch a fish and it is full of tumors. There are game . . . affected as well. People tell me that they find tumors in rabbits, deer, and moose. I don't have to do any study to know that there is something wrong here. And the people don't have to be scientists to figure it out either. And the trees are affected from acid rain. We see stands of maples and birch that are dead, and there goes the production of maple syrup. I speak with my father and he asks, "Where are all the frogs and the snakes?" There are no more snakes and frogs, but we haven't seen the genetically mutated ones. We have been pretty lucky [with the agricultural chemicals]. There is some agriculture on Manitoulin Island, but it isn't good farm land. It is mixed boreal forest. We are right on the Canadian shield, so the soil is rocky, but it is beautiful with crow berries and cranberries. It is God's country!

This is my message to all people: I saw this poster once. [It said] When every leaf is gone, when every tree is gone, when every fish is gone, you can't eat the money!! That is my message.

The Great Lakes Basin accumulates toxics from throughout the hemisphere. Researchers have calculated that a single meal of Great Lakes trout or salmon contains a dose of PCBs equivalent to drinking five liters of Great Lakes water every day for 200 hundred years. (Steingraber, 1997, p. 318)

WINDOW ROCK, ARIZONA: NAVAJO NATION: STORY-TELLING MONTH

In the Navajo Lifeways, "Changing Woman" holds the mysteries of the Earth. The Navajo faith in the cycles of nature has come to them through the generative powers of "Changing Woman," one with the Earth. As a traditional young Navajo woman with whom I spoke expressed it:

My grandmother always taught me to walk in the Beauty Way. Beauty is behind you in the past. Beauty is in front of you in the future. Beauty is under your feet in the way you walk on the Earth. Beauty is above you in the sky. We have the four colors to guide our path: white, black, blue, and red. White is in the east where we greet the day. Black is in the west where the day ends. We have the Seven Directions to guide us and all of the Five-Fingered Ones are our brothers.

The Navajo Reservation straddles land that is dotted with continual movement. Oil wells seesaw boldly and rhythmically among some of the most colorful and majestic rock formations in North America. As the sun travels along her daily path across the sky, a changing of color and movement highlights the land. Sheep herders tend their fluffy flock in the midst of puffy sky clouds and swirling clouds of red dust.

Natahlbah J. Brown writes about Navajo Economy and the Environment

Natahlbahe J. Brown was a student at the Salish Kootenai College at the time he wrote these words:[7]

---

[7] Brown, N. J. (1996). *The Navajo Economy and the Environment:* Pablo, Montana: unpublished paper used with permission.

Navajo women were always the head of the household. I grew up knowing my grandmother and my mother as the matriarchs of our family. The
Navajo Nation, located in New Mexico, Arizona, and Utah, is the largest
Indian reservation in the United States. It encompasses over 24,000
square miles with an additional 3,500,000 acres of Navajo-owned land
next to the reservation. The Navajos also have the largest Indian population of about 150,000 on a Reservation whose agricultural subsistence level is estimated to support only [a carrying capacity[8] of] 35,000
persons. Such a situation has created a state of poverty where, in 1970,
the per capita income was only $831. The Navajo have depended on
raising sheep, goats, and cattle, and more recently, mining activities
on the Reservation to survive. However, this economic system changed
the environment on the Navajo Reservation. . . . the result of capitalism
on the reservation of the Navajo Nation.

Prior to 1600 and Spanish contact, the Navajo depended mainly on
hunting and gathering much like many other tribes in North America.
They also planted corn. In 1600, after contact with the Spanish, who
[also] introduced sheep herding, the Navajo became less nomadic and
concentrated on sheep herding and agriculture for their economic base.
The women learned to weave from the Pueblo [Indian people]. With
wool from their herds and natural dyes from the land, women created a
style of weaving that is distinctly Navajo. Sheep were like gold and each
family's ambition was to have a large herd.

Under the 1868 treaty between the Navajo and the federal government of the United States, each family was provided with a few sheep,
goats, and horses. Over the next decade, the government supplied the
Navajo with 30,000 sheep on the reservation. By 1887, the number of
sheep and goats were over one million. It is estimated that the per
capita of sheep for each family was between 63 or 250 for a family of
four. Distribution of sheep and goats was uneven and up to 24 percent
of the population had no animals while others obtained large herds. In
1933, after a series of long droughts, the Commissioner for Indian Affairs, John Collier, convinced the Navajo Council to adopt a plan for
stock reduction. During the stock reduction phase, the population of
Navajo people on the Reservation grew from 39,000 to 50,000. The
population increase combined with the stock reduction reduced the

---

[8] Carrying capacity: The total number of persons (or animals) that can be supported by resources
within a defined land area.

number of sheep and goats to 20 animals per capita. The stock reduction affected all herd owners, but was most devastating to small herd owners. With their way of life destroyed, the small herd owners were forced to invent new sources of income. By 1940, dependency on livestock and agriculture had declined 58 percent. The remaining income was divided in this manner: 30 percent, wage work employment by the Bureau of Indian Affairs, railroad companies, and various mining companies which exploited the mineral rich Navajo Reservation; 9 percent, sale of arts and crafts; and 3 percent from miscellaneous activities.

With the passing of the Metaliferous Minerals Leasing Act of 1920, the Reservation was opened to mineral exploration. Mineral exploration on the reservation by mineral and oil companies could occur, however, only with approval by the Navajo Nation. . . . Although monies from mineral extraction revived tribal economy, it also had a damaging effect on the environment. Today, the Navajo Nation continues to mine its land, raise sheep, goats, and cattle. For anyone who has been to the Navajo Reservation near Window Rock or Ship Rock, the environmental effects of mining are obvious. Oil drilling rigs are abundant as are the large open pits created by the strip mines for coal. Yet the mineral extraction continues. The Navajo Nation is rich in natural resources, but the health of Navajo men is compromised as they work deep inside the body of Mother Earth.

Navajo Nation: Uranium Mining

Coyote met doe and fawn in a clearing one morning and coyote was envious of the fawn's beautiful spots on her coat. He asked the doe, "How can my coyote pups have spots like that?" Doe answered that she couldn't tell him because it was too dangerous. Coyote begged and begged and finally doe gave in, "Gather dried juniper and make a big fire. Put your coyote pups close to it. The juniper will shoot off sparks which will set their coats on fire. When coyote saw the sparks flying he got excited and made the fire bigger. Happy that his pups would have beautiful spots, he pushed his pups closer. When he looked down at them, they were nothing but skeletons. (Apache legend, told by Joseph Geronimo, MacAdams, 1996, pp. 66–74)

Mining began on the Navajo Reservation in the 1940s with the demand for weapon-grade uranium. Many were small family mines and little was known about the danger of the tailings or the toxic effects in the air and ground water. The companies came in and took uranium. About two-thirds of the 150 million acres guaranteed to Indian tribes by treaty has been taken from them either through allotment, other sales, or seizure without compensation (Grinde & Johansen, 1995). According to a Federal Trade Commission (FTC) report of October 1975, 16 percent of all uranium found in the United States is on Reservation lands. Twenty percent of the national total was mined on reservations in 1975 (Grinde & Johansen, 1995).

Although two-thirds of uranium reserves in the United States are located on Indian lands, 80 to 90 percent of the mining and milling that has taken place in the last 50 years has been on or adjacent to reservations (J. Weaver, 1996, p. 47).

In 1952, the Bureau of Indian Affairs approved a lease for a uranium mine on Navajo lands near Shiprock, Arizona. One of the owners was Robert Kerr, Governor of Oklahoma.

The people who worked in the mines started dying in the 1950s. We tried some traditional ceremonies to cure the husbands. We tried traditional remedies and we tried the Native American Church. They gradually went down. They were usually heavy set men and when they died, they were skin and bones. (Hugh-Benally in Eichstaedt, 1994, p. 173)

The mine closed in 1970. Thirty years after mining began, of the 150 Navajo men who worked in the mine 133 died of radiation-induced lung cancer or had severe lung and respiratory disorders such as fibrosis. As their fathers continued to die of lung cancer, children who played in the waters that flowed through abandoned mines and tailings piles developed burning skin sores (Grinde & Johansen, 1995). Because of the radioactive contaminated waters, birth defects and Down's syndrome, previously unknown among the Navajo, soared (J. Weaver, 1996). Of all infant deaths in the Navajo IHS unit for the years 1990–1992, 35 percent were caused by congenital anomalies (Indian Health Service, 1995, p. 40). The mortality rate attributed to malignant neoplasms as age-adjusted was 78.5 percent for the Navajo IHS unit in the years of 1990–1992 (Trujillo, 1995, p. 65).

A 1976 Environmental Protection Agency report found radioactive contamination of drinking water on the Navajo Reservation in the Grants,

New Mexico, area, near a uranium mining and milling facility. (Eich-staedt, 1994, p. 208)

They left pits with exposed uranium and hazardous waste. Timothy Hugh-Benally, 63-years-old and director of the Office of Uranium Workers, Ship Rock, New Mexico, describes conditions in the mines:

The working conditions were terrible. Inspectors looked at the vents. When they weren't inspected, they were left alone. Sometimes the machines [for ventilation] didn't work. They told the miners to go in there and get the ore shortly after the explosions when the smoke was thick and the timbers were not in place. There was always the danger of the ceiling falling in on them. (Eichstaedt, 1994, p. 173)

Don Yellow Horse began mining in mines operated by Kerr-McGee when he was 18. He describes his main job as a "mucker," taking rocks out of the mine:

When we first came, it was twenty-four hours a day. It was also dusty and no air. We just started to work: sometimes a day shift, sometimes at midnight. They didn't tell us anything [about the dangers of radiation]. They forced them [miners] to get the high grade ore. (Eichstaedt, 1994, p. 189)

Yellow Horse describes how he drank the water leaking from the water-cooled drills:

The water [from the drilling hose] was leaking from the drilling into a pop can wedged under the water hose. [The leaking hoses provided a source of drinking water.] I drank that a lot of times. It was fresh and cold. (Eichstaedt, 1994, p. 189)

Other miners like Cecil Parrish, about age 70, began working the mines in 1952. He remembers:

At Moonlight Mine they used to work with their bare hands and shoveled the uranium into a bucket and hauled it up . . . no coveralls . . . no showers. They worked you like a slave. They wanted the miners to work twenty to twenty-four hours a day. (Eichstaedt, 1994, p. 188)

Not only did exposure to uranium cause health problems in the miners themselves, uranium continues to create health hazards for Navajo families. There are 22 homes in the Red Valley area and several dozen more across the reservation constructed from mine tailings or radioactive rocks—uranium bearing sandstone fractures easily into squares and provides a readily available source of construction materials. With the help of federal assistance, the tribe has replaced 17 of the homes in Red Valley.

> I built this house and I didn't know that it contained high radiation uranium. I still live in this house. I was told it is very dangerous to live in this stone house. I don't have any money. I don't work. There is no way I could get money to build me a house that does not contain radiation from uranium.

When the mines finally closed, millions of tons of tailings were abandon by processing companies and have been blowing in the wind since the 1960s. The tailings contain thorium-230 and radium-226 which are doomed to leach into the ground water for over 1,000 years (Eichstaedt, 1994.)

In a situation that occurred in 1979, 94 million gallons of water contaminated with uranium mining waste broke through a United Nuclear Corporation storage dam. The water poured into the Puerco River in New Mexico, the main water supply for the Navajo Indians who live along the river, and a tributary of the major source of water for Los Angeles. Navajo ranchers, their children, and farm animals waded through the river unaware of the radioactive danger. This tragedy continues to take toll on the health of Navajo people, who lost the use of their water. For the Navajos, this event has become a prophetic warning for all humanity (Keane, 1997).

Navajo Abandoned Mine Lands Reclamation Office (NAMLRO), headed by Charley Perry, whose father was a uranium miner and died of lung cancer, is working to reclaim the land.

> Out of 1,100 abandon uranium mine sites, 314 mines have been reclaimed which cost the Navajo tribe $506 million. There was a large pile of tailings in Shiprock, Arizona. The Project constructed an enclosure. The mill tailings are buried inside a capsule and covered with 3

feet of material. The Department of Energy (DOE) states that it will be safe for 1,000 years—we'll see. We identified a contamination plume in the ground water where the tailings once sat for 30–40 years affected by rain and snow. The surface waters and surface site remediation is almost complete. We had four surface sites: Tuba City, Ship Rock, Halcita, and M.V.

Using the data for tribal remediation needs, students at Navajo Community College are involved in the research of monitoring ground water quality. Students monitor wells and take ground water samples. An additional pile of tailings exists 100 meters from the San Juan River. There are no data predicting the movement of contamination from this pile as it eases its way into the San Juan. However, NAMLRO is implementing an organic trench in hopes that the contamination will be taken up by the plants (L. Martin, 1997).

The testimonies from the 1992 World Uranium Hearings held in Salzburg are revelatory here, and especially in regard to mental retardation in children as a harmful aftereffect of radiation. A third category of documented and scientifically accepted harmful effects of radiation has been discovered in mental retardation in children who were irradiated while still in the womb (Edwards, 1992).

When miners extract uranium from the ground, the rock is dug up and crushed. A finely pulverized rock resembling flour is left. In Canada, 200 million tons of this radioactive waste is laying on the ground, with 85 percent of the radioactivity remaining in the pulverized rock. In 80,000 years, the half life of uranium, there will be half as much radioactivity as now. There are no archeological remains dating human existence back that far. As these tailings are left on the surface of the Earth, they blow in the wind, they wash in the rain into the water systems, and they spread inevitably. If the mining companies close down, who is going to look after this material forever? How will 200 million tons of radioactive sand be safely guarded forever? As the tailings sit on the surface of the Earth, they continually generate radon gas, which is about eight times heavier than air, and so the radon stays low to the ground. In just a few days with a light wind, it can travel 1,000 miles. As it moves, it deposits on the vegetation below the radon daughters, which are solid particulates including polonium. Animals and plants thousands of miles away from the uranium mines are contaminated with radon daughters. This "mechanism" for pumping radioactivity into the environment for milennia to come is one of the hidden dangers of uranium mining (Edwards, 1992).

Winona La Duke of the International Treaty Council may have been speaking for more people than Indians when at an antinuclear demonstration near Grants, New Mexico, she said, "Indian People refuse to become the silent martyrs of the nuclear industry. We stand fighting for our homelands for a future free of the threat of genocide for our children." (Eichstaedt, 1994, p. 211)

All uranium ends up as either nuclear weapons or highly radioactive waste from nuclear reactors. In the process of mining the uranium we liberate naturally occurring radioactive substances, which are among the most harmful substances known to science.

The Great Spirit instructed us that, as Native People, we have a consecrated bond with our Mother Earth. We have a sacred obligation to our fellow creatures that live upon it. For this reason it is both painful and disturbing that the United States Government and the nuclear power industry seem intent on ruining some of the little land we have remaining. (Thorpe, 1997)

In New Mexico, roads to the Laguna Pueblo were resurfaced with low-grade uranium ore. Similar material was used to construct tribal buildings and housing. Birth defects soared as they did in the case of the Navajo. In 1995, the Indian Health Service unit serving Indian people in the Phoenix area listed 27.9 percent of infant deaths as caused by congenital anomalies (Indian Health Service, 1995, p. 41). The age-adjusted mortality rate for malignant neoplasms in the IHS service unit in Phoenix was 76.9 percent (Indian Health Service, 1995, p. 65).

The U.S. Department of Energy (DOE) admits that as many as 5,000 separate locations nationwide [within the Navajo Nation], such as schools, homes, public and private buildings, have been contaminated by the tailings either from dust blowing off the piles or from proximity to large amounts of gamma radiation, or from using the sand-like tailings in concrete for slabs and footings. (Eichstaedt, 1994, p. 129)

Uranium mining has not only crippled thousands of Indian people in the United States, but Canadian Indians as well. Among the Canadian Metis and Chipewyan nations, who both depend on natural foods, radiation contamination has lead to a 600 percent increase in hospitalizations for cancer deaths, birth defects, digestive and circulatory disorders (J. Weaver, 1996).

> Wherever there are uranium mines, wherever there are power plants, and wherever people are downwind of nuclear tests, the cancer rate goes up. As a result of atomic testing, many of the people of the Western Shoshone in Nevada now have thyroid cancer. They are dying younger death. They have leukemia, which was unheard of in earlier times. Pollution and toxic waste from the Hanford nuclear weapons facility threaten all native peoples who live on the Columbia River salmon for existence. (Thorpe, 1997, p. 55)

> The Hanford nuclear plant released more than 440 billion gallons of irradiated water thirty miles upstream from the Yakima Reservation between 1945 and 1989. . . . oysters caught at the mouth of the Columbia River were so toxic that when one Hanford employee ate them and returned to work the following day, he set off the plant's radiation alarm. (J. Weaver, 1996, p. 49)

RADIOACTIVE RESERVATIONS

Despite the uranium mines and a documented increase in the cancer incidence affecting Navajo miners, Mescalero Apache in New Mexico, and the Paiute-Shoshone on the Oregon-Nevada border, the Skull Valley Goshutes in Utah considered allowing the government to build a temporary nuclear waste dump on their reservations.

Oak Ridge National Laboratory head Alvin Weinberg articulated the problems associated with nuclear waste disposal as "transcientific." "The staggering toxic durability of the waste means that the testing techniques of 'normal science' do not apply," he says. Given this toxicity, few communities believe that the benefits of a nuclear dump would outweigh its costs. In lieu of other bidders, American Indians and First Nation Canadians are asked to assume this burden (R. Hansen, 1997).

As the federal government searches desperately for a permanent waste site for high-level nuclear waste, stockpiles of nuclear waste from 100 reactors nationwide continue to grow. In reaction to the NIMBY (Not in my backyard) syndrome, Indian people realize that the general public doesn't want the waste around but federal and corporate bureaucrats continue to try the old trick of dumping on Indian Country. Lance Hughes of Oklahoma-based American Indians for a Clean Environment says, "The general public doesn't know anything about this move, and given the geographic and political segregation, they probably won't hear much about it" (R. Hansen, 1997).

Former Republican lieutenant governor and attorney general of Idaho, Leroy was appointed as the first head of the U.S. office of Nuclear Waste Negotiation in August 1990. To coerce Indian communities to accept nuclear waste dumps, Leroy and other consultants developed "deals" that offer money along with community facilities and improvements to any community accepting a waste dump. Through this policy, the government hoped to force communities to bid against each other to win the compensation packages, thereby reducing the government's ultimate disposal costs (R. Hansen, 1997).

As part of his strategy to enhance tribal cooperation, Leroy attended the annual meeting of the National Congress of American Indians in San Francisco in December 1991, where he outlined the Department of Energy's new management strategy for commercial spent nuclear fuel. At the meeting, Leroy appealed to assembled leaders to draw on their "Native American culture and perspective" and its "timeless wisdom" to seize the opportunity to house the radioactive spent fuel. Quoting the famous Duwamish Chief Seattle, Leroy said, "Every part of this soil is sacred in the estimation of [Indian] people," implying that no matter where the waste eventually ended up, it would still be on sacred ground. He promised $100,000 with "no strings attached" to any tribe considering temporary waste storage. If a tribe opted to offer a temporary nuclear waste dump, the waste would be transferred after 40 years to the permanent storage slated for Yucca Mountain, Leroy assured tribal leaders.

Reminiscent of the heydays of treaty signers and gifts of blankets contaminated with smallpox, the government has downplayed the long-term dangers associated with high-level nuclear waste. Presented to the tribes as "economic development," the plan to use the Mescalero Reservation as a temporary storage site assumes that a permanent storage facility will be established sometime in the future. However, many major unresolved political and technical questions go unanswered. Recently, a sizable earthquake in the Yucca Mountain area raised new safety and feasibility questions. Scientists continue to raise questions over the safety of the geography in the region and whether a "permanent site" could in fact isolate the deadly waste from the biosphere for milennia. "Scientists at Los Alamos Laboratories in New Mexico warned in March 1995 that the planned method of burying radioactive waste at Yucca Mountain could result in explosions" (R. Hansen, 1997). Western Shoshone in the region have organized a resistance campaign.

Mescalero Apaches, whose reservation lies in southern New Mexico, were the first to sign up for the nuclear storage program. As Tribal President Wendell Chino likes to say, "The Navajo make rugs, the Pueblos make pottery, and the Mescalero make money." "The Mescalero can bear this [waste storage] responsibility because of our strong traditional values that favor protection of the Earth. We can serve as reliable, trustworthy, and responsible guardians of the nation's spent fuel," he told a Department of Energy-sponsored conference on high-level radioactive waste. "We believe that spent fuel is a business opportunity, a service provided to a willing customer by a willing supplier in exchange for a reasonable profit. Thirty-three utility companies agree with us."

On January 31, 1995, Mescalero Apache tribal members voted 490 to 362 to halt all further negotiations with nuclear utilities over hosting the proposed private sector temporary nuclear waste storage facility. The results of the vote stunned both the Mescalero Apache Tribal Council (MATC) and nuclear utility officials, who had reached a tentative agreement on the facility. "The voice of the Mescalero Apache spirit has been heard," noted Rufina Marie Laws. "Very few of us will be around 40 years from now," said Joseph Geronimo, great-grandson of the famous Apache Chief Geronimo, in explaining the vote. "Our children would be stuck with it. And what would they get for it? Nothing." In rejecting what many saw as an outright bribe to sell their homeland to the highest bidder, Geronimo said, "Our people have made the choice that their tradition and culture is the most important thing in the world, and Grandmother Earth is not for sale at any price." MATC President Wendell Chino told *The New York Times* that "right or wrong, they [tribal members] made a decision. I don't have a problem with it. I just recognize the fact that the Mescalero people have shut the door on themselves in not accepting a great opportunity" (www. monitor@essential.org. Multinational Monitor, 1997).

It is unclear whether the dump will be built at Mescalero in the face of opposition by tribal members. New Mexicans living along the transportation routes have major problems with the storage facility since highly radioactive waste will be shipped through their communities.

NAVAJO NATION: COAL MINING AND THE POWER PLANT

Emma Yazzie is a Navajo elder who lives 20 miles from Shiprock, New Mexico. Sheep are her livelihood. Her simple lifestyle is based in shepherding economy, much like other Navajo people who take pride when their lands are covered with herds of sheep. But Navajo lands are also home to one of the largest coal mines in the western hemisphere, providing power at the expense of Navajo health, so people in Phoenix can heat their swimming pools and air condition their homes. Without her permission, the mine owners staked a road across her pasture for truck access from the mine to the power plant. "You power people are watching us starve while you make money off coal in Navajo land," Emma said as she threw the stakes across the desk of the plant manager. Today her sheep are sick, bleeding from their noses. Often they die in the first year. Those that survive are thin and give little wool from their dirty brown fleece. But it was not always so. Once Emma Yazzie awoke to clean blue skies and clear air. Today, the air is brown and heavy with coal-laden pollution (Grinde & Johansen, 1995).

> As a mother and grandmother, I am concerned about the survival of our people, just as Mother Earth is concerned about the survival of her children. . . . Is this the legacy we want to leave for our children and for Our Mother Earth. . . ? (Thorpe, 1997, p. 56)

The Diné Alliance: Navajo (Diné Alliance)

Diné Alliance, Navajo Nation, is an organization that represents residents living around Peabody Coal Company's Kayenta/Black Mesa mining operations. The mining complex covers over 103 square miles, making it the nation's largest. Inside the mine boundary, many Navajo try to continue to live a traditional way of life, grazing, farming, and gathering firewood, food, and medicinal plants. However, Peabody Coal Company has been conducting severely destructive mining operations. Before the mining, the air was clean and good.

The following is an open letter written by the Diné Alliance to the Office of Surface Mining to request changes:

Due to excessive coal dust we face endangerment to our health and the health of our livestock. The air is thick with blowing dust and Peabody is stripping away trees and topsoil years ahead of mining operations. By law, mine operators must not cause unnecessary disturbance, must prevent air and water pollution, and reclaim the land immediately. Peabody should not remove trees and soil until they are ready to mine, and be required to protect endangered clay, mineral, and medicinal plant sites.

The Black Mesa issue is the first case of environmental justice brought to the executive branches of the U.S. government since President Clinton issued an Executive Order on environmental justice February 1994. This Executive Order directs all federal agencies to focus on protecting environmental and human health in low-income and minority communities and to give the residents access to public information and the chance to take part in decisions about their environment and health. While we are aware that the mine is presently operating under an administrative block pending no continued use of the Navajo aquifer, we request an opportunity to present public comments on environmental concerns. We believe that we are endangered due to continued drawdown of the Navajo aquifer, toxic contamination of our land and water resources from use of an illegal, unpermitted coal slurry pipeline, unlined and excessive coal stockpiles, and forced and coerced relocation.

We request that all water sources remaining, used by local residents for their livestock, be tested and monitored for selenium, copper, and other toxic forming substances. We also request that this investigation include the interactive toxicological effects of selenium, copper, and other heavy metals. Also a full geophysical study needs to be done pertaining to possible contamination of regional aquifers and water basins.

Certain medicinal plants and culturally significant clays found only on Black Mesa are being eradicated, thereby destroying and endangering

residents' ability to conduct traditional spiritual and healing ceremonies. We request that the J-28 area be preserved. This is the only site
we have to collect "chi" (a soft red clay) that we use for ceremonial purposes and as a medicine. We also use this "chi" as a sunscreen. If this
site is mined, the "chi" will become extinct. We request that Peabody
not be allowed to mine this area and that it be preserved under the Historic Preservation Act.

We request a copy of Peabody's planting plans to ensure that native
species plants, medicinal plants, and trees that originally grew in the
mining areas are re-planted in the reclaimed areas. We see no trees and
request that juniper and pinon be planted. We don't want it to look
green, if this means that it is taking up water and food for plants that
would be better for animals to eat. We also want to ensure that selenium
accumulator plants are not planted in the reclaimed areas; particularly
Indian Rice Grass and Snakeweed. Dr. Jack States notes in his memo-
randum "Statement regarding selenium as a potential and current environmental hazard within the Peabody Coal Co. lease on Black Mesa,
Arizona," dated October 22, 1994: "In earlier research in the vicinity
of Black Mesa (Environmental Impact Studies of the Navajo and
Kaiparowits Power Plants, 1974 Vol.1), our research team verified the
presence of selenium in native vegetation at non-toxic levels (1–3ppm).
These levels were greater than in the soil and were high especially in
Snakeweed and Indian Rice Grass." Dr. David Love, of the U.S. Geological survey, and an authority on selenium toxicity, recently reported
that nowhere was the threat of selenium toxicity greater than "on the
reservations of the Navajo, Hopi, and Apache Indians in Arizona, 60
percent of whose lands are pocked with outcroppings of seleniferous
formations that are actively or potentially dangerous." The reservation
in New Mexico is similarly afflicted. "It is no wonder that the economy
of these peoples is in terrible condition and their health and that of
their livestock is poor. The government has poured hundreds of thousands of dollars into their support, yet it has totally disregarded the fact
that more than half of the land allocated to them is now or probably will
become poisonous."

We request the Office of Surface Mining (OSM) permit plans for
Peabody ensure that Indian Rice Grass, Snakeweed, and other selenium accumulators are not included in mining plant plans in the reclaimed areas. Peabody must be required to pull up all selenium
accumulators that are presently seeded in the reclaimed areas. We furthermore request all mine planting plans in the states of Arizona and

New Mexico be reviewed to ensure that they are not included in mine planting plans for Northern Arizona and New Mexico, as they are noted for greater selenium toxicity. And as Dr. States notes: "Mining stirs it up, in areas where they grow, making the toxicological effects much worse." A former Ranger recently stated that "Rangers in the Four corners area are telling tourists of dangerous levels of selenium, particularly in the Chinle Formation and the Morrison Area."

We request that Peabody stop creating huge coal stock piles and that our concerns about excessive dust and leachades from the piles be investigated. We want to know why these piles are so big and we want mining practices to be altered, leaving much of this coal in the ground until needed. Peabody must not be allowed to overrun capacity. We request that air quality monitoring stations be set up around all stock piles. We also request that water tests be done and monitored, as there is no evidence to show no leachades, and no ground water contamination. And due to this, we request 100 percent containment of all unlined coal stock piles.

We request that local residents have an opportunity to review all locations for replacement of air quality monitoring stations on both the Kayenta and Black Mesa mine. We further request that they review information about the upgrading of air quality monitoring stations on the Black Mesa mine.

It remains our position that neither Peabody Coal Company nor the Navajo Nation has the right to drive the people from their homes. The people who happen to reside in the permit area own their homes, though the homesite is held in trust by the Navajo Nation. At no time have these people given up their right to the structural integrity of their property or their right to enjoy the other usual benefits of having a house. We have concerns that Peabody never obtained the Right-of-Entry and that Peabody never had the right to relocate under its lease. The lease states: "Peabody may occupy that portion of the leased lands necessary to carry on mining operations including the right of ingress and egress. The lease requires Peabody to obtain permission from and to provide compensation for individual Navajo tribal members for damage improvement, customary use, and grazing in the mining area." They have no right to mine until these obligations are met under SMCRA. Peabody does not have the right to mine unless they already made these arrangements. Therefore chunks of mining operations are not valid, and many people relocated without knowing their rights and were never compensated. OSM should never have granted any permit to Peabody for its operation. In order to give a mining permit Peabody needed the right to mine. And under SMCRA it states that no one is to be relocated for coal mining purposes. Otherwise OSM is guilty of taking away the constitutional rights of the individual. We want a full investigation of Peabody's original right to mine and relocation of people done illegally under SMCRA. It also states in the original lease and in the lease amendments that Peabody, in addition to having to obtain permission from the Navajo Tribal Council and the Hopi Tribal Council, needed the individuals' permission. Peabody did not do this.

Peabody must stop harassing residents to relocate, denying them the ability to build new homes as needed if they refuse to relocate. Peabody must stop threatening residents that if they do not relocate that their children working at Peabody will lose their jobs.

Peabody must not discriminate against employees that voice their environmental concerns and provide SMCRA handbooks to all employees explaining their rights. Peabody must stop relocating burial sites and bulldozing human remains. Residents must be informed that they have the right to not have their burial sites relocated. We request implementation of the American Grave Protection Act and the Navajo Grave Protection Act.

OSM must investigate broken promises by Peabody to local residents that have relocated; including their failure to build homes, provide good roads, ramps for handicapped, and provide adequate water sources. And what about the rights of the children to be able to build houses of their own. Denver OSM must stop maintaining two (2) sets of records and stop pressuring Albuquerque OSM to pull letters from their public files. (Sent by dineh@Prime.Net.com for redistribution to Planet Peace: www.planet_peace.org)

Hanta Virus: Navajo Nation

Natural environmental disruptions not immediately caused by human technology can also prove serious in terms of viral infections or disease. Hanta Virus is one example of such a disease. Named for the Hanta River in Korea where it was first reported, Hanta Virus, carried by mice droppings on the Navajo Nation was explained by the Navajo Medicine Men in the early part of this century who observed the increased amount of snow melt cascading to the valleys below. The melting snow combined with a spring deluge of rain reminded them of similar outbreaks in 1918 and in 1933. In 1992, before the outbreak occurred, the Pinion trees produced an abundant harvest. Descending on the increased food supply, mice populations reproduced ten fold in one short season. The rains and snow melt caused flooding, forcing the rodents out of their burrows to seek food and shelter above ground, increasing contact with humans. "When there is disharmony in the world, death follows," said one of the men (Platt, 1996).

POINT HOPE, ALASKA: PROJECT CHARIOT 1959–1996

They say that it will be 250,000 years before the high-level radiation in the water will be safe. In looking at numbers like that it goes beyond what I can relate to in any shape or form. I had to translate it into something that I could understand. So I did it by generations—20 years per generation; that's 12,500. Twelve thousand five hundred generations are going to have to deal with the garbage produced in those times. What a legacy. (Butler, Inuit: Walters, 1993)

Alaskan Roots of Environmentalism

"Ever since the war-time Manhattan Project, the potential for virtuous and constructive applications of the most destructive force in history has enthralled the American nuclear establishment" (Coats, 1984, p. 1). In the late 1950s, researchers began to think of "peaceful" uses of atomic explosions. Scientists believed that nuclear power could be harnessed to propel airplanes, ships, and trains. As a result, the Atomic Energy Commission (AEC) established Project Plowshares to develop and promote peaceful uses of nuclear explosions (Coats, 1984). Cape Thompson, Alaska, was defined and identified as a remote site, 20 miles from human settlement on the mouth of the Chukchi Sea. In this "remote area" 110 miles north of the Arctic Circle and 20 miles from the Inuit village of Point Hope, the AEC proposed to create a massive harbor by detonating two one-megaton and two hundred-kiloton nuclear "devices" just below ground level. Each of the smaller bombs was ten times larger than the bombs dropped on Nagasaki and Hiroshima. The AEC called the plan "Project Chariot" (Coats, 1984). The blast was scheduled for summer of 1959. Behind this project was Edward Teller: "In addition to economic and political objections, Project Chariot faced criticism on social and environmental grounds" (Coats, 1984, p. 7). Although located in the wilderness, "far from White people," the plan did not take into account the Alaska Native village of Point Hope, home to over 500 people who depended on fish, caribou, birds, berries, whales, caribou, ptarmigan, and arctic flowering plants. Environmental Impact Assessments were carried out by Don Charles Foote, a biologist from the University of Alaska, Fairbanks. The president of the university at that time was Donald Wood, a supporter of the project. Foote's data demonstrated that high winds and low precipitation meant that the area around the blast zone was free of snow and ice and Natives hunting on land and sea peaked during the spring. His data indicated a nuclear blast would severly impact the Native People and their resources. The reporting of his truthful data to the AEC caused him to lose his position at the university. State, national, and local people stepped up a crusade to stop the project. The Point Hope villagers sent a letter of protest to then President Kennedy denouncing the project as too close to hunting and fishing areas.

Environmental groups such as Sierra Club, Izaak Walton League, and Defenders of Wildlife emphasized the dangers of radioactive contamination in the Arctic food chain. Strontium 90 causes bone cancer, leukemia, and eventually mutation of the gene structure. Those involved with the project at Livermore Labs and AEC knew that the Department of the Interior was prepared to exercise severe judgment in the case of the project (Coats, 1984).

When the project was canceled, the wilderness areas in the vicinity of Fort Thompson were ruined by the construction of over 40 buildings, including power and radio stations, and two 2,200-foot air strips, not to mention the damage caused to the tundra by heavy transport vehicles. Project Chariot opponents were concerned with the Alaska Native way of life as well as the damage to the Arctic ecosystems.

Although Project Chariot was canceled, in 1962 the AEC transported 5^9 curies of mixed isotopes to a site 32 miles from Point Hope. All of the material is unaccounted for in an area used year round for subsistence hunting

---

[9] One curie can kill 1,250 individuals in an hour if well distributed (North Slope Borough Science Advisory Committee, 1993).

and travel activities (Bowerman, 1996). Today, the people of Point Hope, Alaska, have a cancer rate of 533 per 100,000 (age-adjusted to 1970 U.S. standard population). This far exceeds the North Slope Borough rate of 8 and the United States rate of 9 (Bowerman, 1996) indicating that the odds for acquiring cancer is 17.31 percent if a person resided in Point Hope in 1962.

CANADA

The Last Stand at James Bay

James Bay is an extension of water south out of Hudson's Bay. Long known as a summering ground for polar bears, over 40 rivers flowing northward from Quebec and Ontario empty into its rich fertile waters. Tundra on either sides of the bay provides habitat for caribou, moose, otter, lynx, beaver, muskrat, as well as polar bears. The waters of the bay sustain walrus, belugas, and other whales and seals. The amount of fresh water pouring into James Bay from the adjacent rivers is so plentiful that it compromises the salinity of the Arctic Ocean. Ice break up doesn't occur until mid-July. The thin, nutrient poor soil barely sustains a forest 6-feet tall, stragglely black spruce, and a ground cover of caribou moss. This is the tiaga ecosystem of the Northern Quebec-Labrador Peninsula. It is the "garden" for Naskapi, Cree, and Inuit populations of First Nations' people providing for all of their needs.

An Elder for the Cisabi Band of Cree, Margaret Sam Cromarty is a gentle soft-spoken woman who was born in Quebec in 1936 and has raised five children. Her influence permeates the lives of many more grandchildren who live on the LaGrande River. Margaret's birthplace lies under water now covering sacred places and burial sites.

The Cree versus Hydro Quebec: 1971–1996

Only after the last tree has been cut down
Only after the last river has been poisoned
Only after the last fish has been caught
Then will you find that money cannot be eaten.

(Cree Prophecy)

In April the Canadian winter loosens its grip on the land. Throughout Northern Quebec and Ontario, snow still blankets the muskeg as trappers return home to prepare for fishing season. Snow geese, snowy owls, and tundra swans prepare nesting sites on the snowy muskeg. Meanwhile, arctic water birds dance about with impatient feet on the Atlantic shores of New Jersey and Delaware where they gorge themselves on the eggs of horseshoe crabs preparing to migrate to James Bay. It is a rhythm that has pulsated since the beginning of memories.

It was in such a spring in 1971, with no environmental impact statement (EIS) and over objections of Native sovereignty, that the Provincial Government of Quebec, not the Canadian federal government,[10] announced plans for James Bay I, a hydroelectric development project in the James Bay region. The Cree, whose hunting and fishing lands would be decimated as a result of this decision, were not even consulted in examining the impacts of development on them. When questioned about the effects on the Cree and their rights, government spokesmen simply asserted that the project was "to be built on provincial lands and would benefit the Native People."

> My people have depended for untold generations on the bear, moose, the caribou, and beaver, and they are animals which have always fed our people. . . . The lives of our people and the lives of these animals have been related for a very long time. . . . Our land and our lives have remained largely unchanged for thousands of years. (Speech presented by Matthew Coon-Come, Grand Chief of the Crees of Northern Quebec, 1991 Lummi Tribe Conference, Seattle, Washington) (Grinde & Johansen, 1995)

James Bay I

The James Bay I is a hydroelectric plan developed by the Province of Quebec. The plan conspires to harness electricity by damming rivers and

---

[10] Sovereign Nations such as the Cree do not make treaties with state or provincial governments, nor do the provincial or state governments have jurisdiction over First Nations. Only the federal government can make a treaty with a First Nation because First Nations are sovereign nations. The provincial government has no jurisdiction on the Cree Reserve, but that is exactly what happened in this case!

flooding the surrounding area of 30,000 square kilometers of Quebec, or one-fifth of the province. The first phase of the project began in May of 1972 with construction on La Grande River. Four dams were constructed on La Grande River, Eastmain River, and Caniapiscau.

The Hudson and James Bays are the largest inland seas on the North American continent and together form a critical link between Arctic and sub-Arctic nesting grounds of migratory birds and their wintering grounds in the south. Crops of eel grass meadows located on the shores of the bay provide habitat and nutrients for the migrating birds, brant, insects, and for mammals. With the construction of the dams, the amount of fresh water in the bay will increase substantially, changing aquatic ecology and testing the tolerance levels of the salt water eel grass. Should the eel grass succumb to the inundation by fresh water, it would be one of the most violent ecological disasters in North America.

In the Cree worldview, the damage wrought by the James Bay project was similar to other developments that impacted on their lands. Another special concern for the Cree was the effects of flooding on 50 percent of the wetlands destroying important beaver and game habitat and causing a reduction in the numbers of animals. Fluctuating water levels in the reservoirs restricted the ability of many animals, particularly beaver, to reinhabit the areas. Fish numbers declined. It will take up to 50 years to reestablish the balance of species in the reservoirs. The vegetation destroyed by construction could take 50 to 100 years to return to mature forest, if ever. Hunters suffered serious and permanent loss of subsistence resources, a major threat to the continuity of their culture and society (Feit, 1991). Mathew Coon-Come, Grand Chief of the Cree, calls the development on Cree lands a case of environmental racism (Thurston, 1991). In addition to the destruction caused by the rising waters, the building of a 700-kilometer road across hunting lands belonging to six Cree communities has caused additional destruction. Airports and communication infrastructures were built as were construction camps and a new town to house project headquarters. New mines and forestry operations are planned. In all, the La Grande hydro complex involved diverting three major rivers into the La Grande River to increase its flow by 80 percent—requiring four main dams, 130 kilometers of dikes, and 8 main reservoirs flooding 8,722 square kilometers (5 percent of the land surface). With the reservoirs filled in summer, the water released in winter would produce electricity needed for heating requirements in southern cities, causing major water level fluctuations throughout the winter. Construction of the power transmission lines would require cutting three or four corridors 960 kilometers long through the virgin forest. This was the first of three phases.

After an initial fight, the Cree reluctantly agreed to a financial settlement which amounts to $10,000 a year per family, plus exclusive hunting, fishing, and trapping rights to Cree hunters.

To the Cree people in the villages, the ruling was a great victory, but it was also a straightforward recognition of the truth about Cree lifeways, values, and the dangers inherent in development conducted without Cree involvement and consent.

> We know some development is necessary, and we understand there is value in progress and advancement. . . . We are not trying to live in some distant past. We are not attempting to avoid high technology, machinery, electricity, and other signs of progress. But I must ask if every new structure, every new highway, every dam is really "development." (Speech presented by Matthew Coon-Come, Grand Chief of the Crees of Northern Quebec, 1991 Lummi Tribe Conference, Seattle, Washington) (Grinde & Johansen, 1995, p. 230)

More than 20 years have passed since one-third of the productive lands of the Cree were flooded by Phase I. The ecological effects have been devastating. With the forest flooded, the trees began to rot causing an algae bloom from nutrient buildup in the water. The rotting vegetation also caused an increase in the release of methane gas, one of the greenhouse gases. A 1984 study revealed that 64 percent of all the Cree living in the village of Cisasibi had dangerous levels of mercury in their bodies. While some of the mercury may have come from air polluting sources from the west, it seems that bacteria feeding on the humus in the soil submerged beneath the James Bay reservoirs had formed toxic methymercury which entered the food chain through the fish. The soils which were flooded held a toxic secret: they were rich in inorganic mercury. "When the dams flooded the land, bacteria feeding on the now drowned vegetation released the mercury into the food chain in the form of methyl-mercury, which can accumulate in living organisms" (Thurston, 1991). The mercury moved up the food chain to contaminate the fish, a staple food both for culture and nutrition. In 1985, tests of 1,318 Cree revealed that 47 percent of women, children, and men had mercury levels above the World Health Organization standards, and 10 percent had levels high enough for them to develop neurological symptoms of mercury poisoning, called Minimata Disease.[11]

The project caused enormous societal problems and changed the lives of those Cree who were separated from their traditional ways. The project brought the 20th century crashing down on Chisasibi. Before the project there were no roads, and no cars or trucks. There was little store-bought food. In Chisasibi, where once people caught whitefish along the rapids, the river sluices through rapids which are now under water. Children hang out in dayglow clothing and high-top sneakers; the men play checkers. Traditional fishing and hunting activities have disappeared. With the breakdown in family structure, frustration mounts, especially in young people. In 1990, there were suicides, attempted suicides, and drug overdoses. Health has changed. Although infant mortality has been reduced, and there is longer life expectancy, hypertension, obesity, and alcoholism are common. Chief Coon-Come puts it this way: "People in Quebec are going to say, 'Those lazy Indians, now we have to pay for alcohol treatment programs, housing, and health programs.' That's because they have destroyed our economic base" (Ulbrich, 1991). It is a scathing example of environmental racism, environmental injustice, and collisions of cultural values. The land is fragile in these Northern ecosystems. It takes 100 years to grow a tree the height of a man's thigh.

While the Cree have clearly come through the events of the last two decades a united people, more autonomous and better able to achieve their goals, it is also clear that their relationship to the governments and project developers is an ongoing problem. The process has strengthened the Cree ability to confront the problems that threaten them, but it has not fundamentally resolved those problems or provided a mutually acceptable new relationship between the Cree and the governments. The Cree hunters have hoped for a new relationship with Euro-Canadians, based on mutual respect for each other's needs, or a reciprocal and responsible sharing of the land and resources. That has not been forthcoming.

---

[11] Minimata disease: See Glossary.

I find that most development projects are not driven by wisdom and intelligence. They are driven by greed. Governments decide what they want to do . . . because of economics and politics. . . . They say, "We need jobs," or "We must not let this water go to the sea and be wasted." (Speech presented by Matthew Coon-Come, Grand Chief of the Crees of Northern Quebec, 1991 Lummi Tribe Conference, Seattle, Washington) (Grinde & Johansen, 1995, p. 231)

MOHAWK NATION

Lorraine Canoe: Wolf Clan, Mohawk Nation

Lorraine Canoe is an Elder in the Mohawk Nation. I imagine what it would be like to be in her presence. From recent photographs, she looks out with a deep gaze, reflecting the pain of her people, contemplating the future for her grandchildren. Her long, grey grandmother hair is worn straight, pushed away from her face. From other photographs, I see she rides a bike, sells vegetables in the marketplace, and smokes cigarettes. As an Elder and revered grandmother, it is her right not to grant interviews. I know her words through the writings of others. Her name, for example, comes from her great-grandfather, Canoe. Lorraine Canoe lives in Brooklyn, New York. She teaches at Hunter College in New York City but summers are spent on the reservation.

Non-tribal members are not allowed in the Longhouse, the traditional gathering place for tribal members. "I have two daughters. Should they ever get married in the Longhouse, I have friends all over the country, non-Indians, Jewish friends, I have Black friends, and they're not coming into the Longhouse at all. No White people, no Black people in the Longhouse. . . . everybody has their own way. It's hard for us to maintain our way if everyone can just come in" (Canoe, 1993, p. 276).

Her Words

When we dance, the men dance on the outside of the Circle. The inside of the Circle is to honor women. When you dance to the ceremonial sounds of the earth, you are tickling Mother Earth and giving her joy for all the things she gives us to stay alive. When a tree moves and it gives you oxygen, you breathe. Without water we wouldn't be alive. We come from water; we live with water; our bodies are water. You can't buy that kind of spirituality—it comes from inside; it comes from the earth itself. (Lorraine Canoe)

In precontact times, the Five Iroquois Nations of New York (later the Six Nations with the addition of the Tuscarora)—Seneca, Onandoga, Oneida, Cayuga, and Mohawk—located along the eastern border of Canada and New York State, supplied most of their food by planting crops of squash, beans, and corn. Taking advantage of moderate climate and soils, their populations concentrated in the St. Lawrence River Valley and southern Ontario. Remnants of their loose confederacy remain today with a matrilocal and matrilinial line. The women chose the men to make decisions on war and peace and to settle disputes among villages and clans (Conrad, Finkel, & Jaenen, 1993). The confederacy had no permanent officials and decisions required the consent of the tribe to be put into effect—a most important aspect of tribal government that, in the 20th century, makes it difficult for the tribe to deal with environmental issues.

After the American Revolution, the Treaty of Versailles in 1783 ceded all British territory south of the Great Lakes to the Americans, but pressured by their Native allies, the British remained in the lands north of the Great Lakes and granted 300,000 hectares of land in the Grand River Valley to the Mohawks. The original land was part of a much larger land purchase arranged by Governor General Fredercik Haldimand with an Ojibwe group called the Mississauga (Conrad et al., 1993).

Many of today's Mohawk live on the Akewesasne Reserve spanning the border of the United States and Canada. The Mohawk territory, called Akewesasne or *Land Where the Partridge Drums,* is home to 10,000 people divided into two federally recognized jurisdictions: the St. Regis Mohawk Tribe and the Mohawk Council of Akewesasne. The St. Regis Mohawk Reservation is located adjacent to a Super Fund site.[12] The Jay Treaty of 1794 exempts the Mohawk from the boundary considerations (Morrison & Wilson, 1992) of the U.S.-Canadian border. Other Reserves of Mohawk Territories in Canada are the Kahnawake and the Kanesatake.

---

[12] Super Fund site: Recognized by the EPA as a highly toxic area and allocated millions of dollars in funding to remediate.

In the 1950s, industries such as General Motors, Reynolds Metal Corporation, and Alcoa Aluminum developed along the river and near the reservation. Waste from the industrial complexes including PCBs, mercury, mirex and other toxins was discharged into the river. By the 1980s, the amount of toxic contamination reached serious levels. Turtles contained 835 parts per million (ppm) of PCBs. Three ppm in poultry fat is unfit for human consumption. Since then, the Mohawk Nation's environmental department has recommended that fish from Mohawk waters not be eaten (Tosee, 1996).

In February of 1996, local health officials and community leaders met to discuss a plan proposed by General Motors (GM) to store untreated PCB-contaminated materials on the shore of the St. Lawrence River. The plan is designed to save GM $15 million dollars and would place 1,712,000 cubic yards of toxic waste on the shore of the river. The plan, opposed by the Mohawk leaders, would subject the Mohawk community to PCBs indefinitely. Tribal environmental scientists and the New York State Department of Conservation Wildlife Pathology Unit demonstrated that contamination is leaving the site and migrating into the St. Lawrence River.

Driven by the plague of toxic waste from GM, the environmental division of the tribe has developed into one of the most advanced tribal environmental programs in the country. GM industry along the St. Lawrence is based on resource extraction, pollution, and profit. Because the Mohawk people are strong-willed, believe in a spiritual, social, and cultural relationship with the natural world, and have persisted in carrying out tribal culture, their current environmental status could have been much worse. The tribe developed and implemented its own water quality standards for the St. Lawrence River by negotiating with the EPA. But it may be too late for some Mohawk women as carcinogens and PCBs may have contributed to the rise in breast cancers among Mohawk women and in populations of beluga whales living downstream (Steingraber, 1997, presentation to the World Breast Cancer Conference, Kingston, Ontario). Aluminum smelters and other industries have added to the contamination of the St. Lawrence with yet another toxic chemical called benzopyrene, a potent and well-known carcinogen (Steingraber, 1997). Additionally, a vegetable soup of PCBs, DDT, chlordane, and toxaphane, all banned but carried by the

winds to reside in the sediments of the St. Lawrence, continues to contribute to these problems. Mirex especially is now carried in the flesh of
eels migrating through these waters, the same eels that belugas use as a
food source and in which Mirex has been found at toxic levels. It is thought
that the presence of Mirex is the result of a pesticide spill near Niagara,
New York (Steingraber, 1997).

> To date, cancers in the belugas include bladder, stomach, intestinal,
> salivary gland, breast, and ovarian. Of 73 stranded whales which were
> autopsied in 1983, 15 had cancerous tumors somewhere in their bod-
> ies. No cases of cancer have been reported in belugas inhabiting less
> contaminated waters from the Arctic [in Canada]. (Steingraber, 1997,
> p. 133)

It is not surprising then that breast cancer incidence is increasing in
the members of the Mohawk tribe (Young, 1994) who live on lands adjacent to these once life-giving waters.

Effects of PCBs on the Health of Humans

Polychlorinated biphenyls (PCBs) belong to a class of chemicals containing a variable number of chlorines. The degree of toxicity varies with the
position of the chlorine atom on the basic structure. Although there are
more than 200 isomers (forms) of PCBs, commercial mixtures are composed of 40 to 70 PCB compounds. PCB production was discontinued in
the United States in the 1970s, but PCBs escaping from abandoned insu-
lation materials, transformers, hydraulic fluids, plastics, dyes, inks, pesticides, and adhesives. PCBs persist in the environment and are linked to
extensive global contamination. By the late 1960s, significant levels were
being detected in fish, water, soils, wildlife, and human tissues. "In mice
assays, PCBs have been known to cause liver cancer, pituitary tumors,
leukemia, lymphoma, and intestinal cancers" (Steingraber, 1997, p. 126).
Humans ingest PCBs by eating eggs, meat, dairy products, fat, fish, and
shellfish.

Release of dioxin follows the burning of PCBs. Dioxin is highly carcinogenic and can cause immune suppression, liver tumors, and birth

defects (Schmidt, 1992). Most carcinogens disrupt the genetic DNA by breaking it down, altering it, or disabling it. Women in Japan who work in the chemical industry and were exposed to PCBs generally exhibit an elevated rate in breast cancers (Davis et al., 1993).

As the endocrine system regulates hormonal activity, it can be adversely affected by toxins that tamper with hormones. Recall that hormones are essential for the regulation of a number of biological processes in the body, as messengers that relay information to cells about growth, division, and cell death. To act, hormones link with cell receptors, much like a key in a lock. The result binds to DNA within the cell nucleus and activates specific genetic codes. Hormone mimics, such as the organochlorines PCBs, and dioxins, have been shown to disrupt endocrine function. The result is not genetic damage but inappropriate activation of genes either by blocking biological response or by activating the cell at an inappropriate time. Dr. Theo Colburn, world-renowned for her work in this area, stated recently:

> We are certain of the following: A large number of man-made chemicals released into the environment . . . have the potential to disrupt the endocrine systems of animals including humans. . . . Unless the environmental load of synthetic hormone disrupters is abated and controlled, large scale dysfunction of the population level is possible.

Much like contageous diseases once thrust onto Indian people, PCBs, immune depression, and diseases such as diabetes continue to affect populations of Mohawk people.

> The stuff that's leaking into the St. Lawrence River from the Alcoa plant . . . the river is trying to fix itself. The fish who go to the bottom to clean it, they're coming up with their bodies upside down, the belly is up. With that kind of sign they still miss how bad the pollution is. . . . I'm afraid to eat the fish from that river. . . . I won't eat seafood because most of them are scavengers, and what they're eating on the bottom and I'm going to put that in my body? No! (Lorraine Canoe, 1993)

Helen Hill, member of the Mohawk Tribe and author of *Shaking the Rattle: Healing the Trauma of Colonization,* spoke to me about environmental problems on her Reserve across the River New York in Canada. She is a student at State University of New York, Buffalo.

When I was growing up there, we had a farm and my Dad used to grow grain and cattle, cows and pigs and horses, chickens and geese and ducks in southern Ontario. There is still quite a bit of farming going on the Reserve [today] that I come from. The guys get together at haying time and they all help each other with the harvesting. I remember . . . they used to . . . have threshing bees and haying bees. The farmers used to get together at Joe Blow's farm over there and then go down the road to Sam's place and then over there to George's place to help him bring in his hay or grain. It was like that. My brothers are trying to revive that, so there is a lot of help for each other. There is quite a lot of hunting on the Reserve. When I was a kid, we had rabbit. My dad never hunted deer too much, but he hunted rabbit, pheasant, and partridge. Because we had the farm we also had chickens, pigs, and cows, so we had meat in that way, too. My mom always grew a garden. My family was a combination of traditional and nontraditional because my mom is mixed blood. My grandma was, and my dad's mother was Scotch English; my dad's father is Mohawk. So I come from a mixed blood family. My grandma was Anglican; she was kind of the leader of the family. I didn't get to go to the traditional teaching in the Longhouse until I was 17. So I said, "I'm not going to church anymore, I'm going to the Longhouse." So it was a combination . . . when I was growing up. There's a lot of people in our community fighting to keep out the pesticides and the chemicals. They want the land to go back to the natural way. And there are some farmers in the surrounding area who want to use chemicals and there are still some of the men in our area Reserve who use chemicals in their gardening and growing. There are people growing soybeans, they need to use the sprays for that. So, there is conflict. I think there have been studies of pesticide levels in the game animals— not big studies. My sister, Hazel, is part of the protesters up there who don't want the pesticides. She is very actively involved in the grass roots movements—to stay traditional, to stay as a sovereign nation, when there is anything that comes along, she usually has contact with people who do the studies.

We don't really have an [environmental] organization [as such], but there are little cliques going on in a lot of territories. There was at one time I think an organization called Six Nations Environmental Protection

(SNEP) or something like that. There was a big to do a few years back when they were trying to bring in big truckloads of hospital waste into our Reserve and dumping it in the sewer or community dump. There were one or two houses where they found hospital waste in somebody's back field near their creek. The guy had been paid big bucks to use his land as a dump and the money meant more to him than the land, so there was really a big to do at that time. I think it was either somewhere between 1990 and 1994. As a matter of fact, now on our Reserve, you need to have your Indian Status Card. You have to show that card in order to take the household refuse to the dump. See, because I live in Buffalo, if I were to take my stuff to the dump now I would have to show my Status Card to the guy at the gate—if I wanted to dump. So that is the only way we have protection. There are waste management trucks, there's two of them, now on the Reserve. They provide the 50-gallon drum to the household and the people. The people put the bag of garbage in the drum and the guy comes along and picks it up and takes it to the dump. The other waste management thing has these big dumpsters and they are set up for business. My daughter has one at her house; once a month the guy comes along with his big truck and hauls it off to the dump. They tell me the population of the Reserve is 11,000 to 13,000. It is a big Reserve. I'm not sure how many enrolled [tribal] members there are, but it used to be 6 miles on the Grand River from the source to the mouth that was the original Haldimand Deed, but now it is down to 6 miles square. But you know stealing and selling [the lands] left us with very little land. Because of the Grand River we have a lot of [health] problems with the water. Upstream there is a tire factory and a couple of other different things that go from Paris, Ontario, to Branford, Ontario, and so there are problems with the water. They are spraying chemicals on the surrounding areas because of the farmers. Right now Branford is negotiating with the Band Counsel to put a sewer pipeline across an island that is still in our territory. And that sewer pipeline is a big bone of contention with the Native People. Because it is sewer. It is supposed to go under the Grand River and supposed go across our land but the people are saying, "No, that's not right. What if there's a leak and what if . . . you know." So that is a big fight that is going on [between the tribe and the non-Indians].

I wish we had the same kind of people [to fight it] in our Territory [that you have in your area, to reject the Yellowstone Pipe Line coming across the Flathead Reservation]. See in our Territory we have the elected Band System, like the Band Counsel system, we've got the confederacy system. The government only deals with the elected Band system and the land is still supposedly owned and controlled by the confederacy system and we've got people that don't believe in either system, because neither system is working for the people, but they are working for their own profits. There's lots of problems in that way. In the environmental stuff, the factories have pretty much closed down around Branford, that's the closest town [to the Reserve] and what I did notice, when I was home last, they have a big sewage plant or a big landfill and it is on the Reserve land, on this other tract of land that is supposedly Indian land that hasn't been taken over by Branford; Branford hasn't bought it or whatever, there's these big things, huge tanks like storage tanks for oil, but I don't know what's in them, but they are right along this canal. My sister said it is full of toxins from some factories from previous years. So we don't know what is going on as far as that is concerned. There's still some pieces of land [in the city limits of Branford] that belong to the Reserve and the only people protecting it is my sister and her friends and the few people that believe in the land and want to make sure that it is not stolen or sold. And they are doing that because they believe that there's a lot of dumping on that land and they don't want the land contaminated. The road salt has been stored in tanks that had carcinogens in them and that is being spread across the land [in winter to control the snow and ice].

A lot of bad things are happening on Reservations and Indian Territories. To prevent bad things from happening, Indians need to say "no" more often and be united. What is happening in our Territory, it is sad to say is this: There's only a few people saying "no." Those getting the good publicity are those trying to promote economic development for the Reserve. So it is the same no matter where you go [in Indian Country]. I am an advocate for natural living and healthy lifestyles. I am having a hard time eating meat. I am trying to be a vegetarian. I'd advocate organic gardening and eating foods that your parents and grandparents were eating long time ago before the Europeans brought in the other foods.

> Maybe the Earth is telling us something. How much have we learned from processing uranium and what they use uranium for and how the water tables are destroyed just to get uranium out of the ground. . . . How well do you respect your environment? The spirit of the water, the air, and all those things that you need to live . . . the life that supports you. (Lorraine Canoe, 1993)

ATHABASCANS: THE PEOPLE OF THE CARIBOU:
THE MONTH WHEN DUCKS PUT THEIR YOUNG IN THE WATER

> The country knows. If you do bad things to it, the whole country knows.
> It feels what is happening to it. I guess everything is connected together
> somehow, under the ground. (Koyukon, Athabascan; Nelson, 1983,
> p. 241)

Early morning: The mist hangs in a ragged veil low over the face of snowy
mountains to filter the sun. A fragile tundra ecosystem with specially
adapted plants holding moisture and warmth stretches far to the northern
horizon. For protection against the winds, some plants, miniature trees,
grow sideways across the tundra, rather than upward to the sun. Intimate
friends, arctic willow, dwarf birth, crowberry, and lingonon berry, jostle for
position with mound-like plants of saxifrages, arctic poppy, and cotton
grass. My boot prints leave deep, watery impressions on this ancient tundra and will remain for hundreds of years as harsh evidence of my en-
counter. This is the border where the Northwest Territories and Yukon
Territory converge, an ancient wintering ground where Porcupine River
Herd of barren ground caribou (rangifer tarandus) come to nourish themselves during the long winter of arctic night. It is late August. I hike across
a seemingly barren tundra, caribou and wolves long absent. They have
journeyed north in early spring on ancient migration trails—the stimulus
to give birth urging them on to summer grounds on the shores of the Beau-
fort Sea. They begin their return in September, often arriving in late October or November. But like all nomads, the caribou are unpredictable and
may not return to precisely this particular place.

> . . . the annual migratory cycle is anything but predictable, and wide
> variations in timing, route, destination, and numbers are the rule. (Nel-
> son, 1983, p. 170)

In the ancient language of my grandmothers, caribou[13] translates to
the word "shoveler." Unlike most members of the deer family, both male

---

[13] Before the 1950s, scientists separated the Eurasian reindeer and the New World caribou into
separate species. Fortunately, today we recognize them as the same species.

and female caribou have antlers. The central plate on caribou antlers acts as a scoop which they use to shovel snow away from their forage. Here, irreverently scattered about on the open tundra, I discover old caribou antlers, some covered in moss, others silently attached to skulls, others fresh and white. Fractured skulls, rotting fur, leg bones and hoofs are carelessly strewn about. The evidence relates an ancient and contemporary story of hunting and predation, for this place, this fragile place, is a primeval hunting territory of wolves and Athabascan Indian people. Wolves are efficient predators, but lack ceremonies of respect and thanks for their kills as the Athabascan people have. So it is wolf who has strewn these bones about.

Known as Athabascans,[14] or People of the Caribou, there are nine distinct groups in all dispersed throughout the central part of Alaska, Yukon, and Northwest Territories. Athabascans believe they were the first people and that it is the anthroplogists who retain the myth of an ancient crossing of Athabascans across a land bridge in Beringia. These ancient lands are the lands of grandfathers and grandfathers before them, all trusting on the migrating caribou for their principal food source. The cultural connection of the Athabascans to the caribou has deep spiritual roots. Stories of distant time reveal how the people lived in peaceful harmony and intimacy with all the animals. For modern Athabascans, the manifestation of that belief is illustrated in that each caribou has a human heart within its breast and every human has a bit of caribou heart. As such, humans will always have the spiritual knowledge of what the caribou are thinking and feeling; and the caribou will also share in the thoughts and feelings of the people. With the exception of hunting bear, no animal is given higher recognition by the Athabascans than the caribou (Nelson, 1983).

Hunters of caribou move across the land in dog sleds or snowmobiles, chasing them across naked tundra or into mysterious boreal forest, until the hunters have a good shot. All parts of the caribou are used but the front feet, which are never eaten for fear of contracting rheumatism. The head is a special delicacy and the meat is extremely rich. Soup is often made from the head or "head cheese." As a small child, I remember eating head

---

[14] The nine groups are Ingalik, Koyukon, Gwich'in, Tana, Holikachuk, Han, Upper Tana, Ahtna, and Tanaina.

cheese made by my grandmother. A cardiologist's nightmare, it was luxurious and rich with fat, spread in slabs over thick pieces of fried bread. She called it "couton." One year, while researching on Labrador's North Coast, roasted caribou ribs, also a delicacy and reserved for potlatches, were served to me as the hunter's greatest gift. I don't eat mammals, but these gifts, freely given have become part me and I part of the caribou. Caribou is to northern Indian people as the bison is to Plains Indian people—nutritious, ceremonious, and spiritual.

The hide is a thick brown color with a wide creamy neck stripe. It is the warmest fur in the world according to the Elders and is used even today as an important clothing material for hunting jackets, boot covers, and camp mattresses (Nelson, 1983). In 1994, I was privileged to videotape a fashion show of traditional caribou clothing presented by Dr. Jill Oakes of University of Manitoba at the Churchill Northern Studies Centre. The characteristic and magnificent patterns of stripes, diamonds, and placement of contrasting furs sewn into each parka, mukluk, kamik, mitts, or leggings designate the area where the clothing was made. When hunters were found frozen to death, the search party could name his home village by the pattern on the clothing.

Antlers of caribou are also important to the Athabascans. Rivaling antlers of elk and moose in size, they are crafted into awls, tool handles, and a variety of other useful and breathtaking works of art.

HEALTH AND MEDICINE

The spiritual relationship that Athabascans have with their environment is set forth in an elaborate code of rules emanating from distant time. Honor is shown for everything in the environment, through gestures of etiquette and by avoiding waste. Several years ago on the Yukon River an ice jam formed during breakup threatened the area with a flood:

From a near-by military base, airplanes were sent to bomb the ice in an attempt to dislodge it. This violent effort to overwhelm nature was regarded as extremely disrespectful by the traditional people, who customarily pray to the river ice asking it to flow away and cause no harm. (Nelson, 1983, p. 241)

For many years after the bombing, the Yukon River continued to flood. People said it was because of the disrespectful bombing.

For these traditional people, the environment is both a natural and supernatural realm. Nature is impregnated with portent and power and shamans of old sought medicine, prescience, and power from the spirit forces of nature (Nelson, 1983). Most shamans had special affiliations with Ravens as messengers. Raven is trickster, liar, creator, king court jester, and powerful spirit helper.

Before World War I, Athabascan shamans and medicine people in Alaska worked their power together in a collaboration to help America win the war. In so doing, they shifted their power away from the Earth to the battlefields across the oceans. After the war, they were unable to get the power back and the shaman's power began to wane (Nelson, 1983). Although shamanism is seldom practiced by today's Athabscans, many still believe that Ravens impart signs from nature. Traditional people feel that since the shaman are no longer practicing, Raven has abandoned them resulting in adverse health effects, environmental degradation, and human intervention.

Young people in the Northwest Territories face greater health risks than other young Canadians. The stress of cultural contact has taken a severe toll on youth in the Aboriginal populations. Students in grades 7 to 10 have suicide problems. "[They suffer from] inadequate diets, drinking and smoking patterns, and high levels of sexual activity (Kersaw, 1997). Cervical cancer is highest among Aboriginal women. In Saskatachewan between 1967 and 1971, cervical cancer rose among Aboriginal women to 52 percent (Young, 1994, p. 104). Young also notes that incidence of lung cancer is one of the fastest rising among Aboriginal people in Canada.

Depending on geographical location of the group, there are many contemporary issues of health and ecology affecting contemporary Athabascan people. I begin with the Alaska-Canadian Highway.

THE BUILDING OF THE ALASKA-CANADIAN HIGHWAY: PROJECT WASTE

During World War II, to protect North America from invasion by the Japanese, Canadians and Americans collaborated in this remote area of the

Military Waste Dump in the Arctic.
Photo by Frank Tyro. Used with Permission

north to build the Al-Can highway as an avenue to move troops and supplies to the North. Creating the highway amidst the wilderness, quagmires of permafrost, and mosquitoes is a marvel of engineering and a tribute to the stoicism of the military forces. When the war ended, the departing troops abandoned hundreds of military and construction vehicles, barrels of toxic waste, and other military debris to the People of the Caribou. Not only do these materials create an eyesore on the "pristine" landscape, the barrels of toxic waste are leaking in the permafrost and the ground water.

THE HUMAN GENOME PROJECT AND THE
PEOPLE OF THE CARIBOU

The U.S. Human Genome Project, initiated by the Department of Energy and the National Institutes of Health in 1987, is a multidisciplinary effort to understand the basis of human heredity. In the worldview of Western medicine, the focus of the Human Genome Project concerns the characterization of the human genome—the complete collection of human genetic material, including the estimated 50,000 to 100,000 genes contained in human DNA. A variety of other countries have undertaken the study of human genomes including Great Britain, France, Italy, and Japan. Projects are also under way to describe the genomes of bacteria, yeasts, crop plants, farm animals, and organisms used in medical research. For the medical community and generally for populations at large, the Human Genome Project and other genome projects will result in an unprecedented understanding of the basic biochemical processes of living organisms. The Human Genome Project, in particular, will enable the creation of a new "molecular medicine" based on early detection of disease, effective preventive medicine, efficient drug development, and personalized therapies.

During the Rio Summit on the Environment in 1992, the International Convention on Biological Diversity (CBD) was drafted by the United Nations member countries. The document directly addresses international concerns for conservation and preservation of the world's biological diversity, the sustainable use of its components, and the fair sharing of benefits arising from the use of living resources. Athabascans and other Aboriginal people oppose the Human Genome Project fearing that it will suppress biological diversity (Personal conversation with Jude Gobert, Salish Kootenai College, 1997).

In 1996, the people of Kitimat Village, British Columbia, were approached by six prestigeous Canadian universities plus the Canadian Ministry of the Environment to participate in a health project involving collection of blood samples from the tribe. The researchers noted that susceptibility to environmental contaminants varies between ethnic groups, and between individuals in an ethnic group. Over five years, the project is designed to assess the present and future health impacts associated with environmental contamination by local industry (Johnston, 1996, personal communication).

> Of particular concern [to the tribe] is the portion of the project involving blood samples. It is a well-documented fact that aboriginal communities elsewhere have had negative experiences with blood research, especially when that research is undertaken by outsiders. (Johnston, 1996, p. 1, personal communication)

141

For the Athabascans, objections stem largely from the lack of controls for the future of the blood samples themselves. Once in the possession of the researchers, the donors discovered that they have no authority over their blood samples. Other concerns include communication with the community, spiritual and cultural considerations, community participation in decision making, and the right to refuse to participate in projects that allow removal of any genetic materials.

Nuclear Contamination in Caribou

Recall that the principal food source of the Athabascan people are barren ground caribou which are strict herbivores and have a winter diet consisting primarily of lichen (Kelsall, 1968; Parker, 1978). Lichens have a long-lived surface and accumulate atmospheric contaminants in a non-selective manner resulting in a contaminant load similar to atmospheric input over the long range. The lichen-caribou-human food chain makes it ideal for studying contaminants in Athabascans whose primary food source is the caribou (Elkin & Bethke, 1995).

Direct absorption of radioneuclides is the most important process by which fallout from above ground weapons testing is concentrated in Arctic flora (W. Hansen, 1993). Two major periods of fallout affecting Alaska during 1953–1959 and 1961–1964 reflect the atmospheric testing of Great Britain, the United States, and the former Soviet Union. During the 1970s, nuclear testing by China and France also contributed to overall fallout (Hansen, 1993).

During the autumn, caribou shift to their winter diet composed mainly of lichens where concentrations of cesium[15] have collected. Cesium concentrations in caribou flesh thus increase at the end of winter. Athabscan people generally hunt caribou during this period, before the animals migrate north again. In addition, scientists have found that strontium-90 levels in the bones of caribou are also elevated at this time. When animals are hunted in the north, before the fall migration, they have lower levels of radionuclides (W. Hansen, 1993). In addition to increased levels of radionucleides, Bethke and Elkin (1993) discovered

---

[15] Cesium-137 and strontium-90: Radioactive elements of decayed Plutonium.

increasing concentrations of all classes of organochlorines, but these levels were lower than levels found in marine mammals.

For Native People and others, consuming game meats contaminated by radiation can compromise health. However, there is a dearth of research with the Athabscan people concerning issues of cancer incidence as a result of nuclear radiation in meat.

Thoughts from an Anonymous Cree[16] Elder

Her long, colorful skirt moves gracefully as she steps into reality from a Carol Grigg's painting of Indian Woman. Wearing beaded moccasins on her feet, black and grey hair drawn back and knotted at the nape of her neck with a large beaded barette, her smile is wide and dimpled. She works as a teacher and counselor with Aboriginal people in Edmonton, Alberta. When I speak with her in Canada about her Cree people, her smiling face becomes grave and serious. She does not speak with me for very long. Out of honor and respect, I will not use her name.

> I worry about our people, our women, our young people. I try to help them. I wish people in Edmonton would hire them for jobs. There are so many talented native teachers, but no one hires them. We have talented lawyers, nurses, and other professionals who also find difficulty in locating work. A few years ago I was diagnosed with breast cancer and had a mastectomy; now in addition to my work I also volunteer for our breast cancer group, Reach for Recovery. I am the one who speaks with our native women. It is so hard. They come in from their villages by bus for their surgery or chemotherapy or treatments. Many times I have put them on the bus after their treatment, knowing they are so sick I will never see them again. Sometimes I challenge the bus company to let them have their ticket at the price of an advanced fare, which is cheaper. The young people I worry about, too. They need their culture. I don't know so much. But I try to help them learn the ceremonies. I am a baby when it comes to knowing all of this [ceremonies], but I try, and I think they like it. I know more and more of my people are getting cancer and it frightens me. I know it is coming from the contamination in the environment. The Elders tell me that the meat doesn't look the same as it did when they were

---

[16] Cree people are members of the Athabascan language group.

young. But there are so many other problems for my people, that sometimes this [environmental health issue] is ignored.

UPPER SKAGIT TRIBE (COASTAL SALISH) WASHINGTON: THE MONTH OF THE BUTTERCUPS

Laughing gulls, clams, breaching orca whales, temperate rain forests, salt spray air, rolling oceans, calm bays and inlets, water—all of these elements guide the lifeways of the Upper Skagit people in northwestern Washington where rivers met the sea in ancestral tribal time. In ancient times, migrating salmon cascading through the rivers and neighboring oceans provided foods for Native People during the long wet winters. Life centered on the coming of the salmon, picking berries, and ceremonies. As a result of language loss and tribal land loss, the population among the Upper Skagit Tribe has been declining since the 1800s. In 1855, there were 300 and, in 1984, there were 233 tribal members. Descendents from the group of Indian people of Puget Sound, the Upper Kagit, Swinomish, and Sauk-Suiattles are closely related (Ruby & Brown, 1993). In their language of Lushootseed, the suffix "-mish" means "people." The Puget Sound area has many place names that incorporate this suffix—Snohomish, Skykomish, Duwamish, and Sammamish, among others. The original significance of Skykomish is "upstream people"; likewise, Duwamish is "inside people," referring to those who lived not along the shores of Puget Sound, but in the region inland, or "inside."

The land of the Upper Skagit Tribe was impacted upon by surveyors from the Northern Pacific Railroad in 1870 and encroached upon by White settlers, the "Changers," who trespassed on the graves of the dead. In 1889, after a massive smallpox epidemic, the bodies of dead Upper Skagit people lay unburied for a long time.

Vi Hilbert is one of the last of her tribe who speaks the Lushootseed language. An elder, 80 years old, she is preserving her tribal history, language, stories, and ceremonies. " It is a big responsibility," she says. Teacher, storyteller, translator, researcher, tribal Elder, great-grandmother, Vi appeared in the world in 1918 in the Skagit Valley of Washington state. Charley Anderson, a medicine man and historian, was Vi's father, and Louisa Anderson, a vivacious tribal speaker, was Vi's mother. Vi grew up speaking her tribal language Lushootseed, which is roughly translated as "the way people speak along the bounded salt water of Puget Sound." Unfortunately, to many of her generation, the language was lost. During her childhood, Vi joined her parents as they traveled throughout the Northwest picking berries. By the time she received her high school diploma, Vi had attended 15 schools, including government boarding schools where the speaking of Native languages was not permitted. When not in school, however, Vi was raised according to the traditional ways, attending tribal ceremonies, learning standards of behavior, and hearing the stories through which her tribe's history was passed from one generation to the next.

Trying to support her children as a single parent, Vi worked as a hairdresser, welder, managed a gas station/luncheonette/billiard hall, and ran a sandwich cart at Boeing. It was in the 1960s that concerns over the rapid decline in Lushootseed usage prompted Hilbert to begin to preserve the cultural and oral traditions of her people.

She began the study of linguistics and spent countless hours recording, interpreting, and transcribing stories from tribal Elders. The culmination of this work came together in three volumes of Skagit legends. Because the language was handed down orally without written words, Vi and Thom Hess, an associate professor of linguistics at the University of Victoria, developed an alphabet so the language could be written and created the Lushootseed dictionary. Because of these efforts, Lushootseed is considered to be one of the best-documented Native languages in the Americas. Dialects of Lushootseed have traditionally been spoken along every river in the Puget Sound area of Washington state, from Suquamish in the west to Snoqualmie in the east, and from the Skagit River in the north to Squaxin Island near Olympia in the south. Implicit in Lushootseed language is the idea that every person has a duty to participate with a good heart in the world around him or her.

Vi Hilbert finally became an associate professor of American Indian Studies at the University of Washington for 15 years, where she taught courses in Lushootseed language, culture, and literature. She founded and is the director of Lushootseed Research, a nonprofit organization dedicated to promoting and providing research support for the Lushootseed language and literature of the Salish people of Puget Sound. She established Lushootseed Press, whose first publication was *Aunt Susie Sampson*

Peter: The Wisdom of a Skagit Elder, based on the teachings of her aunt, a tribal historian and medicine woman.

Vi Hilbert has earned several major honors, including a Washington Centennial Commission Ethnic Heritage Award (1989), a National Endowment for the Arts National Heritage Fellowship (1994), and an Honorary Doctor of Humanities degree from Seattle University (1994). In 1989, Vi Hilbert was declared a Washington State Living Treasure.

I am Vi Hilbert, Elder of the Upper Skagit Tribe. The Upper Skagit Reservation is located in the Skagit Valley on the Upper Skagit River in Washington State. There are about 50 homes in the area and more are being planned. I was born in the Limon Hamilton Area, the ancestral land of my people. The land was part of the people and the river was their highway, which took them wherever they wanted to go. My dad was a canoe carver and he used the river as his father and grandfather had used it before him. I was taught by my ancestors the way we honor and respect it, because the teachings from the culture allowed us to know many things about our world. The land we lived on was alive—the creator had given the land and this place life and had given us life. We were taught to respect every part of it. Everything that grew had life and had spirit. So for that reason we were taught to show respect to everything that had been placed here by the creator. Everything had spirit and if you respected everything . . . it would serve us, but we had to show respect first. So this is what all generations were taught and the people spoke of this in their everyday life, as they worked, as they ate, as they communicated with one another. This was the philosophy the people lived by.

My people traveled from the mountains up to the Skagit River, across the [Cascade] mountains into eastern Washington into Lake Shalan and were comfortable finding a path for themselves across the mountains into Shalan Country. They intermarried with people across the mountains in the Shalan Country, and then the cultures were intermingled. Then they went down river to trade for saltwater foods using the game from the mountains to trade with the people from the coastal saltwater areas for clams and seafood that were plentiful in those areas. And the plants that were honored in eastern Washington were used as barter goods, so our people traded salmon for plants that were plentiful in eastern Washington. So, [the area] from the mountain to the saltwater areas were all familiar to our people and they honored all the gifts that each area had to share. And sharing was the predominant word and bartering was the way they helped one another. Money was not an issue.

People went from the Skagit River to the Columbia River and this was a route they were familiar with. They traveled south to trade and to barter for things in the Columbia River area that outsiders had brought. Invading new peoples brought things that were unfamiliar to our all people, things like whiskey and chickens . . . that . . . came from the Columbia River area. Then they went to Victoria [Canada] to get things that were being brought from Hudson's Bay area from people who were invading that part of the land [of North America]. They [our people] knew many new things would be available if they crossed the waters to that part of the land. So it was a common route that people took to go bartering, and they intermarried. So east and west, north and south, were territories that were not uncommon to my dad's people and my mother's people.

My mother's people came from the American San Juans,[17] and they were quite comfortable traveling into Canada across the border. They traveled back and forth across the border into the Frasier River area and they honored and respected the cultures in each of these areas and familiarized themselves with the language of each area. Language is not a barrier. My mother could speak and understand vocabulary that was used in all of these areas, in eastern Washington, in Victoria, Canada, and the Puget Sound area. . . . It was mutually understandable in each area, so they showed respect by communicating in all of these languages. They knew there were differences, but they were not insurmountable differences.

My dad was a marvelous hunter. He knew how to provide for the table and for the community because he was a hunter who knew where to find game in the mountains and in the lowlands and when he was on the river because his father before him was called "head man" on the Skagit River. The river was as familiar [to him] as the back of his hand. The areas where the fish tended to rest were deep eddies where a man could put in a dip net and always find a salmon resting there or a place where there were schools of fish that traveled from one part of the river to another—a net or a weir[18] could be created out of cedar and set there. So these things were part of my dad's vocabulary. He knew in the

---

[17] American San Juans: Islands located in Puget Sound.
[18] Weir: A trap to capture fish. In the Northwest, they were generally made of cedar.

language what [vocabulary] to use to hunt for any of these things. To hunt ducks, our people knew how to use nets to capture flying game that was used as food for the table. They knew what kinds of roots were edible and where to find them. They knew about marsh keys. They knew about what was used for cultural use and what were medicinal because generations before them learned to use things from the land. The green things were known by my mother and were used as medicine for colds, for TB, for female problems. These things were all pointed out to me as I was growing up—this is for this, this is for that. And the literature, stories of our people encompassed many things of that nature and you had to read carefully to get the message from the stories. Oh, these things were used as medicine and when you were familiar with the stories, the message is right there! Berries were another important part of our diet and they were found in many places on our land from the late spring to early fall. So they utilized the gifts that had been placed here over the centuries. They knew how to and utilized all the things that were placed at our disposal and were part of the culture itself because they had been used for many generations.

Conditions have changed over the generations because "the Changers," what people called the newcomers to our land, have pushed our people away from familiar territories and have placed themselves along the river in our normal, natural camping areas, and the places that were open meadows where we gathered [medicinal roots] and things are no longer available to my people. The mountains can still be forages for some of the berries—the blueberries and the huckleberries. Our people know where to find those. Those roads have not been closed to us. So those things are still available. But those places where I went as a child to hunt things with my parents are no longer available. There are signs "Private Property, Keep Out." It hurts me deeply when personal places have barriers to us and I can't step on the land where my grandfather had his Longhouse and there is a sign, " Private Property. Keep Out." The Longhouse and the lands where my people's Longhouse existed are no longer available [for us] to even walk on.

My people were there to sign the Treaty of 1855[19] and they thought they had secured land for themselves. They were told to go in and move in with the Swinomish. When they went there to move their Longhouses to the Swinomish lands, they found that their Longhouses were too big to be accommodated by lands that were set aside for them at Swinomish.

---

[19] Treaty of 1855: Port Elliott Treaty.

So there was no room for them [my people] at Swinomish. So they put their Longhouses across two boards on the canoes and pulled themselves back up the Skagit River and found wherever they could put themselves, and that was up into the mountains. So they were told to go up into the hills and they stayed there until about 17 years ago—I can't remember the year the Skagit Tribe was granted a Reservation. They were granted 50 acres to establish a Reservation. They purchased the land and it was put in trust then and became a Reservation because the leaders, the Elders at that time, felt that being on a reservation would give them more advantages than just being a tribe. Aunt Susie said [that] the reasons our lands were taken over by settlers from the outside is because we are a compassionate people. And we have always been a compassionate people. [When] we saw poor people who needed help finding a comfortable place to live, we just invited them to come and we showed them how to use the land, and they just pushed us aside. That's what Aunt Susie said, one of our historians. And she laughed as she said it. She didn't have [the word] "naive" in her vocabulary and this is what she meant in the Lashootse language." We became naively impoverished, by our naivete. By helping people, they just took over our lands. This is the way these Changers have done during Chief Seattle's time. He helped people who just moved in on his land and now his people have no land. So what is fair? The Nooksacks had a different history, but a similar one to the Skagits.

When I was a little girl, I loved to be on the river with my dad because we could go into the shell canoe, one that he had made himself, and he could take us anyplace he wanted on the Skagit River—I loved the skill he had to do that. I had to coax him to ride in the canoe because my mother was worried about it. But when my dad went to fish and I would coax [him] to go, I would be allowed because we were just going across the river to the deep bay, where he would tie the canoe to a tree that was near-by and then he would take his dip net and pull the dip net through the water time after time after time; and this was probably the time of the year when the big run of salmon had already gone up the river to spawn and these were the stragglers that were tagging along behind; and that's why there weren't a lot of them sitting in the eddies. But he patiently sat in this one spot hoping to catch just one salmon so we could have food for our table, and I would sit quiet with him, not talking, not jiggling around in the canoe but sitting there learning how to be patient, learning how to be still, learning how to be quiet. This was the lesson I learned when I sat with my dad. We watched the water. We watched the sky. And he would lift his dip net up, one that had a long pole and a drag net at the end. He'd put it in the water and pull it slowly down, inch by inch through the water. He would make a sweeping motion with his dip net. His hands were very sensitive to what was on the other end of the pole. And if he sensed the body of a salmon touching it, he would quickly pull the net up and maybe manage to catch one salmon. He would put that salmon in the canoe and take us across the river. My mother would be waiting on the bank there, waiting for the arrival of my dad's catch. She would greet that salmon with lots and lots of enthusiasm, holding her hands out to receive it from my dad. She would hold it up and greet that salmon and sometimes kiss it on the nose because it would be such a welcome gift to our family. She knew that we would have food for the table, and what we didn't eat she would take and barter it for something like milk or eggs. So that meant a lot to the household that we lived on the Skagit River.

As I watched men and women share their lives in the community that I grew up in, I observed the way women honored their men and vice versa. Men were so proud of the handiwork of their women and the women who could put a meal on that could be enjoyed by the whole community—and you could see the pride on the husband's face. And the woman proudly would cut the food that her man had provided for the table because her man had been a good hunter. There was a mutual respect and a mutual responsibility even if the man, in my own opinion as a child, was kind of a worthless "dufus." The woman in his life could see the qualities that I, as a child, did not see, and I honored that. And I observed that and I thought about it; and as a child, I couldn't see any-thing a woman could be proud of in what seemed as "dufus" to me, but there were qualities there that I knew nothing about. And so as I watched my mother and my dad respect one another; and my dad always encouraging my mother to be a speaker and encouraging her to be in the forefront. She would do as he asked and be the speaker for any occa-sion. But when it came to something that was very deep, and wise words were needed, my mother turned to my dad and said, "Charlie, I want you to talk." So my dad would quietly respond and he would do what she asked him to do because these were words that came from the wisest place in a culture that needed wisdom. My mother respected my dad and he loved her irrepressible ability to be a clown if that was what was needed to lighten any occasion. She could bring laughter to a group at any time at a funeral, or a Shaker meeting, or in places that were very spiritually special. My mother could address each of those issues and my dad would stand in the back there and beam with pride. He knew that was his wife and she could speak any where and be heard. Her voice was very strong. They sang together and they were members of the Longhouse as well as the Shaker Church. This is the world I remember. The strength that men and women gave to one another and the respect that they showed for one another by silently applauding. You could see the pride on their faces when someone had a beautiful song and the song was shared in the community. You could see the pride if the song belonged to her husband or vice versa; when a woman's song was picking up a whole community. So these are good memories of people respecting one another and sharing the gifts that were respected by an entire community.

The women collected the berries and the cedar and the men were the hunters. The men went up into the hills to hunt for the big game, and also pheasant and grouse, animals that were edible. The gun was already a part of our culture in my time. But before that, the men used a bow and arrows. My dad used a gun and used a spear when he was fishing for salmon. During my Aunt Susie's time, fishing weirs[18] were constructed. There were some men who loved to pick berries and were very fast pickers, and they would bring down gallons and gallons of berries for the home to use. So there were exceptions [to men's and women's work]. The men and women collected cedar. Men who helped their wives would go up and gather roots—they knew where to find them during high tides or when flood waters would wash the roots clear of the land.

Cedar bark is still available up in the mountains for our people to use. Cedar bark is used for spirituality, for head dresses, and for winter time in the Longhouse. People who practice their spirituality in the Longhouses need the cedar for their regalia. So they go up into the mountains and ask the cedar to share some of its bark. They always do this [ask permission]. It is part of the ritual. The cedar is asked for any part of its sharing, its roots or its bark. The people never fail to do this in my memory. And the bark is only used on the east side [of the tree]. My cousin Minnie said, "You look for a tree that has a great strong limbs and go to the east side of it and ask for bark from the east side of the tree. And you do this with the roots also. You look for a tree that has very straight limbs and its roots will be straight also. Then you go out several feet from the base of the tree and then you dig down to find its roots. Then you cut some of the root . . . and take the heart out, and you use the heart of the root as the inner core of your basketry." You never took enough of the tree to kill the tree. You just took some of it. Then you went to the east side of the tree to take the little bit of bark.

The land has been impacted in many, many ways since the Changers have come here. The people have used and abused our land. They have polluted with pollutants that maybe they didn't realize how greatly this could impact all of life by using poisons to spray on all the land, on the greenery that is part of the world that we live in. They have used poisons in the work to earn money and have made that, in fact, their priority to get a product out regardless of how much damage it did. Maybe in the beginning they didn't realize that there was a lot of damage being done. Pollutants. Pollutants. Everybody has to get there fast so they can't use the old-fashioned methods. . . . I don't know if we have a way to reverse all of this. I think that people are becoming aware of things they have done in the last 100 years that have not been beneficial to the land. I think, "Better late than never that they are taking a look at ways how not to continue polluting the water and the air." So now that people are aware that they have been doing this, they can stop doing as much as they had been doing. Maybe our land can be a little healthier because of it. But the damage has been done in many places. The Skagit River can no longer be used as drinking water. When I was a girl, I went down to the river to get pails of water that we used for everything. And it was safe. And I think it has only been in my lifetime—I am only 79 years old—in less than 100 years, many things have changed and not necessarily for the betterment of the world.

With the mills polluting the water, the salmon have been impacted to the point of being a thing of the past, and the water is no longer drinkable. So I think these things are being tended to because now people are aware that there needs to be a concerted effort on the part of everyone, even the greedy ones, to pay attention. The dams have been a great detriment to my people, all of the dams. In order to create a technology for so many people to live on our lands, they had to make dams to create electricity because people are not content to use candles and kerosene lamps, the way we were. They have to have electricity to do all of the high tech stuff that needs to be done now. Because the high-tech stuff requires more of this and more of everything, the dams have created that kind of power. The dams have impacted our salmon to the point of extinction. There are still a few salmon trying to find their way up the spawning grounds. But when they get to a certain place up the Skagit River, where they would lay their eggs, then the dam would open its waters and wash all those eggs away. So the salmon that had come there to spawn were spawning to no avail.

One of the Elders would watch that happen and would cry in despair over the salmon trying futility to lay their eggs to spawn. That was Walter Sam who told me that, it brought tears to his eyes watching that happen—for no purpose now. So I think the dams along with the large polluting fish canaries have impacted our fisheries to the point of extinction. This greed has to come to an end. I don't know what my tribe is doing about it. I'm not that knowledgeable about the structure that tries to deter some of this. But I think the world should pay attention because the world depends on fish for the kinds of protein that are not available in any other form. Not all people are fish eaters, so they don't give the respect to the salmon that my people have. They have a different feeling about it because they have not grown up in a culture that respected the presence of salmon for a culture to live and be sustained by the use of the salmon. It was just a way of life with my people. They considered the salmon a part of their world and they considered them to be respected "people."

The Words of Okie Joe, Chief of the Upper Skagit Tribe

People who fight and die for their country should be citizens. Indians in World War I were not citizens, but we fought and died for what we got now. During the early 1920s, 1930s, 1940s, there weren't any Reservations here. We didn't even have Indian land to claim as a Reservation. Well, they took everything away from us and we may as well say we were second class citizens. Our Elders, Ray Boome and Bill Morton and them, they didn't even have a house for our meeting house. They had to go rent a house. We had no Indian lands, not even buildings. When we first started fighting for our Indian rights, my cousin Ray Boom and I, we told the Elders we were going in for our test case to let them people know there was a tribe of Indians up here, the Upper Skagit Indians. We owned all this valley at one time and we owned our fishing rights and hunting rights and everything like that. So they agree [the Elders]. So my cousin and I set a net out and we caught one fish: we had a test case. And the judge had to agree that we were entitled to our fishing rights and our hunting rights. It must have been in the late 1940s and early 1950s. We had to keep running and hide from the game wardens when we wanted to fish. And I finally got tired of running, so we told them we wanted a test Indian fishing case and we were going down to set and net and to come pick us up. We wanted to go to court over the fishing rights and the hunting rights. So we went to court and we beat the state for our hunting rights and our fishing rights, and they had to agree that we owned that a long time ago and they took it away from us, and later on the judge confirmed that we owned, all the tribes around the state of Washington, owned the fishing and hunting rights. Well, we won our rights before that, but the judge confirmed that we owned them.

It was not legal then in the old Elders' time [for Indians to fish and hunt]. You had to hang around to do all that kind of stuff. I remember when I was a little kid that my grandfather just sent me down the river after dark to throw a net in to catch fish; you couldn't just go out in the open to catch fish. If we wanted to fish, we had to go up to the spawning area and gaff and spear fish. It was the only way we could get our fish. All the three different tribes were in the same boat. All the three tribes were part of the Upper Skagit Tribe at one time and they all moved to different rivers or formed their own Reservations [after they got a Reservation]. But they couldn't hunt or fish either and they had to sneak around about their fishing. We were chased by game wardens a lot of times and so we got tired of that. We was just fishin' for our own use, but after we got our fishin' rights, we started selling them. We didn't have to hide any more. We had fishin' boats we could use. My cousin Ray Boome and I started the Indian huntin' and fishin' rights on the Skagit River and we started gettin' our land for our Reservation. Andy Fernando went to Washington DC to verify that we were entitled to a Reservation. That's how come we got it.

We used to hunt elk and mountain goat. I remember when I was about 6 years old my grandfather and my uncles took me up the mountains to go huntin' and pick berries at the same time, huckleberries. The women who picked huckleberries camped out up there. We had an old pack horse that we used to pack all our gear and stuff on. Nobody seems to want to go out and do any extra work or go up into the mountains any more. They'd rather hunt along the road. All you need [to hunt] is a hunting card and a tag, so you can keep track of how many goats you got. The white-colored hair on them is what the women weave clothes out of. You have to plan ahead to form a party of several different men and women if you want to go out and hunt or pick berries and stuff like that. They had Indian baskets made out of roots and cedar bark to carry the berries back in. The men always did the hunting and the women always picked the berries. The men would spot the berries for them and then the men would leave [to go hunting] and the women would be left in the berry patch. The men would go higher up into the mountains and hunt. It is too hard work for our younger people to go out and there are very few who would go out and pick huckleberries and stuff like that. It is easier now with the logging roads all up and through the mountains. They just need to drive around and park and go out and pick berries. It's easier for huntin', you don't have to pack your game so far.

Clear-cut logging is taking everything now. It used to be just big logs that they'd take. Now they're takin' all stuff that we wouldn't even look at when I was up logging. They're logging everything . . . little cedar poles, and fir and hemlock, even that cotton wood now. They grind up most of that stuff and make paper out of it. Everything will be cut-clear now. They're gonna hafta start replantin'. Some of the boys are tryin' to help by replantin' trees. Some of the boys told me that they are plantin' trees now. It's not the company that's plantin' trees. It's the state of Washington or the tribe. The tribe will get the contract to plant and they'll send our young men out to plant them. A lot of my grandsons around here are out plantin' trees. They make good money doin' that . . . so much a tree . . . they're all wrapped up in a bundle, you know, so much a bundle. If you're a good planter, you can make a lot of money. This is the tribe's way of gettin' work of the young men and doin' somethin' for the Earth. The tribe works on a lot of different areas where the trees have been cut. They send the tree planters in to plant the new trees.

They [the government, or the White people, environmental activists] blamed us for takin' all the fish, but after they shut us down so we couldn't fish no more and the sportsmen were fishing and they shut the sports fishermen down, and now they are working on the gill netters in the salt water. They are shuttin' them down now. They are getting the blame for takin' all the fish. But really, it is that there's not enough fish, now. When they started takin' all the fish in the saltwater, they didn't just take one kind. They just scooped up everything. And that wiped out certain species and there are not enough fish that escaped. They logged everything up there like that and they ruined all the spawning grounds [on the river]. So logging did quite a bit of that, too.

When you get down to the mouth of the river you get into farming and you look down there—there is nothing but cow poop down there and in the creek. It used to be a good spawning area down there and a good fishing area down there. Then they just wiped that completely out. It is the chemicals and a little bit of everything. It don't even look like water down there any more. You have to go way up in the mountains to find clear water. A lot of that time, they sprayed way up in the mountains and they pollute the creeks that way. They claim that bugs are eating up all the trees, but it gets into the water that stuff. What they're doin' is pointin' fingers at everybody else. And nobody wants to take the blame for that stuff. We say it's the loggers and the loggers say it is somebody else, and they say the state is to blame for spraying the chemicals on everythin' and killing everything and we don't know who to blame any-more. Cuz they're all to blame. When they logged they took everything. They killed everything that was there and now they have to figure out what to do now. They are replantin' now. You got different people comin' in and changin' things and different governments comin' in. You can't never say what's goin' to happen cuz you never know who is goin' to be runnin' things anymore.

We should have claimed half of the Upper Skagit Valley as our Reservation and that would have protected our rights more. We don't even have enough room to turn around on this Reservation. Why did you guys ask for such a small Reservation? You look around you and see how much land other tribes claimed for their Reservation. The Muck-leshoots claimed their land. They didn't just claim a small Reservation, they claimed a lot of land. They got young people growin' up there and they need room to turn around in. When they grow up and they and their kids grow up, they can't be stuck in a little place like this. I think we need to form a powerful group and let the committee know what we want for the tribe.

CONCLUSION

In 1975, the U.S. federal government formally recognized its responsibil-ity to American Indian people and guaranteed them the right to live ac-cording to their own customs and moral order, free to develop their own culture under the Indian Self-Determination Act. However, Indigenous people across much of North America continue to experience the arro-gance of conflicting lifeways in which nature, Indian People, and their lands are still considered as wild things to be harnessed and tamed.

Chapter 5

RELATIONSHIP WITH THE LAND: GLOBAL

To know the wisdom of the Elders, you must know patience.

*I*n this chapter, the global chorus of voices from Indigenous people come alive, people whose lives and cultures have been fragmented by environmental contamination, people who have maintained their cultural identity in spite of the toxic racism and environmental health problems they face on a daily basis. Two hundred and fifty million Indigenous people occupy this fragile Earth. They are in a daily struggle to maintain healthy lifeways in the face of conflict over their lands. In this chapter, I highlight issues of health and ecology affecting Amazonian miners, Zambian Tribes people in Africa, Small Nations of Yakutia in the former Soviet Union, Siberia, Maori of New Zealand, and the Sami in Finland. In many cases, the voices of the people are heard. In other situations, there is only documentation of the issues. There are many, many more from Papua, New Guinea, to the Inuit of Arctic Canada. I begin with the poisoning of the Amazon in Brazil.

BRAZIL: THE POISONING OF THE AMAZON

Ancient Amazonians were a fabled tribe of South American women warriors. In their quest for perfection as archers, Amazonian warriors excised their left breast. For today's Amazonian women, the breast has become a toxic waste dump for chemicals that reside in fatty tissues.[1] It is not a symbol of excellent marksmanship, but a symbol of rising increases in breast cancer.

My experiences in rain forests come from living for two years in the central islands of the Philippines, and from studying in the rain forests of Trinidad and Puerto Rico. For the past 10 years or so, much has been written about rain forest ecology and preservation; therefore, it is not my intention to duplicate that effort here, but to provide a brief overview.

Although differences in rain forests exist, there are many similarities. Rain forests are dark magical places filled with thick vegetation, very little sunshine, and long shadows filtering through thick canopy. Gaps exist where light enters, tracing stream beds or where a tree has fallen. To an ecologist nurtured on the hardwood forests of Pennsylvania or the coniferous needle leaf forests of the north, the tropical rain forest appears as a jumble of vegetation. Lianas or vines and epiphytes[2] such as orchids, and bromilliads[3] all contribute to the chaos. Over millions of years, plants in the rain forest have adapted unique features to support their survival, such as thick waxy leaves to store nutrients and retard dehydration; long drip tips on the points of leaves that lead water off the leaf to prevent algae, moss, and lichens from colonizing; and butresses that hold large trees steady.

Rain forests are noisy places with insects calling day and night. Luxuriant and flamboyant birds make their presence known with unique cries, such as the tonk-tonk-tonk of the bearded-bell bird. Mosquitoes, flies, wasps, hummingbirds, leaves dropping, and moving water all contribute to the cacophony.

As in the stratification structure of the temperate forests or the boreal forests, rain forests are also divided by ecologists into distinct layers.

---

[1] Breasts are noted for their high fatty content and often serve as repositories for synthetic organic chemicals circulating in the female body. Many of these compounds are carcinogenic (Steingraber, 1997).

[2] Epiphytes: Plants that live on the nutrients found in the air and on other plants. They have no roots, but use the trunks of other trees for support.

[3] Bromilliads: Living high in the forest canopy, these members of the pineapple family with thick, waxy leaves forming a holding tank for water provide niches and nesting spaces for frogs, snakes, and salamanders. Many of these species never leave their bromilliad homes.

"Each layer—the floor, the under story, the canopy and the giant emergent trees—is a distinct habitat, each with differing conditions" (Caufield, 1989, p. 50). Few animals move between their distinct niches in the canopy to the forest floor.

The upper canopy of the rain forest receives the most rain and sun. Being exposed to the highest level of sunlight, it is in the canopy where the greatest levels of photosynthesis occur. It is also at this level that more than half of the animals live. High above the forest floor, they are free from predators and most, being herbivores, find an abundance of food.

High humidity and low light create the peculiar characteristics and habitat of the forest floor. Here giant blue morpho butterflies, rainbow beetles, ticks, colorful birds, large animals such as deer, sloths, and striped cats share food, space, and nesting areas. From the forest floor where human trails are shared with the trails of animals to the canopy, the rain forest is the pantry for Indigenous people. Tribes harvest nuts, resin, gum, rattan, in addition to finding a variety of foods. For example, one tribe in the Philippines can divide their plant species into 1,600 categories while professional botanists can distinguish only 1,200. The rain forests' strength is in its biodiversity:

Land is the most important element of any forest tribe's survival. . . . Once deprived of their land, forest dwellers can only look forward to being absorbed into the lowest level of the dominant culture, as landless peasants, low-paid laborers of peasants. (Caufield, 1989, p. 100)

Rain forest nutrients are bound up in a complex relationship with the vegetation. Once the vegetation is destroyed, areas cleared for farms or industry or mining, the red clay of the rain forest is soon compacted and transformed into unproductive desert.

In its ever-widening circle, seeking locations for materials to exploit, the industrial world is focusing on the remote Fourth World[4] areas of the tropical rain forests where Indigenous people have maintained their lifeways through isolation. Mining in a rain forest brings threats to the culture of a people who rely on the natural resources around them for food and medicine.

---

[4] Fourth World: The world of Indigenous people.

Ganika

Ganika describes herself as a political refugee "with a very big mouth."
Originally from Surinam, she lives abroad in an undisclosed European
city. We meet to speak openly in the student lounge of a prestigeous Canadian university. The windows are open to a breezeless, humid summer day.
Like women in a Rousseau painting, Ganika's face is the color of burnt
umber. Brass circles dangle from her ears and flutter in the breeze from an
electric fan. Her thick black hair is tied up in two braids. She sips a bottle
of Evian water. With infectious enthusiasm, she speaks to me of contamination and destruction of the rain forest in her native Surinam. Her accent
has an unfamiliar dialect:

> My name is Ganika and I am from Surinam, once called Dutch Guyana.
> My mother is an Arawak Indian and African, my father is Chinese and
> Dutch. I am living abroad at the moment as a political refugee. I am liv-
> ing without a job. I had a job, but I got fired because my mouth is too
> big. I am surviving, living. It took me a long time to admit to myself that
> I actually am a political refugee. But I am. I was teaching at the Uni-
> versity of Surinam, the biggest country of all three Guyanas. I have a
> big mouth and I tried to open my students' eyes to the politics of the
> rain forest. One morning I came to my office and I found a bullet hole
> in my wall. On my desk was a decapitated Iguana, so I knew "they" or
> someone was going to kill me. My name means "Troubled Waters."
> Anyway about my country: First the British had it, then the French,
> then the British again, and finally the Dutch had it for over 500 years.
> We are a protectorate of the Dutch. My country is geographically linked
> to Latin America, but culturally we are closer linked to the Caribbean.
>
> Everyone thinks that rain forests are all the same all over the world,
> but they aren't. Ours is the most beautiful of the three Guyanas and has
> many unique plants and animals not found in any other rain forest.
>
> In Surinam, there are only about 2,000 Aboriginal people left. They
> are from four tribes. One of the tribes is Arawak. That is my mother's
> tribe. Most of them live deep in the rain forest away from the White
> people. They know how to survive in the rain forest so as to preserve it.
> They are logging, but in a good way. About 100 years ago, the Dutch
> government brought Indonesians here to be laborers. These Indone-
> sians now feel they are Surinam nationals. Now the president of
> Indonesia wants to come in and ally himself with these Indonesian

nationals to log our rain forest. He thinks the Indonesians will help him, but they won't. He wants to destroy our rain forest with this logging. They have already destroyed theirs; now he wants to destroy ours. Well, there is a big war going on in our rain forest. When the government officials come in, their cars get shot. There are African ex-soldiers collaborating with the Aboriginals for the preservation of the rain forest. You know, the Aboriginal people can make their living in the rain forest without destroying it. There are gold and diamonds in there being mined, but not destroying the environment.

Next door to Surinam is British Guyana. There was big mining there using mercury. A big dam collapsed and the mercury water behind it spilled out and contaminated the waters and poisoned all the fish. Animals and people were poisoned, too. And some got Minimata disease. The people were told not to eat anything, but it was too late, many got sick. Now no one can eat anything there. The water went down to Brazil and continues to poison.

Our Aboriginal people are trying to preserve what they have left of their culture. The Catholic Church destroyed it. Even in my mother's time, people were forced into the boarding schools. Now the people are trying to remember their Aboriginal ceremonies, religion, and way of life. The kids are learning their language. It is through language that culture is passed on to the next generation. The Aboriginal women are working in a kind of ecotourist business. They have a van and they allow only 16 persons per group to enter and to learn and observe their culture and their rain forest. It is strictly controlled. [The women feel] if people come to observe, they will understand better and help to preserve it.

IN BRAZIL

Twenty thousand Yanomami (also called the Yanomamo) people live in scattered villages on the border of Brazil and Venezuela. In 1987, gold was discovered in this region, home to 8,000 forest-dwelling Yanomami Indians. Thirty thousand Brazilian prospectors invaded their territories seeking gold. The Brazilian government admits that since the gold rush began at least one Yanomamo Indian a day has died (McElroy & Townsend, 1996). As mercury was used to extract the gold from rocks, the waters became mercury polluted.

Mercury has been used in gold mining in Brazil since gold was first discovered in the Amazon basin in the 18th century. In the last 10 years,
between 1–2,000 tons of this highly poisonous liquid metal have been
released into the Amazon Basin. (Greenpeace International, 1997)

Mercury levels are increasing as more gold is mined. For every kilo of
gold produced, four times that amount of mercury is released into the
environment. Concern over the contamination of the Amazon River and
of local populations is escalating with hundreds of thousands of people
living in the region thought to be at risk. (Greenpeace International,
1997)

Begun as a trickle in 1979, the current gold rush is a result of rapid
increases in the price of gold in 1987. The gold fields of the Amazon involve over one million miners or *garimpeiros*. Although 90 percent of the
mercury used in Brazil is imported from Mexico, there has been a significant increase in imports from Holland, Germany, and the United Kingdom
(Greenpeace International, 1997). Metallic mercury is not produced in
any of these countries, but rather, these are the countries where exporting
companies have their headquarters. Mercury used in Brazil is produced in
Spain, Italy, the United States, and Mexico:

Metallic mercury is used as an amalgam to separate particles of gold
from river sediment. During the simple process of adding liquid mercury to filtered sediment, some of this highly toxic substance escapes
directly into the water and soils. . . . Mercury in the amalgam is later
burnt off, releasing a toxic white vapor and leaving near-pure gold ore.
About three-quarters of the mercury used in gold mining is released
into the atmosphere, where it is absorbed by plants and soils in contaminated rain. (Greenpeace International, 1997)

As we have seen in the case of the Cree peoples of James Bay,
Canada, metallic mercury escapes into the rivers where it is transformed
into the highly toxic and persistent methyl mercury which builds up in the
food chain, ultimately accumulating in high concentrations in fish, the staple diet of local people, causing Minimata disease:

The gold-mining activities themselves also dramatically change the river
environment; as the sediment is disturbed, clear waterways turn to

rivers of opaque golden brown. However, the ecological effects of this stark alteration of the river environment have been poorly studied. (Greenpeace International, 1997)

Added to the accumulated contamination of the Amazon ecosystem (both aquatic and aerial) is the serious risk posed to the health of hundreds of thousands of people living in the region. People are exposed to mercury both directly in mining operations and indirectly as it moves through the environment into the human food supply. (Greenpeace International, 1997)

The elderly, children, and pregnant women, whose health is more vulnerable, are particularly at risk from poisoning by inhaling the mercury vapors when it is released into the open air in the mining process. Researchers have found that levels of mercury found among people in gold-mining areas are high enough to produce clinical symptoms of mercury poisoning such as birth defects, brain damage, and death. Less severe poisoning may result in tunnel vision, instability, and neurological disorders (Greenpeace International, 1997).

Recent surveys in the gold-mining town of Itaituba, which has the largest concentration of gold traders in the Brazilian Amazon, show that up to 37 percent of miners have excessive levels of mercury in their blood. Itaituba is in the Tapajos valley, the largest of nine major gold-mining regions in the Amazon Basin. (Greenpeace International, 1997)

Distance from mining operations is little protection as mercury moves widely through the environment. Blood and urine samples taken from individuals in the fishing village of Jacareacanga, . . . 100 km from the nearest mining camp, had significantly elevated levels of mercury, with 16 percent showing exceedingly high levels in their bodies. Kayapo children have also been found to have average blood levels more than twice the acceptable upper limits. (Greenpeace International, 1997)

Samples taken from the floor dust of gold workshops in Itaituba show dangerously high levels of mercury in gold workshops which are a major source of atmospheric mercury and human exposure.

Prostitution, violence, and alcohol were partners in the invasion. Rain forests were cut down to create airfields leaving huge scars. Other epidemics soon followed the miners affecting Whites and Indian People alike. Diseases like malaria, influenza, and other respiratory diseases ran rampant because of non-existent health care. Pollution killed fish, shrimp, and by the early 1990s health officials documented over 20 percent of the population had died from diseases or environmental pollution introduced by the gold miners (Gomez, 1993).

> In Brazil alone, an average of one Indian culture per year has disappeared since the turn of the century. The survival of such groups depends on the survival of the forests and the policies and lifestyles of the dominant cultures are destroying both. (Head & Heinzman, 1990, p. 106)

The invasion to destroy Indigenous cultures around the world is not an accident of development. "Modern civilizations" and the people who hold power in them covet land held by Indigenous people. Since they have the power to persecute and claim lands, they destroy Indigenous cultures that stand in their way (Head & Heinzman, 1990).

Modern technology such as helicopters, satellite surveying systems, and telecommunications have helped to create the most detailed surveys of remote areas of the Earth. Resources are identified and extracted in a one-sided invasion. Amazonia, Brazil, boasts the largest contiguous rain forest in the world with the highest diversity of 300 species of trees in a single hectare.

In the early 1970s, the World Bank financed the building of Highway 364, known as the Trans-Amazon Highway, so the Brazilian government could penetrate the rain forest. Rondonia Province at the end of the highway continues to be deforested at an alarming rate. By the year 2000, at the rate of current destruction, only 20 percent of the forest will remain intact. Indigenous people living inside those forests have been decimated by forced removals, settler-borne diseases, and armed raids (T. Weaver, 1997).

Colonists chose to establish their farms where the trees were thick and the land seemed rich. Today, lacking the balanced agricultural skills of the forest dwellers, two hundred million colonists on the fringes of the rain forest practice slash-and-burn agriculture, destroying as they do so over half the primary rain forest each year (Caufield, 1989). The soils are so poor that they cannot sustain slash-and-burn agriculture even for 5 years, let alone more. So the settlers, who pour in at a rate of 13,000 a month, move into new areas where the cycle is repeated (T. Weaver, 1997). Rain forests, the world's oldest forests, have existed for over 60 million years and they are disappearing in a heart beat.

Contact with outside people and technologies often results in disaster for Indigenous people. For example, the Nambiquara Indians in Brazil were poisoned by drinking water stored in contaminated herbicide cans sold to them by neighboring ranchers for the purpose of storing water. The containers carried herbicides of 2-4-D and 2-4-5-T (Head & Heinzman, 1990). These herbicides are code named Agent Orange.

In addition to effects of mercury, mining exposes miners to the dangers of silica and silicosis.

Silicosis

Silicosis, caused from inhaling small particles of free silica (silicon dioxide) in industries such as gold, lead, silver, and coal mining, is the oldest known occupational lung disease. Every year 2 million workers in the United States are exposed to crystilline silica with 300 deaths annually (U.S. Department of Labor, 1993). Silicosis can develop in as few as 10 years in industries where the dust is extremly high, such as in sand blasting, foundary working, and tunneling. Symptoms are shortness of breath, coughing, and reduction of lung volume. Scarring of the lung tissue results when dust from mining and other industries is significant. There was no effective treatment for silicosis at the time of this writing (Berkow, 1992).

In 1993, Hnizdo and Sluis-Cremer published data on more than 2,000 African gold miners, 14 percent of whom had developed silicosis. Research by Steenland and Brown (1985) documents the risk of silicosis as 68 to 84 percent in miners who were exposed to silica with more than 4mg/m3 years of exposure:

> Because the Earth is our mother, the liver of the Earth is coal, the lung is uranium, earthquakes and tornadoes are her breath. Now she is in pain. When the government takes her organs, she will die. The government only wants money. (Navajo, Burger, 1990, p. 104)

Africa: Zambia

Zambia, once the British colony of Rhodesia, is situated on the interior plateau of southeastern Africa. Because the central plateau is only 1 kilometer (km) above sea level, the climate in Zambia is warm but not humid. There are two seasons—the wet and the dry. Rains usually begin in November and last until June. Much like other tropical countries, the rain can be seen from vast distances before it actually arrives. When it does fall, the air smells sweet. Thunderstorms are common during the rainy season and often electrical storms knock out power.

There are 8 million people in Zambia. The Indigenous people are the Bantus. The 8 nations that surround Zambia have been in political turmoil for many years. The borders of Zambia are difficult to patrol. As a result, Zambia's economic resources are 1,000 km from the nearest seaport. Zambia's wealth is tied to copper, her greatest natural resource. The country remains largely unspoiled by environmental pollution, but there are problems with the colonial mentality of the non-Bantu in areas of land use.

When independence from Britain was granted in 1963, English remained the language of education, law, and commerce. Environmental poverty was a pressing issue. During the colonial era, migration to the city of Lusaka was limited to those men who had jobs in the urban area. The population of Lusaka was 123,000. After independence, the population rose to over 400,000. Squatter settlements sprang up everywhere, on private and public land. Thousands of poor people shared pit latrines. Clean water was a commodity (Dankelman & Davidson, 1993).

Progressive development on land traditionally occupied by Indigenous people caused ecological destruction in the building of roads, dams, canals, waterways, resource extractions, logging, and land use changes from urbanization, agriculture, and migration. As humans change the environment in the name of progress, we become more vulnerable to opportunistic species such as pathogenic microbes. Many infectious diseases seen around the globe today are related to disruptions in the environment (Platt, 1996). Pathogenic diseases such as malaria, dengue fever, and cholera developed near irrigation projects, dams, construction sites, standing water, poorly drained areas, and contaminated drinking water.

Problems in health and lifeways for Indigenous people are exacerbated when major changes are forced on them through mega industries and government.

Kasama, a village in the Northern Province of Zambia, sits on a high plateau with incredible views and cool breezes. Once land of the Bantu who occupied all of South Africa before the Europeans came, Kasama is now a sleepy town boasting immigrants from England, Norway, Pakistan, and elsewhere. Europeans who live in Kasama live the life of the privileged. It was for them that the Kasama International School was founded. The school boasts a swimming pool, small classes, and dedicated European teachers. A Bantu woman washes the clothes for the household staff. Her skin is blue-black and her smile is filled with even white teeth. Her dress today is printed with green and black leaves. Far away at a meeting in Canada, her Zambian "sister," a nurse, speaks for her:

I trained for my nursing in the UK. They have the same system here [in Canada]. My family is still in Zambia, and my parents, but I could never go back. I have been away for 8 years. Some people in Zambia still practice the old religion, but many are Christian and others combine Christianity with the traditional religions. For me, Christianity works. I grew up in the city [Harere]. The economy of the people [in Zambia] depends on copper and agriculture. But the copper mines are running out of copper. People of Zambia have a relatively good life compared to the political upheaval of neighboring people in Zimbabwe and Zaire. The U.S. government has been interested in our copper and our government is stable. But there are problems. The mines are especially destructive of the land. And when the copper runs out? Who will clean up? Not the owners of the mines. Our land is good. We have good soil. The plateau has nice weather most of the year. We grow some coffee to sell on the world market, but we need to find ways to grow more and to sell more. There are not enough doctors or health care workers to take care of sickness. I feel guilty because I left, but I am helping my parents have a better life by sending money home. The White people [government workers, teachers in the International School] can get airlifted to Johannesburg

[South Africa], but the regular people don't have that kind of money. It costs $10,000 for the life flight to take you to Johannesburg to be treated for severe illnesses. We need more health care workers. We have 2,000 refugees living in Kasama now because of the fighting in Zaire. There are Red Cross and United Nations' people setting up hospitals, but these facilities are for the refugees of the war in Zaire.

Conclusion

Mining is one of the most destructive of the resource extraction pursuits of non-Indigenous people. Mining industries decimate lands and cultures in South American rain forests, in Africa, and in North America. But, for Indigenous people, the health of the land is the health of the people. It is the place where the ancestors are buried, where we grow our food, and hold sacred ceremonies. As implemented on much of the Indigenous lands today, mining affects the culture, people, and the land. Although protocols exist for safe mining practices, greed and ignorance usually prevail, preventing such protocols from being implemented.

NEW ZEALAND: MAORI

The Maori are the Indigenous people of New Zealand. Their experiences parallel the experiences of First Nations in North America. For the Maori, to speak of the land is to speak of a spiritual relationship or union. To them, land is not an economic commodity to be bought or sold. It is a sacred heritage passed down from tribal ancestors. It is their cultural heritage. That close bond with the land was established in time when the world was taking shape, when the loving Sky Father and the Earth Mother reparated. After the separation of the Earth and the Sky, all the life forms began to live on the Earth. Mountains are especially important to Maori people as symbols of the power of the tribe from which they were born (Doig, 1989).

In 1840, perhaps 1,000 settlers, traders, and missionaries shared New Zealand with the 100,000 Maori people who accepted them into their country to trade for new manufactured goods and muskets. By 1858, with the White population rising to 48,000, the population of Maori decreased due to fighting and disease. The Maori were being displaced in their own country.

Conversations with Maori Health Educators

It is a humid July day in Sioux Falls, South Dakota. A blazing sun forces us to the shade where we sit munching white-bread American sandwiches. We have been together for two days. We will be together for one more day. Kuini, Olive, and Tania are nurses; Bella and Phillip are the Elders, Ngaire is a health care worker. They have come to America at the invitation of Jo Ellen Koerner and the Healing Web Project[5] to share knowledge and culture. Their language is a song, lyrical with hints of Hawaiian phonetics. They are my new relations, my sisters . . . bonded together last night in a sweat lodge with the Lakota people of Vermilion, South Dakota. We laugh . . . we learn . . . I am a remora, sucking in everything. In a travel guide to New Zealand, Kuini points out the sacred places in Aukland. "This is my mountain. . . . this is where Bella and Phillip live. . . . this is our Marae."[6] I ask focused questions, but all of the women are eager to answer:

> Men are the leaders in Maori culture, and the role of women is that of discreet advisor. The man walks past the Marae and listens to the gossiping women. He pretends to stop, to tie his shoe so he can listen better. If he is careful, the women will speak loud enough and voice opinions so that the man will know how to decide in the council. When visitors go into the Marae they must be led by the eldest woman. Only a woman can lead into the Marae. (Tania, interview, 1996)

For the Maori, conflict and struggle have been present since the first Europeans settled in New Zealand in 1841. For 155 years, the real struggle

---

[5] Healing Web Project. A program implemented by Sioux Valley Hospital to improve the dynamics of nurse to nurse relationships.
[6] Marae: Land owned by the Maori people; similar to a Reserve. It includes the ornately carved ceremonial home building of a particular clan of Maori; similar to a Longhouse.

between the Maori and the government is not the land nor the war, but the relationship itself:

> The New Zealand government continues to grab our lands for public works or government-supported industrial schemes. It happened as recently as in the 1970s and 1980s with the land taken for the New Plymouth airport and various major economic projects in the north. For over 155 years, we Maori protested the government's right to administer lands reserved for the Maori, or lease those lands without Maori consent. The grievances built up over time. Harvesting of natural resources ended because the government took the good productive land. They are also interested in the rivers, bush country, lakes, and seas. (Bella, interview, 1996)

The Treaty of Waitangi: 1840

> In 1840, Maori gave up their lands to the Queen of England so that we could have the Queen's protection as our chiefs performed their duties over the lands and the people. But the new settlers wanted more land which the Maori didn't want to give up. As a result, we had the Maori Wars of 1860–1865. We were not as strong as the *Pakeha* (Whites). We had guns, but not good ones. The government took back the treaty and our land was open to the *Pakeha*. But our Elders are persistent and for the next 100 years, they kept the terms of the treaty before the *Pakeha* government. In 1985, some tribes were paid for the lands that were taken unfairly. Two years ago, the New Zealand government offered the tribes a $1 million package, but the young people rejected it and more and more of our youth are becoming militant as a result of unemployment and frustration with land loss. (Maori elders, 1996)

The Taranaki Maori were plundered of their resources. The little land they have cannot sustain their cultural lifeways and cultural survival. The Maori feel that the government should compensate them for loss of land, social and economic destabilization, and affronts to the dignity of the culture and people. "The army marched through the lands of the Taranaki Maori and destroyed every village along the way" (Phillip, interview, 1996). The people feel that the taking of the land constitutes a record of continual repression and denial of human rights. Over time, the Maori have endured poverty and the ensuing health effects of that poverty. Today, their argument concerns not the wars of the past, but the relationship between the government of New Zealand and the Maori themselves. The Maori, who see health care as a treaty issue, require much persistent aid to cure health problems. Maori health statistics generally show a lower life expectancy than for Whites. The following excerpts concerning health of the Maori are from noted health care professionals in Aukland, New Zealand. Head of Maori studies at Massey University, Mason Durie, indicates:

> The time is now for the government to have a treaty policy rather than the current "Treaty settlement policy." A major breakthrough in health will come when fundamental issues like poverty, unemployment, and housing are addressed.

Professor of Maori and Pacific Island Health at Auckland University, Colin Mantell, agrees:

> Poor Maori health indicators can be viewed as a treaty issue, split into poverty on one hand and difficulties in accessing health care on the other.

Because the Maori are guaranteed the same rights and privileges as British citizens, the safeguards of their treasures (*taonga*) includes health of the people (Paul Stanley, Aukland University's Alcohol and Public Health Research Unit member). Sue Crengle, a Maori physician in general practice, says, "Article 3 guarantees Maori equity, which should include standards of health. Because Article 2 of the treaty was not honored, the effects of loss of land and possessions resulted in hardships with a negative impact on Maori health. The Crown has a duty to improve Maori health and make sure it is acknowledged. I personally believe health is a *taonga*."

However, some of the astonishing facts are:

- Maori face twice the normal risk of alcohol-related disability or death. Far more Maori abstain, but Maori drinkers have heavier sessions than non-Maori.

- One in four adult Maori alive today can expect to die early because of smoking.
- Britain's National Asthma Campaign found clear links between asthma and poverty. One census study found 86 percent of people disabled by the disease were in the lowest three social classes.
- Up to 18,000 of the estimated 40,000 hepatitis B carriers could be Maori.

Other health issues affecting the Maori people include:

- Mainstream health services give mentally ill Maori patients more drugs than other patients to make them easier to handle.
- The Core Services Committee recommended regional health authorities fund traditional healers where this was likely to improve Maori access to health care. Kim Workman, deputy director-general of health, said the recommendation recognized the value of nonconventional medicine. It was a useful first step which would also affect Asian and Pacific Island traditional practices.

The Health Ministry's Report include findings that 38 percent of Maori referrals come from law enforcement agencies and welfare services. Drug psychosis admissions make up 21 percent of Maori admissions for drug and alcohol disorders, compared to 5 percent for *Pakeha*. In the midland region, young Maori women are 20 times more likely to be admitted to hospital for drug and alcohol problems than non-Maori women. Maori males are seven times more likely to be admitted than non-Maori. The report figures demonstrate a culture under siege.

We are beginning to have our children schooled in the Maori language. My children have been in Maori language school since they began school. They are in what you call high school in the States. It is better for their generation now. Not like when I was in school, people made racist remarks and harassed me. But the young people have a lot of anger. As they become empowered, they want things to change for the better. There is a lot of unemployment, but that is the case all over New Zealand. There are a lot of suicides in the adolescent population.

(Conversation with a social worker from Aukland, World Conference on Breast Cancer, 1996, Kingston, Ontario)

The White man says there is a bloke named Jesus Christ and a god in the sky. And there's a devil down in the ground. They build their cities. They destroy the land, the forests. They pollute the water. I worry what is to become of all the Black fellas. Will our kids be forced to accept whatever the White man says? The White man says we must forget our rituals, our religion, our cultures, our roots. (Robert Bropho, indig .rights.oz@gynosys.svle.ma.us)

ROVANIEMI, FINLAND (FINNISH LAPLAND)

Dalle son navt
go bohcco borra
ja go gearga
de lahttesgoahta
uoa uoa uoa

Then he goes out like this
when he eats reindeer
and when he has time
he begins to sing
uoa uoa uoa

From *A Hunter's Bestiary*, Lapland

An eagle makes its nest on the knee of Vainamoinen, the Creator, who is floating on the sea. As its egg rolls into the sea, it breaks up into the sun, moon, and stars and creates the universe of the Finnish-Estonian people (Honko, Timonen, Branch, & Bosely, 1994). Creation myths are nonexistent, however, in explaining the Sami migration into Finnish Lapland. In 555 A.D., the Byzantine historian Procopius wrote one of the first sources in which the country of Thule (Scandinavia) was referred to as an island with a large number of tribes. The people were hunters, not farmers, and called themselves *skridfinnarna* (Baer, 1992). In the 11th century, historians record the work of the *skridfinnarna* as hunters.

Some anthropologists feel the *skridfinnarna* moved westward from the Ural Mountains, others feel they moved northward with the reindeer as the ice receded from the last Ice Age. Thule (*skridfinnarna*) people bringing their culture migrated across the circumpolar north into Arctic Canada and the Northwest Territories where they have been replaced by the Inuit. The last Thule in Arctic Canada died in the 1940s in the Northwest Territories.

The people of Lapland, Finland, tell of Biegolmai, a monstrous figure, the Mythical Wind Man, who dropped snow onto the land with two huge snow shovels. No living thing dared enter his kingdom. Once in the midst of his fury, in a raging snowstorm, one of his shovels broke. When the storm abated, living things were able to take hold on the land (Beach, 1993). The myths also tell of the Sami relationship to the land. Across the circumpolar north, cultural similarities exist with the Siberians and other people who hunt today as an ancient circumpolar culture, long since splintered with the coming of Indo-Europeans and Slavs (Beach, 1993). The Sami are the Indigenous people of Norway, Sweden, Finland, and Russia. Originally known as the Lapps by the Scandinavians, they are the earliest reindeer (rangifer tarandus) herders. Today, Sami hold minority status even in their own lands and reindeer have been almost eliminated from the market economy. Lapland (Sami Land) transcends the borders of Sweden, Finland, and Russia's Kola Peninsula. It is land adjacent to and above the Arctic Circle.

The basic worldview of the ancient Sami, the spirit world, and the peoples' relationship with the spirits is comparable to American Indian philosophies. Traditional spirituality involves shamans and spirit or totemic animals. Shamans have the power to move between the upper (sky), middle (Earth), and lower (hell) world at will. Often they use birds to move souls between the three worlds. The traditional drum of the Sami shaman, made of reindeer skin stretched over a circle of birch wood, portrays the three worlds painted in hieroglyphics, which include deer, hunters, symbols for wisdom, snow crystals, supreme god, and hundreds more. Before contact with Europeans, Sami believed in shamans and the abilities of spirits to assume many forms. Some of the more worshiped and powerful spirits were the Sun, the Thunder, the God of the Underworld, and the Goddess of Childbirth (Beach, 1993). Although many Sami were converted to Christianity, traditional beliefs continue.

The traditional clothing of the Sami resembles that of the Lakota with the use of spirit animals drawn on hides and skin drums. More well-known is the colorfully embroidered tunics of men and women. Much like American Indians in North America, the Sami have suffered language and land losses and attacks on Sami villages by the dominant cultures. The price of economic development in Sami lands is high. The cultural lifeways of the Sami are threatened by lumbering, mining, and dam construction for electricity demanded by industries in the south.

The roles of men and women in traditional Sami culture differ in their relationship to the reindeer herd, but they seem to share a partnership. The women are responsible for bringing up children who will be the next generation of reindeer herders. Women convert raw reindeer material into food, clothing, and equipment as well as participate in the slaughter of the reindeer. Many Sami women are employed in a cash economy outside the reindeer herding society, helping to subsidize their husband's reindeer herds. The men tend the herds and breed the reindeer (Eikjok, 1992).

Of all nations outside of Russia which were affected by the nuclear fallout from Chernobyl, the Sami homelands and Sami reindeer herders suffered the most. The historic catastrophe of April 1986 discharged over 100 million curies of radioactive gases and particulates contaminating much of eastern Europe, Russia, and the Scandinavian countries. Because lichens, which are the principal dietary food for reindeer, actively take up the radionucleide isotopes, all of the reindeer herds in Lapland were contaminated as were the water, soil, fish, vegetable gardens, and wild foods. Transfer to humans is through the lichen-reindeer-human food chain. Exposure to radiation, which destroys the immune system and increases susceptibility to infections, can lead to cancer and death (Chessworth, 1996).

It has been 12 years since the Chernobyl accident, but the incidence of birth defects and deformities in animals continues. The most common genetic mutations documented in animals are those born with an absence of one or more extremities, deformities of the skull and spine, absence of eyelids, absence of hair, exposed internal organs, or absence of an anus (Chernousenko, 1991). Today in the Midwest and in other areas of the United States, we are seeing similar defects in frog populations. *The Washington Post,* on September 30, 1996, reported that herpetologists have discovered frogs with missing legs, extra legs, and paralyzed legs sticking out of the body at odd places. One frog had an extra eye found in its throat. Environmental Science students at Salish Kootenai College report similar findings in their research on the Flathead Reservation.

The term *shaman* comes from the Tungus people of Siberia. By controlling their state of consciousness, shamans interact with spirits, traveling outside the body in an ecstatic state between three worlds: sky world, middle world, and lower world. The spirits he controls are helping spirits or spirit guides, also known as power animals. Many are animal forms such as bears, wolves, stags, and a variety of birds (Walsh, 1990). Power animals travel with the shaman and provide strength, guidance, and teaching. In shamanism, there is a greater emphasis placed on personal experiences than in many other religious traditions and which confers extraordinary status. "To the people of their tribe, shamans are figures of awesome power whose help can mean the difference between health and sickness, life and death" (Walsh, 1990, p. 21).

An Experience and Conversation with the Sami Shaman

We travel by snowmobile deep into the forest of Arctic Finland 65 km above the Arctic Circle and 150 km from the Russian border. The forest is dark, foreboding in the gloom of Arctic winter. Ice and snow chips, thrown up by the forward propulsion of my guide's snowmobile, reflect fire in its tail light. At 3:00 P.M., the darkness of Arctic night engulfs us as we move northward toward the *Kota* (camp) of the shaman.[7]

---

[7] Shaman: Hultkrantz defines shaman, a term that originates in Tungusic language, as a social functionary who, with the help of guardian spirits, attains ecstasy in order to create rapport with the supernatural world on behalf of his groups; a specialist who enters into an altered state of

The shaman meets us at a predetermined place known only by the guide. We cache the snowmobiles and hike into the forest for another half mile. The trail is uncharted and I follow blindly, trekking through 2 feet of snow in the footsteps of the guide and shaman to a small canyon of rock formations, the shaman's "power place." Strength purifies me and I feel courageous, the only woman in this Arctic wilderness. The shaman appears in his "power clothes," a fur-trimmed leather robe and hood. It is difficult to determine his age. He wears thick glasses, his dark skin is rough with pox-like scars. We work our translation through three languages: Finnish, Sami, and English. Interpretation and understanding requires concentrated attention by both of us. He has prepared a place of reindeer skins and invites me to sit on them closer to the campfire. "Before we go to the power place, we make meal of reindeer. While cooking, we go to top of canyon."

From his backpack, the shaman removes a black cast-iron pot into which he places a healthy chunk of frozen butter, onions, and about 2 kilos of chopped reindeer meat. He takes three little bottles out of his pack and sprinkles their contents over the meat. My suspicions are on guard for hallucinogenics or some other drug. When it sizzles, he stirs it with his long Lapp knife and wipes the blade in the snow. "Come, we go to rock," he says, "bring reindeer hides and sit for a while." I gather up my hide and follow him up to the precipice of the rocks where we place the hides on the snow and sit in silence. "What you feeling now, Lori? You feel your power animal?" he asks. I tell him about the sea otter[8] which has been my animal for half my life. He explains that his is the sea eagle.[9] Both have been brought back from the edge of extinction and both linked to the sea. He asks me to lie on my back, so he can place his hands on my forehead and neck. As he does so, I feel heat energy, an aura coming from the palm of his hands. In my analytical mind, I wonder if it is a trick. I wonder if he has hand warmers in his pocket, but then I notice he has no pockets. He

---

consciousness to mediate between the spirit and human realms and facilitates access to sacred knowledge and power on the part of his or her clients.

[8] Otter medicine is woman medicine. Otters live near female elements of water and Earth. Always adventuresome and curious, otters assume that all animals are friends. Otter people express joy for others in their achievements, not jealousy (Sams & Carson, 1988).

[9] Eagle medicine is close to the heavens where the Great Spirit lives but remains connected to the Earth (Sams & Carson, 1988).

lays his hands on my forehead, and slides them over the sides of my face and down my neck to my throat. I remember his long Lapp knife and the ability of the shaman to take souls to the underworld and the sky world. I become uneasy. My heart races. His hands encircle my forehead, "I feel you are strong woman; big energy, big power. I feel no holes in this power. You must use this power in a good way, not a foolish way. [The whole experience from sitting in silence on the rocks to the laying of the hands lasts about an hour.] I go now and finish [cooking] the meal. You come when you are ready." He disappears into the darkness. I remain on my back in his power place, staring up at the misshapen spruces against a black sky, long shadows in a moonless night. I close my eyes. Time passes. My mind and body relax from the touch and warmth of the shaman's hands. Although the air temperature is probably below 0 degrees, my body is very warm. My mind wanders. I become one with the reindeer on whose hide I rest, one with the rocks on this cliff, one with the Earth. I have been here since the beginning of time. Because never before this moment have I experienced the healing rituals of a shaman, I wonder later if my spirit/mind left my body or if I was in a state of hypnosis. It seems tame, but I accept it, not as a healing ritual but as some form of hypnotic state. "You come when you are ready." The words echo in my mind. Did I travel to the Sky world or the Low world? When I stand, I see the brightness of the campfire. I am ready. My hunger calls and I trudge back to the orange light of the campfire following my own trail through the darkness in knee-deep snow. I think about Micmac ancestors and their snowshoes which made winter travel easier.

From reports on shamanism, I know that shamanistic power is passed from father to son, or grandmother to son or daughter. I ask the shaman how he received his shamanistic power. Peetra tells me that when he was a teenager, he looked up at the ice ring around the full moon. The ring began to change colors and pulse. The moon grew very large and seemed to come toward him, then it retreated, but the ice ring continued to pulse. After that night, he knew he had some kind of power in his hands. He began to live in the woods and study with a Sami shaman.

The hot reindeer meat he has prepared is delicious. As I eat the reindeer, thoughts of cesium and strontium contamination in reindeer meat pass quickly. He serves it with lingon berry preserves (Arctic cranberry), unleavened dark bread, and hot black tea. "You come to me to search something. Tell me what you feel in power place on rocks," he asks.

I tell him of my feeling of being one with the Earth, reindeer, and rocks. "It is good," he tells me. He removes his drum from another pack. "This drum I start to make, but not finish, you take it to your home in Montana. But first we meditate." I don't believe he is giving me the drum and I ask for clarification. "You give me the drum? To keep?" "Yes," he smiles. "It is yours, but first you play for me."

I pray silently to the Creator, my ancestors. I have never learned the traditional songs of Indian people and I feel afraid to make a mistake. I bring the drum closer to the fire to smudge it in the manner of my ancestors and other Indian people. With my free hand, I turn it to the four directions and bring the smoke closer to the face of the drum. It is made of reindeer hide and birch. I have seen similar drums among the Athabascans of Northern Canada. When it is smudged, I pray that the spirits will guide my song. I return to sit on the reindeer hide. The glow of the fire lights his face and I see he is smiling. I begin to chant a song for the Earth. I remember it from years past. It seems appropriate and the words and rhythm flow naturally from my mind, spirit, and voice:

> The Earth is our mother,
> we must take care of her.
> *Hayana hoyana hay ya na.*
>
> With every breath on Earth we take,
> We must take care of her
> *Hayana ho yana hay ya na.*

The chanting lasts for several verses over and over and when I finish I look up at the shaman's smiling face, his eyes glistening with tears. His eyes stare into mine. "It is good, thank you. You are strong, power woman, beautiful woman." He holds my gaze for a long time and then begins to speak about his past.

Long time ago, my grandfathers come to this place to live here and herd reindeer. Not far from here. It is holy land. Now when the Chernobyl comes, the reindeer get sick, we have to kill all. Fish too we cannot eat. My family . . . my kids are young. There is no milk for them. It is big problem. Many Lapps are angry and sad. Reindeer are our life. Finnish government monitors land and meat. Still after 10 years, we cannot eat livers and kidneys of reindeer. This pollution spreads from Murmansk, Russia, even today.

When he finishes telling me about their experiences with the nuclear power plant explosion, I ask him to play the drum before I take it home. He smiles sadly and beats out a rhythm with his thumb. It is the fast rhythm of a frightened animal.

"I hope you find what you search for," he says as he hands me the drum. "Peetra, I cannot take this drum without giving something to trade," I respond. I take my beaded elk tooth necklace from around my neck and place it over his head. "Take this beaded elk tooth necklace. It is a symbol of endurance and longevity like diamonds; the blue beads are the sky and the orange and yellow are fire symbols. You must have it. It is my way. My man gave it to me." "This is great," he says in perfect English. "We are connected to the power. Do not destroy it in a foolish way." He holds out his arms and asks for a goodbye hug, "May I?"

It is late and dark. My guide and I have to ride over an hour on the snow machines in the dark. I thank him for the meal and his wisdom. He holds the elk tooth in his hand. "I not forget you. Good bye, Lori. I walk you to snowmobile." He gathers up the lantern and leads us back up over the hill to the trail, the soft candlelight from the lantern illuminating our way over the frozen snow. The forest is eerily quiet. The sounds of wolves and owls blatantly absent, unlike winter forests of Montana.

On the way back to Rovaniemi, I ponder his love for the land, the reindeer, his ancestors. I wonder about his power of living in the Arctic winter wilderness. We pass foraging reindeer along the way. They are ghost spirits in the black polar night, moving against white snow, turning their antlered heads to note our passing. I remember the reindeer shared with the shaman: fattened by rich vegetation, the lichens and mosses of the Finnish forest; bathed in starlight and sunlight; father of many fawns, now part of my own body and blood. It nourishes me, one who vowed never to eat mammals; I give thanks for its strength, for its spirit. I am connected to the reindeer's awesome, but gentle power.

The evening experience moves me spiritually. I am drained, but sleep is elusive as the memory lingers of wilderness forests, reindeer spirits, and shaman. Tomorrow, Tatiana from Murmansk in Russian

Siberia will tell me about pollution and health of the people in her area of the Kola.

KOLA PENINSULA, ARCTIC SIBERIA

Siberia, stretching across the north from the Finnish border to the Kamchatka Peninsula and from the border of Kazakhstan to Sakhalin Island in the south, is both Europe and Asia. A huge barren land covering more than 5 million square miles, it is the tundra home of reindeer, Arctic fox, lemming, the Siberian tiger, sea mammals, and a vast number of migrating waterfowl. Siberia is an Arctic researcher's dream with terrain resembling that of Arctic Alaska or northern Canada. Similar plants carpet Siberia's tundra, barren land beauties with ethereal names such as jewel flower, cloud berries, antler lichens, Arctic willow. It is a delicate land, some call it pristine, where plants, animals, and humans survive through biological and behavioral adaptations. "The natural wonders of Siberia inspire the imagination of scientists and tourists; its vast riches inspire others" (Linden, 1995, p. 47). Archeological evidence points to humans living in Siberia more than 20,000 years ago.

Three hundred and sixty years ago, Russians from the west invaded the lands of Siberia much like the European invasion of North America. Once in Siberia, the Russians did not root out and segregate the survivors of the Native People they found, although they did rule over and exploit them. Like the French in Canada, the Russians intermarried into the cultures[10] around them (Weir, 1991). But during the reign of the Soviets, Siberia was synonymous with exile, the gulag, death and deprivation in the labor camps, and exploitation of Siberia's people and treasured resources.

Of all the countries included in this work, the small people republics of the former Soviet Union have experienced the most horrific ecological destruction to their land and lifeways. Within the past 70 years, the Soviets, in their rush for economic development, compromised the lives and health of these proud and independent people. I begin with a discussion concerning conditions for the Yakut people.

---

[10] Also known as the Small Peoples' Republics.

Yakutsk, capital of the Yakut-Sakha Republic (Yakutiia), is a sprawl-
ing city of 250,000 people above the Arctic Circle in Siberia. In summer,
the Lena River is the lifeline in and out of this autonomous republic within
the Russian Federation. During the long, dark Arctic winter, the tractor
train, run over highways of ice, is the conduit of the republic's business to
the "Outside."

> Our health problems in this region are dreadful. Infant mortality is the
> worst in the USSR. (Vadim, Krivoshapkin, medical professor at Yakut
> State University)

All abiotic elements—air, water, soil, and land—are affected by biocides, radioactivity, and pathogens as whole areas have been laid waste.
Commenting on the coal-mining region in Siberia, Boris Yeltzen remarked
in 1990: "People are being poisoned by . . . tons of pollution hazardous to
humans. It is suicide" (Linden, 1995). In addition to affecting the indus-
trialized areas of the southern Urals, hot spots are also found in remote
areas of the country such as Irkutsk and Sakhalin Island, across the straits
from Alaska.

Within the former Soviet infrastructure, reports of things breaking
down or blowing up were frequent. Trains derailed, spilling dangerous
cargo; storage lagoons filled with toxic waste leaked; and sewage systems
broke down, casting sewage into rivers and lakes. In Russia alone, 700
large leaks occurred along oil and gas pipelines resulting in a loss of tens
of millions of tons of all oil produced.

As a result, the cost of environmental degradation in terms of human
heath has been high. Nearly 20 percent of illnesses are caused by the de-
teriorating state of the environment which includes the mental health of
the people.

> Yakuts suffer from alcoholism because of little historical exposure to
> spirits. We become drunk four or five times faster than Russians.
> (Vadim, Krivoshapkin, medical professor at Yakut State University)

Air

The worst air is in the Siberian city of Norilsk, above the Arctic Circle.
Two hundred and sixty-seven thousand residents were subjected to

2,368,700 tons of industrial atmospheric pollution in 1990. The men in the city are said to have the highest rate of lung cancer in the world (Zaridze, 1990). The children of Norilsk held fourth place in the former Soviet Union in incidence of blood and kidney diseases and sixth place for skin diseases (Salop, 1990). In the last 10 years, there has been an increase in children born without eyes, without skin, babies with severe developmental defects, and lowered immunity (Feshbach & Friendly, 1991). From 1975 to 1990, nearly 2 million retarded babies were born. The factories in Norilsk represent the largest point source of sulfur dioxide emissions in the world and the single largest stationary source of air pollution in Russia. The pollution in Norilsk is 222 times more than in São Paulo, Brazil, considered severely polluted because of 350,000 tons of particulates and smoke emitted each year by industries (Feshbach & Friendly, 1991). In the Siberian city of Kemerovo, discharges of sulfur dioxide, hydrogen sulfide, sulfuric acid, and nitrous oxide enter the atmosphere at 5 tons per hour (Feshbach & Friendly, 1991).

The accumulation of industrial pollutants, such as zinc, copper, cobalt, and cadmium, has been the greatest near the metallurgical centers of the Kola Peninsula and southern Urals regions. In neighborhoods adjacent to large chemical plants, spontaneous abortions occur 12.5 times as frequently as the average. Premature birth is 5.4 times the average, and infertility is 3.8 times the national average. Three massive smelters producing refined nickel, copper, and cobalt on Russia's Kola Peninsula discharged 1 million tons of pollutants per year. The fallout has eroded the delicate Arctic flora and fauna for hundreds of miles (Radio Moscow, September 13, 1991). For the Sami people living in Finland, across the border, their forest lands have been reduced to a lunar landscape, according to one Finnish diplomat. (*The Wall Street Journal*, European Edition, October 24, 1989):

> Smokestack filters never work 100 percent of the time, in order to save electricity, they are often disconnected. (Liubomirski, 1991, p. 34)

Water

As the water supply in the former Soviet Union becomes more contaminated with industrial and agricultural pollution, it is more difficult and costly to purify. Lake Baikal, the deepest, largest, and oldest freshwater lake in the world, covers an area the size of the state of Maryland or larger than Belgium. Formed 25 million years ago, it holds 80 percent of Russia's freshwater. Today, it is threatened by three types of pollution: industrial, agricultural, and airborne, which include formaldehyde, benzopyrene, nitrogen oxides, and particulates. In 1988, 7,000 freshwater seals were found dead from a mysterious viral infection (Peterson, 1993). In 1987, the health of 8,000 residents of the Siberian city of Irukutsk were affected by factories piping untreated water into the city's drinking water. Pesticides and herbicides in the rivers flowing north into the Arctic have affected the drinking water, so that child mortality is 50 per 1,000 live births:

> Restless exploitation, skewed priorities and pernicious neglect have depopulated rural Russia. . . . These forces have laid waste to productive fields and forests, poisoned foods, water and people, and denied the rural people adequate medical care. (Feshbach & Friendly, 1991, p. 49)

Other problems with drinking water include massive phenol and dioxin contaminations in the Belaya and Volga Rivers. Fish stocks are contaminated and the salmon, sturgeon, and perch have been reduced from dams, over fishing, and contaminating substances. In 1987, almost one-third of all the fish in the Volga basin died of pesticide poisoning. Tainted from above with chemicals, groundwater is also being assaulted. In the Aral district, four-fifths of the women and children suffer from anemia, and mortality has risen to 90 deaths per 1,000 births. Chemical wastes have been dumped into the drinking water supply so that mothers cannot breast feed their babies without poisoning them (Feshbach & Friendly, 1991).

Soil and Land

The land in Siberia, composed of rocky, barren tundra, tiaga, thick forests, mountains, and semi desert, appears limitless. Protection of wild animals and birds began in the 11th century (Stewart, 1992). In 1667, Tsar Aleksei Mikhailovich ordered coastal areas set aside for gyrfalcon habitat and issued a decree against over hunting. His son, Peter the Great, introduced forest management practices and conservation techniques to preserve the fur-bearing animals, as well as elk. Other rulers followed, writing their own conservation laws; for example, Catherine the Great (1762–1796) banned hunting during the breeding season (Stewart, 1992). But even before the 1917 revolution and modern capitalism, an outraged Anton Chekhov wrote:

> Cut forests when it is a matter of urgency, you may, but it is time to stop destroying them. Every Russian forest is cracking under the ax . . . the abodes of beasts and birds are being ravaged, rivers are becoming shallow and drying up, wonderful landscapes will disappear without a trace. . . . One must be a barbarian . . . to destroy what we cannot create.

Today, vast wastelands, once thick with forests, can be seen. Forests, coveted by wood-hungry nations like Japan and Korea, are just one in Siberia's portfolio of resources, with oil and gas deposits rivaling those of the Middle East. Siberia, rich in diamonds and gold, is more recently rich in poachers thriving on the Amur tiger whose body parts are used for medicines in Asia. The Russian government sees its resources, especially timber, as a quick cash crop to prop up an economy that continues to founder (Linden, 1995). However, not all Russians feel that selling off the country's resources in a capitalistic surge of democracy will compensate for communism's punishment. Vasili Alekseev, Minister of Ecology, Yakutia, pioneered the development of the Lena Delta Biosphere Reserve to protect an area rich with gas and oil reserves which was horribly devastated by radioactive fallout and chemical pollution. Within the biosphere, animals and plants are suffering through loss of habitat, air and water pollution, but Indigenous people have also suffered from the effects of environmental catastrophe.

The condition of agricultural land is another cause for much concern. Erosion, over-irrigation, pesticides, fertilizers, and a lack of ecological literacy by many of the agricultural specialists and managers are the fundamental cause of the poor state of the land today (Peterson, 1993). Not only does pollution by heavy metals affect the land, pollution from fertilizers and pesticides is also a major problem. To make up for inefficient farming practices, Soviet farmers spread tons of DDT on their fields even after it was banned in other countries. Nearly 25 million acres of crops are still contaminated. Nitrates appear in more the 40 percent of the baby foods produced (Feshbach & Friendly, 1991). The incidence of cancer among children living in areas with high pesticide use, such as the cotton belt, increased by 50 percent over the last 5 years as their immune systems weakened. The fields are attacked by more the 6,000 banned toxic chemicals without instructions on how to apply them. According to official data, over 1.8 million tests were conducted on food items in the Soviet Union in 1988, with one-fifth failing inspection.

Nuclear

Novaya Zemlya, a frozen archipelago in the Barents Sea near the Arctic Ocean, was the Soviet's atmospheric nuclear weapons test site. Since the break up of the Soviet Union, reports have surfaced concerning the dumping of chemical weapons, nuclear waste, and nuclear submarines into the Barents Sea.

In the period 1966–1986, sailors from the Murmansk shipping lines regularly deposited radioactive waste near Novaya Zemlya. A large number of containers of radioactive waste were sunk in the bays of the northern archipelago along the Kara Sea. In one of the containers was the reactor of the atomic icebreaker Lenin, which was decommissioned in 1969. After being dumped, several containers remained floating. Sailors had to punch holes in them and wait until they sank . . . spilling radioactive waste into the Barents Sea where trawlers fish. (Peterson, 1993, p. 6)

When the tests were to be carried out, we were driven from our houses to the riverside . . . the light [from the blast] was so bright, you could see a needle on the ground. I saw the yellow and red mushroom and felt the earthquakes. On one occasion, the roof fell in, and crushed to death a young woman. (Peterson, 1993, p. 114)

In Siberia, five nuclear reactors buried 33 million cubic yards of liquid and 127,000 tons of solid radioactive waste in an underground sandy bed located 12 kilometers from the Orb River. In May, 38 people were contaminated after eating wild game tainted with radioactivity. The waste facility was not fenced off or marked and wild animals frequently came there to drink. Radioactive wastes from other facilities have contaminated the silt bottom in rivers. (Peterson, 1993)

In 1991, chronic food shortages and high prices meant that the public had no choice but to eat food contaminated with pesticides and radioneuclides:

> It is dangerous to grow fruits and vegetables in our land today. . . . The land that once fed us has been poisoned and destroyed once and for all. . . . If you take the soil into your hands, it does not smell like soil, it smells like pesticides, herbicides, and fertilizers. There is a sharp increase in deformed babies and cases of cholera. (Izvestiya, May 29, 1985, p. 5)

Among the native reindeer herders of Chukota who live east of the Urals in Siberia, across the Bering Strait from Alaska, gamma measurements have revealed maximum levels of cesium-137 and strontium-90, annual doses that are higher than in populations that do not eat reindeer meat (Doudarev, Miretsky, & Popov, 1996). On the other side of the Bering Strait, Alaskans in Point Hope who eat caribou have demonstrated a cancer incidence of 533 per 100,000 (Bowerman, 1996), a higher cancer rate than in the rest of the United States. Life expectancy for the native inhabitants of Chukota, which has been assessed since 1961 by means of ecological investigations, is only 43 to 45 years (Peterson, 1993).

> . . . a strange blight crept over the area. . . . mysterious maladies swept the flocks of chickens . . . cattle and sheep sickened and died. Everywhere . . . a shadow of death . . . farmers spoke of much illnesses among their families . . . doctors . . . puzzled by new kinds of sickness . . . sudden and unexplained deaths . . . among adults . . . among children . . . streams . . . lifeless . . . white powder . . . fallen like snow upon roofs, lawns, fields and streams . . . the people had done it to themselves. (Carson, 1962)

Environmental Pollution and Human Health in Murmansk

Because the water never freezes, even in the deepest Arctic winter, the area of Murmansk, located on the Kola Peninsula bordering Finland, has been exploited as a naval port and industrial site since Soviet times. The city itself has over 450,000 residents with no major industries. However, Arkhangelsk, south of Murmansk, and almost the same size, has five paper and pulp mills. Apitity, also located in the Kola area, has nickel mines. For the past 20 years, 600,000 to 800,000 tons of particulates enter the air over the Kola Peninsula every year, 70 percent of it resulting from nickel production (Sukanov, 1996). Forty percent of the purification systems are inoperable. Of 110 reservoirs for clean water in the area, only six are clean. Eight thousand square kilometers of forests are under extreme ecological deterioration. Because of soil contamination, natural foods such as berries, mushrooms, or agricultural products are contaminated and unfit for consumption. Nineteen percent of newborns die. Physicians are documenting an increase in respiratory diseases, cancers, bone and muscle diseases, pregnancy complications, and birth defects. Fifty-two percent of all children are affected with some type of health problem. The life expectancy for men is a brief 57 years. The cancer rate is 252 per 100,000 (Sukanov, 1996). In the Murmansk area, Sami, Nenets, and other Indigenous people are affected by the contamination. In its quest to manufacture industrial goods from natural resources, the former Soviet government left a legacy of environmental destruction in its wake.

Seven hundred large leaks occurred along the oil and gas pipelines resulting in a loss of 7 to 20 percent of all oil produced. At low temperatures, oil persists over a long period of time because of low rates of evaporation. The frozen permafrost, which prevents it from seeping into the ground, allows it to travel over long distances. Tundra environments are very susceptible to disturbance and its effects remain visible for many years. Lichens, which are the main source of food for reindeer, are highly susceptible to contamination by cesium.

Scientific papers have emerged documenting the pollution and environmental health problems in Siberia and northern Russia. Volumes could be written. This section will document the feelings one Russian woman has for her country, the land, her people, and their health.

Tatiana is a physician who lives in the city of Murmansk. Her practice is limited. She is also director of a secondary school of health sciences in Murmansk. She is lithe, pale, and blonde, a classical Nordic woman. During the middle of the Arctic winter, she wears a white suit with a string of cultured pearls. Her long blonde hair is stylishly arranged in an up sweep, fastened with a barrette. We meet in the cafeteria of The Lapland College of Health in Rovaniemi. "I love America; I love the American Cowboy. I tell you all how I feel." Our interview lasted over an hour and, when it was over, I was in tears for the Russian Indigenous people of the Kola Peninsula. "Don't cry for us Lori; Russian women don't like to cry. We like to be strong. We live in spite of the misery of our people":

What can I say about Russia? Our Russia has interesting, clever, scien-tific people, but now our life is very difficult. But it is because we are a strong nation, a great nation, because we are Russian people. We have no salary for more than three months, but every man, every woman, every day is in the workplace. This is our character. And we hope our government is open to this situation, and we hope we will live better than we live now. There are many shops in last time [Soviet times]— these shops are closed. Now many shops in Murmansk, many clothes, many products, many kinds of products. We can buy things, but be-cause we have a small salary . . . [things cost more than they can afford because they have no money]. In the North, in Murmansk, every woman has a fur coat, because winter is very cold. Woman like nice dresses, like bright colors, like leather, like many pretty things, gold and silver and other metals. Now what can I say about our Russian people? We have tight connections to our parents, our children, our grandmother and grandfather . . . close ties with family connections and this situa-tion in Russia shows particularly. Our lives are very difficult. After *peristroika*, we lived as in Europe and in America and we want to have the foreign culture, but we need the Russian culture, our traditions. We hope that our Russia will be the old Russia with our old traditions and culture . . . old museums, I want old connections with family and old Russia. I love old Russia.

I have a small daughter and a family. My mother died in October, and this is my cross, but we help each other in our family. My husband is an engineer in computer systems. I love my daughter, Tasha. She is 10 years old and she loves me and I love her. She is a beautiful princess girl, very fair. We are a happy family. I can tell by your face that you are a happy woman also and maybe you are more passionate; but I don't show it because I am Russian. You are a free woman. Russian woman are more strong, but we love people, all people. Now I can meet with people who left our country and they say they want Russian traditions and they love Russia, but they like foreign countries better, more rich. I don't cry because I am Russian. We are different. I have many friends and they love all people. In the world, we are two great countries and we must cultivate our friendships. [I ask her to tell me about the environmental problems in Murmansk. It is difficult because of our limited common languages.]

It is a difficult [environmental pollution] problems. We have cooperation with other countries and they help us in these problems. If we can go to these enterprises[11] [in Russia] and tell them we want a more better environment, if we ask for a better environment, then all the enterprises would close. In Murmansk, there are cleaner enterprises and we hope with your [United States, other countries] help, will be better, cleaner. We hope that the environment will be better with your help. Now . . . at last . . . there are new facilities, new equipment from Norway, from Finland, from Germany. New milk factories, new agricultural enterprises . . . and all this will help to better the environment.

I ponder her words about the pollution of her arctic world with my own experiences in the arctic:

The Harp seal adults swam under the sea ice in a world of malachite green. Their world is the world above and below the water . . . populated below by plankton, whales, other seals, fish, and numerous species . . . populated above by ravens, eagles, polar bears, humans. The seals were noisy . . . all speaking at once. It is a watery world connected to industrial development across the circumpolar north. (Journal, 1990)

In early March of 1990, I lead a group of Arctic ecology students to Arctic Quebec to witness the birth of Harp seal (Phocea Greenlandica) pups. Harp seal pups, white at birth, were the subject of intense arguing between animals rights' groups and native hunters. The "whup whup whup" of the helicopter signaled our arrival as cautious adults disappeared into their breathing holes, leaving their pups on the ice. Our whole world lay in the whiteness of ice ridges and blueness of sky. In this seemingly desolate place in March, two populations of Harp seals migrate from Greenland to whelp their pups. Within two weeks, the pups have doubled

---

[11] Enterprises: Businesses and factories.

their birth weight feasting on the thick rich cream of mother's milk. Adult mothers mate within two weeks of giving birth. Because of delayed implantation, they don't gestate until returning to Greenland without their pups. The young Harp Seal pups, 4-weeks-old, remain on the ice crying for their mothers. As hunger drives them into the sea to forage for themselves, they make their virgin voyage to Greenland, a trip they have never made, except in the haze of evolutionary forces. We returned again and again to watch the miracle of birth. Under the ice, another event was taking place. I lay down to peer into one of many breathing holes. It revealed a secret, underwater world of malachite green animated with swimming seals, a world unseemingly connected to the industrial pollution of Arctic Russia.

> To contemplate what people are doing out there and ignore the universe of the seal, to consider human quest and plight and not know the land [or the sea] . . . seemed fatal. (Lopez, 1986, p. 13)

Conclusion

The northern areas of Russia are subjected to intensive pressure from mineral, oil, and gas extraction. These processes cause transfer of pollutants by water and atmosphere, cause degradation of key wildlife habitats, affect the health of all Russian people and Indigenous peoples across the region of the Kola Peninsula. Because Russia's infrastructure is financially unstable, the Russian people look to the world nations, especially America, for help in the restoration of their environment.

OWLS AS MESSENGERS

Owls are unique predatory birds. Acting to reduce friction and produce soundless flight, the serrated edge of their flight feathers is one distinctive adaptation that sets owls apart from buteos, hawks, and falcons. As biological markers in their position as the top predator in the food chain, the health of owls forecasts evidence of a clean environment or one contaminated with pesticides, herbicides, and PCBs. In Russia, great grey owls and eagle owls have a similar morphology and habitats as our great horned owls and great grey owls. Owls continue to be important animals in the myths of Indigenous people. For example, the tribes from the Columbia River Basin in Washington and Oregon believe that the owl is the messenger of the shaman. They forecast the health of the Columbia River by establishing themselves at points on the River where the salmon run. On the Flathead Reservation, some people think of the owl as the harbinger of death. In Sami mythology, owls are messengers of the shaman.

When I returned home from Finland, the snow fell in thick, heavy flakes all day and night. At dawn, two great horned owls slipped silently into the snow-filled pine woods behind my home. While they called to one another with their distinctive "hoot," I thought of these two as voices from the Sami shaman with a message of expectation for Russian people. Although degradation of their environmental health seems dismal, there must be hope.

Chapter 6

EXPANDING CONSCIOUSNESS FOR HEALTHCARE PROFESSIONALS

Gathering: many Indian people call it the "coming together time"; gathering for ceremonies, celebrations, sorrows, and problem solving; gathering, sharing ideas, knowledge, planning; gathering berries, bitterroot, gathering medicine; a gathering of all nations for pow wow; gathering in village squares as protesters, gathering in silence on the steps of the university, in the dean's office, on the mall of the nation's capital. In this work, I gathered healthcare professionals and Indigenous people to examine challenges in environmental health and justice and to discuss patterns of behaviors among governments and corporations dealing with land ethics on reservations and reserves. I described and discussed a gathering of tribes in patterns of cultural regeneration and survival. Through this work, I hope to have expanded the consciousness of many. As we have seen, healthy lifeways for Indigenous people interconnect fully with the health of culture and the environment. These poignant themes continue to circle and surface in conversations with Indigenous people around the world.

Initially, I sought to examine issues of environmental health under the guise of the medicine wheel-medical ecology model. Because not all cultures and nations embrace the medicine wheel, I now find such a model limiting and ineffective for all Indigenous people. As a result, I suggest a new model of environmental health, a model proposed by the chorus of voices heard across Indian country, a global model created with the words of the Indigenous community. *The Indigenous Model of Environmental Health* is a model under which the healing professions can come together with Indigenous people, not only in examining issues of environmental health and justice, but in accepting a model that embraces the natural world and culture of person as integral to health. Although embracing aspects of the medicine wheel-medical ecology the new model of environmental health is more simply individualized, yet encircling, demonstrating the vision and wisdom of Indigenous people that humans are members of the natural world much like the eagle, bear, otter, and wolf. It is a simple model open to the lives and culture of Indigenous people enmeshed in healthy environment—fluid, clear, circular, global, grounded in honor of each person's way of being, doing, and understanding; rooted in human individuality and communal needs that unfold within the context of community and nature.

In this regard, and to further the model's relevance among healthcare professionals, I turn briefly to Margaret Newman's Theory of Expanding Consciousness. Taken together, the concepts of Person, Environment, and Health in Newman's Theory of Expanding Consciousness depict humans as open energy systems in continual interconnectedness with a universe of open systems known as the environment (Marchione, 1986). Synchronizing with ideologies of health for Indigenous people, Newman's (1988) theory states: "The pattern of environment-person interaction constitutes health." For the health of Indigenous people, the missing key component in Newman's model is the aspect of culture.

For many Indigenous people, disruptions in the pattern of environment, health, and culture occurred over time. When life space decreased in historical circumstances of conquest resulting in loss of traditional lands and culture, Indigenous people focused on movements for change, as seen in the American Indian Movement (AIM) and the Indigenous Peoples Environmental Network (IEN). Consistent in Newman's theory is the concept that time and space have a complimentary relationship with movement a means by which these become a reality. For Newman, movement is the change that occurs between two stages of rest and is an essential property needed for change (McQuiston & Webb, 1997). Newman also points to the need for relationships when an individual seeks through his or her suffering some form of meaning. Today, Indigenous people urgently need such relationships with others to make meaning of the historical losses they have suffered. Relationships with government agencies and grassroots environmental organizations are forming slowly. Via transcultural care agendas, healthcare professionals are beginning to partner within the paradigm of healing practices of Indigenous people. But a further strengthening of relationships is needed to champion the notion of healthy environment, culture, and person.

Nursing theories such as Newman's, grounded in phenomenological thinking, capture an illumination of the lived experience, a praxis that depicts both the struggles of the people who are researched and the theory used to define and structure the research itself as adequate to change the world, open-ended, nondogmatic, informing, and grounded in the circumstances of everyday life. It is a theory which is open to embrace the new paradigm of environmental health.

Mending Fences: The Moon of the Buttercups

The power of the land in Montana emanates from forces sweeping skyward in massive rocky mountains, giant lodgepole pines festooned with lichens and mosses, and formidable animals embracing sacred spirits of grizzly bear, wolf, wolverine. Long gone in late spring, are snowy owls gorging on voles and meadow mice. Evident are buttercups on south-facing slopes, lending color to the brown forest floor. Rough legged hawks, once plentiful as winter visitors, soar on thermals above the mountains on their way to summering grounds in the Arctic. Escorting red-winged blackbirds are buttercups and yellow bells, true harbingers of spring. Shooting stars[1] come forth later in pink-purple masses under moist shadows of lodgepole

---

[1] Shooting stars: (Dodecatheon meadia) Nodding pink flowers with flower lobes bent backwards like a shooting star.

pines. Soon camas and bitterroot, the traditional plants of the Salish people, will complete the cycle as a sign from the Creator that spring is here.

Round Butte, Montana, on the Flathead Indian Reservation, is home to about 135 ranch and farm families. Non-Indian people were the first homesteaders on the land in 1910 because of the Dawes Act which opened the Flathead Reservation to non-Indians. Senator Dawes, as did the rest of the U. S. government, believed Indian assimilation into lifeways of farming or ranching would be accelerated if Indians were forced to share their life-ways and lands with non-Indians. Today, decendents of both cultures live side-by-side with Indian families working as farmers and ranchers. The land is agriculturally rich. Crops vary little. Some concentrate on potatoes, others on alfalfa, hay, or grains. In every family, the woman plants her garden for kitchen vegetables, for canning, or freezing.

Lying between the Flathead River and the foothills of the Mission Mountains, Round Butte is named for an obscure geological formation created in the times of the glaciers. Geologists think Round Butte is the remnants of a Pingo, others feel it could have been a pile of gravel and rock carried off ancient glaciers. Ten miles west of the "Missions," the road to Round Butte cuts a sharp left off Highway 93 at the only stop light in Ronan. Carrying school buses, farm machinery, pick-ups, cattle trucks, and an occasional lost tourist, Round Butte Road was paved in the late 1950s giving easier access to town. Riding out along Round Butte Road, rolling hills come alive with grazing horses, Hereford, Black Angus, Charlois, dairy cows, an abundance of hungry coyotes, voles, barn cats, and ranch dogs. Out here, barns come in two colors, red and not red—most are red. Folks living out here evolved from tough, independent stock, with the nearest neighbor perhaps a mile away or more "down the line." During raw winters, ranchers waken early in the black of morning to drive tractors across snow-filled pastures bringing hay to pregnant cows. The cows gather round, waiting patiently under clouds of warm steam emanating from their own breath. Calves usually drop in January and February during the coldest part of the winter and ranchers are awake at all hours of the night tending to their births.

In spring, Barn Dances occupy many a Saturday night for ranch families. Fascinated with western-style dancing, easterners in New York pay hefty sums of money to learn the Texas Two-Step as performed by the ranchers and farmers in Round Butte. Every Sunday morning the church is filled with these same families.

While "visiting" over weak Montana coffee, conversations with folks from Round Butte naturally focus on the price of beef, dropping calves, getting spring crops into the ground, and worrying about adequate irrigation water. It's a hard living where many ranchers have extra jobs off the ranch to make ends meet, hoping that fall sales will bring more than 53 cents a pound for calves.

In Round Butte, "good fences make good neighbors" (Frost, 1964) whether used for keeping things in or out of pastures. When cattle escape from pastures, they become a hazard, falling prey to vehicles on Round Butte Road or to dogs and coyotes. It's good money gone. Ranchers comment fiercely on the safety of theirs and their neighbors' fences, miles of barbed wire laced and stapled together to posts, and stays[2] of various woods. "Juniper posts are best. They never rot" (conversation with Round Butte Rancher). Most juniper fence posts have been in the ground since the 1920s without a trace of rot.

Mending fence is a skill I learned from my husband, Frank, who grew up on his folks' ranch in Round Butte. In the month of the buttercups, on a breathtaking, sunny spring day, we set off to mend a fence on his father's ranch which had been damaged one night by a young driver "looking for the road." Mending fence takes teamwork; it is an art with a culture unto itself. The principal member of the team, the fence-post-setter, has the most experience. As we collected the equipment from the big red barn, sunbeams from the open door carried dust skyward. In the dark, with sunlight streaming in, Frank walked confidently to the corner of the barn where the fence-mending equipment had been kept for over 40 years, a rusty paint bucket filled with heavy duty staples, most battered out of shape and recycled to mend other fences, special heavy duty barbed wire cutter, post-hole digger, wire stretchers, extra barbed wire to make the mend, good leather gloves and patience. As the assistant, I carry all

---

[2] Stays: It looks like a fence post, but is not dug into the ground. Used to maintain the tightness of the barbed wire.

the equipment over the pasture to the edge of the "home forty" while Frank drives his pick-up carrying the posts. It is freedom to walk. The sky above the mountains is crystal-clear blue, not a cloud fluttering across the horizon. Rough-legged hawks soar on open wings. The sun is warm on my face, my feet slipping and sliding in cow dung, my "wellies"[3] covered in thick Round Butte clay.

Besides teamwork, patience and strength are other important qualities needed in mending fence. Strength is needed to handle the post-hole digger and dig the hole. When the hole is the right size and depth, Frank sets up the post as I maintain the integrity of the existing fence line by keeping the post straight and the barbed wire tight. Patiently, walking backwards along the existing line of barbed wire and old fence posts, he stands with practiced eye to determine if the new post is set along the same line. If satisfied with the position of the post, the hole is filled, ensuring the post sets straight and tight. With experienced hands and a few simple twists of barbed wire, he creates the mend, hammers the crimp out of the used staples, and drives them into the juniper post. While mending fences in Round Butte one must allow "visiting" time with neighbors who travel Round Butte Road to various ranches or to town. Ranchers and farmers, Indian and non-Indian people, often stop to wave or chat as they make the turn to Sloan's Bridge, smiling as they go, "Good fences make good neighbors and it is wise to keep our fences mended" (Frost, 1964).

HONORING IS THE KEY TO HEALING

Forces from Europe 500 years ago set about proving to the Native People of the Americas that their land, animals, waters, clouds, plants, and mountains were not sacred. To prove this, they despoiled the land, colonized the people, and eliminated plants, insects, and unwanted predators with pesticides, herbicides, and nuclear waste. As descendents of both Indian and non-Indian lifeways, we examined the health effects on Indigenous people as land is relinquished, not only in Montana but across the Americas and the globe. We witnessed changes in land-use practices that introduced foreign

---

[3] Wellies: Wellington boots or irrigation boots made of rubber. They cover the leg up to the knee.

plants and logging rituals to native soils. We observed changes in environmental health of the land, people, and culture. Throughout these changes, the power of and connection to the land for Native People remains a strong and serious fusion to health, culture, and the ancestors.

In the culture of the Cree people, it is known as *Meegwitch*, a word of politeness, with a broader meaning that implies honoring people, showing great respect (Morton, 1996/1997). "Honoring is the basis of human growth and so, health" (Morton, 1996/1997, p. 15). The Ojibwe believe that Nanabush or Winneboozo, the cultural trickster, brought illness to the people and, as we have seen, the health beliefs of the Crow are the result of bad medicine from the mantos or the spirits. It is through legends and stories that Native People transmit their histories of survival. Stories focusing on issues of environmental health and justice have been unknown, until recently. But heroes are emerging. They are honored by the tribes and are beginning to mend the fences. They are strong, patient, united, and collaborative.

Across the globe, Indigenous people speak of cohesion and solidarity. We need Indian People to be united in our territories to protect the land. We need to collaborate with others who share similar problems. We need to mend fences with those who don't agree. We need to develop the holistic Indian way in preventing environmental health problems before they become catastrophic problems.

In 1975, the U.S. government passed the Indian Self-Determination Act. The act reaffirmed the federal trust responsibility to the Indian people and rejects the policy of termination and assimilation into the mainstream culture. It offers tribes the freedom to choose their unique lifeways and to perpetuate their culture and traditions (Therriault, 1997, personal communication). Under this policy, tribes may take control of any reservation project operated by the BIA including schools, law enforcement, road construction, and assistance programs. Today, 20 years later, with the Indian Self-Determination Act, tribes are stronger, some manage and operate their own health care systems, most manage a tribal police force, operate tribal colleges, govern high schools, and celebrate their religious freedom. Indian students are emerging as an educated force retaining traditional Indian ways with a diversity of skills to strengthen their tribe's position for the next century. Indigenous people elsewhere may not have the legal position within the dominant culture to strengthen their activities.

HEALTHY ENVIRONMENT, HEALTHY CULTURE, HEALTHY PEOPLE

Indigenous people around the world define environmental health in terms of harmony with nature. It is harmony that connects self, spirit, and culture to the environment. Spirituality and culture have been compromised in cultural transformations forced by the dominant culture. We have focused on Native People as nations and as individuals dealing with issues of health, ecology, and environmental justice. We embrace a vision for the future where modern cultures begin to capture the ecologically sustainable orientation of Indigenous people so desperately needed. It is an orientation which has been long absent from the spiritual and social consciousness of modern societies (Cajete, 1994).

Since 1975, tribes have progressed in returning to cultural ways and maintaining a healthy environment. Examples of such success follow:

- Concerned Citizens of Choctaw defeated a plan to locate a hazardous waste facility on their lands in Philadelphia, Mississippi.

- In South Dakota, the Rosebud Sioux Nation has the lowest per capita income of any area in the United States. Despite their low economic status, Rosebud Sioux leaders have declined invitations by mega companies for toxic waste dumps and incinerators. The Good Road Coalition, a grassroots organization based on the Rosebud Reservation in South Dakota defeated plans by a Connecticut-based company to build a 6,000 acre landfill on the Rosebud Reservation (Bullard, 1994).

- Recently, the Bureau of Land Management (BLM) recommended to withdraw nearly 20,000 acres in the Sweet Grass Hills, Montana, from possible mining.

- Indian people in the state of Washington are fighting nuclear exposure testing without their knowledge from the Hanford Nuclear facility. A lawsuit was filed in U.S. District Court in Seattle on April 3, 1997, on behalf of six Indian tribes alleging that the Hanford Nuclear facility has subjected Indian people to "systematic experimentation on the hazards of radiation exposure by the government and agencies such as the former Atomic Energy Commission, the Department of Defense and the Department of Energy." The lawsuit further alleges that Hanford released radiation to monitor the effects of exposure on vegetation, fish, and humans. As a result, thousands of Indian people in the surrounding towns have suffered thyroid cancer and reproductive disorders. Because of their lifestyle of eating natural foods, Indian people were more at risk, and they were studied without consent. Furthermore, the government did not take steps to protect them from harm (Char-Koosta, 7/18/97, p. 11).

- In Minnesota, the Ojibwe of White Earth Reservation[4] lost their lands during the 1800s as a result of the Dawes Allotment Act. They were given the "opportunity" to gain an allotment on their otherwise community-held lands. Today, the people of the White Earth Reservation have formed the White Earth Land Recovery Project: "Native lands and issues will always remain a prime consideration of the White Earth Reservation. HONOR is an organization currently working with the White Earth Project in land acquisition" (Bosewell, 1993).

- Lee Lone Bear, a healer from Northern Cheyenne, works with health care providers and physicians from Lame Deer to incorporate traditional healing with Western medicine at two hospitals in Billings, Montana—St. Vincent's Hospital and Deaconess Medical Center.

Traditional healers approach their patients with a different point of view. They explore the whole person. They work to heal the patient from the inside out. A holisitc approach is critical to solving our problems. It involves culture, environment, person: mind, body, and spirit (Merriam, 1997). In this book, I have only grazed the surface of health and ecology issues affecting Indigenous people—there are many many more. Globally, every tribe, every group faces their specific challenges. For more information or to become involved, please see the Appendix for names of groups working with or working by Indigenous people around the world. Also investigate Indigenous Environmental Network and Indigenous Women's Network on the World Wide Web.

---

[4] The White Earth Reservation is located in northwestern Minnesota. Most of the 837,120 acres are held by non-Indian interests including state, federal, corporate, and private entities. Seven percent of the land is owned by the White Earth Bank and the Minnesota Chippewa Tribe (Mino-Bimadiziwn, 1993).

Like the Thunder Bird of Old, I shall rise again out of the sea; I shall grab the instruments of the White Man's success—his education, his skills—and with these new tools, I shall build my race into the proudest segment of your society. . . . I see our young braves and chiefs sitting in the houses of law and government. . . . so shall we shatter the barriers of isolation. So shall the next 100 years be the greatest in the proud history of tribes and nations. (Chief Dan George, Coastal Salish, Honorary chief of the Squamish tribe, B.C., 1967)

AFTERWORD

*T*his book began with the description of the Central Fire. It completes the circle with my connection to Mohawk women living in Canada. Recall that the Mohawk tribe, a member of the Iroquois Confederation, is one of the Keepers of the Central Fire. We met at the World Breast Cancer Conference in Kingston, Ontario. Six of my Mohawk sisters live on the Kahnawake Reserve adjacent to the toxic St. Lawrence River. They are cancer warriors and survivors. I would like to honor them by writing their names: Charlotte, Myrna, Helen, Brenda, Eva, Anna. They connect me to my Micmac heritage. They know my grandmother's name, our healing plants, our remedies, our traditional foods. They have listened to my grandmother's language. In an ancient ceremony, we gathered in a small circle with other Aboriginal women from Cree and Maori tribes. An Elder from the Cree tribe in western Canada led us. Her name is Eva, the First Nation's woman.

Grey clouds, pregnant with unborn rain, mark the horizon where sky meets the lake. It is a little after dawn and a pale yellow sun bursting from the depths of the lake gives birth to a new day. The waters of Lake Ontario are cleaner now than they were in the 1960s and 1970s. Wavelets wash up upon the bank and splash over black rocks. Gulls cry out overhead. My Mohawk sisters are water people. They pray to the Great Spirit, the Creator, giving thanks for the moon, the sun, the four leggeds, the winged ones, the air, the soil, and the plants. They give thanks for the clean water.

Eva removes wooden matches from her beaded moosehide bag. The moosehide, with its characteristic aroma, has been smoked and tanned in the traditional way. We know from the style of beading—the flowers, the colors, and the shapes—that this bag was beaded by a Cree beader. Eva carefully brings the lighted match to the tip of the sweet grass, braided in a circle. It is lighted. Eva moves the end in a fast rhythm to keep it lit. The smoke rises in circles. The smell is sweet and familiar. I take it in my hands and it cleanses me. My mind wanders into the past. It is 1640. I dream of birch bark canoes skimming across a pristine Lake Ontario paddled by strong, clever men, lead by insightful, adventurous women. Eva's voice brings me to the present. The women in the circle pray for all women. We pray for the men. We pray for the earth. We pray. We pray. We Keep the Central Fire.

Appendix A

RELEASE FORMS

I teach at Salish Kootenai College in Pablo, Montana. Last year when I taught students in courses of environmental health and justice, there were no texts which addressed issues affecting American Indians or First Nations people. I hope this project will fill that void.

This work is meant not to romanticize nor perpetuate the stereotyped images of First Nations in the media as they emerged in the 1800s, but to demonstrate that modern tribal sovereignty is strong in the face of harassment from mega business and federal government policies, and that Native People can assert themselves in solving issues of land and conflict.

You are being asked to talk to me about the roles of men and women in your culture, Mother Earth, and the problems that are caused when big government or big business try to control the land and the resources. I understand that you may not tell me everything about the roles of women or their special powers as you see them, I understand the need to preserve your culture and these special parts of it. I respect and honor that. I want to know the issues that you personally are interested in and that affect the health of your people. The information I am collecting may be used in a textbook to help First Nations' students and non-Indians learn about environmental health and justice issues affecting reservations and reserves across North America. I will not use your name without permission, but I may use the name of your tribal affiliation. For taking part in this interview, we will not exchange money, but your information will be used to help others understand what is happening to Indian people and their lands.

Your name will not be used or the name of your Reservation or town, but I would like to use the name of your tribe. For your name, I will make up a different name. You may withdraw from the interview at any time and I will not use the parts of the interview that you do not want me to use. I agree to be interviewed _____

Name: _____

Interviewer: _____

You have permission to use my name _____

You have permission to use my research paper or excerpts from it if you give me credit _____

You have permission to use my photograph _____

Questions

Can you describe what life was like for you as a young child? _____

_____

Would you tell me a little about your people's relationship to the land?

_____

_____

Can you tell me a little bit about the roles of men and women in your culture? _____

_____

Can you tell me about the land or hunting territories where you live? ____

_____

What are the environmental issues affecting your people? _____

_____

Appendix A

Are there corporations or big businesses trying to reduce the size of your reservation/or are they trying to create economic developments with the tribe? _____

_____

What do the words "environmental justice" mean to you? _____

_____

What do you think is the most important environmental injustices affecting your tribe today? _____

_____

As a people can you tell me what this means to your future? _____

_____

How has this affected the people of your tribe? _____

_____

Has the tribe organized to work on the issues? _____

_____

What would you tell other women or men who have similar problems affecting their people? _____

_____

Is there anything else you'd like to say? _____

_____

_____

_____

_____

_____

_____

Appendix B

Report of the United Nations Conference on Environment and Development[*]
(Rio de Janeiro, 3–14 June 1992)

ANNEX I
Rio Declaration on Environment and Development

The United Nations Conference on Environment and Development, having met at Rio de Janeiro from 3 to 14 June 1992, reaffirming the Declaration of the United Nations Conference on the Human Environment, adopted at Stockholm on 16 June 1972, and seek to build upon it,

With the goal of establishing a new and equitable global partnership through the creation of new levels of cooperation among states, key sectors of societies and people,

Working toward international agreements which respect the interests of all and protect the integrity of the global environmental and developmental system,

---

[*] Adopted by the United Nations Conference on Environment and Development, June, 1992.

Recognizing the integral and interdependent nature of the Earth, our home,

Proclaims that:

PRINCIPLE 1

Human beings are at the centre of concerns for sustainable development. They are entitled to a healthy and productive life in harmony with nature.

PRINCIPLE 2

States have, in accordance with the Charter of the United Nations and the principles of international law, the sovereign right to exploit their own resources pursuant to their own environmental and developmental policies, and the responsibility to ensure that activities within their jurisdiction or control do not cause damage to the environment of other States or of areas beyond the limits of national jurisdiction.

PRINCIPLE 3

The right to development must be fulfilled so as to equitably meet developmental and environmental needs of present and future generations.

PRINCIPLE 4

In order to achieve sustainable development, environmental protection shall constitute an integral part of the development process and cannot be considered in isolation from it.

PRINCIPLE 5

All States and all people shall cooperate in the essential task of eradicating poverty as an indispensable requirement for sustainable development, in order to decrease the disparities in standards of living and better meet the needs of the majority of the people of the world.

Appendix B

PRINCIPLE 6

The special situation and needs of developing countries, particularly the least developed and those most environmentally vulnerable, shall be given special priority. International actions in the field of environment and development should also address the interests and needs of all countries.

PRINCIPLE 7

States shall cooperate in a spirit of global partnership to conserve, protect and restore the health and integrity of the Earth's ecosystem. In view of the different contributions to global environmental degradation, States have common but differentiated responsibilities. The developed countries acknowledge the responsibility that they bear in the international pursuit of sustainable development in view of the pressures their societies place on the global environment and of the technologies and financial resources they command.

PRINCIPLE 8

To achieve sustainable development and a higher quality of life for all people, States should reduce and eliminate unsustainable patterns of production and consumption and promote appropriate demographic policies.

PRINCIPLE 9

States should cooperate to strengthen endogenous capacity-building for sustainable development by improving scientific understanding through exchanges of scientific and technological knowledge, and by enhancing the development, adaptation, diffusion and transfer of technologies, including new and innovative technologies.

PRINCIPLE 10

Environmental issues are best handled with the participation of all concerned citizens, at the relevant level. At the national level, each individual shall have appropriate access to information concerning the environment that is held by public authorities, including information on hazardous materials and activities in their communities, and the opportunity to participate in decision-making processes. States shall facilitate and encourage public awareness and participation by making information widely available. Effective access to judicial and administrative proceedings, including redress and remedy, shall be provided.

PRINCIPLE 11

States shall enact effective environmental legislation. Environmental standards, management objectives and priorities should reflect the environmental and developmental context to which they apply. Standards applied by some countries may be inappropriate and of unwarranted economic and social cost to other countries, in particular developing countries.

PRINCIPLE 12

States should cooperate to promote a supportive and open international economic system that would lead to economic growth and sustainable development in all countries, to better address the problems of environmental degradation. Trade policy measures for environmental purposes should not constitute a means of arbitrary or unjustifiable discrimination or a disguised restriction on international trade. Unilateral actions to deal with environmental challenges outside the jurisdiction of the importing country should be avoided. Environmental measures addressing transboundary or global environmental problems should, as far as possible, be based on an international consensus.

PRINCIPLE 13

States shall develop national law regarding liability and compensation for the victims of pollution and other environmental damage. States shall also cooperate in an expeditious and more determined manner to develop further international law regarding liability and compensation for adverse effects of environmental damage caused by activities within their jurisdiction or control to areas beyond their jurisdiction.

PRINCIPLE 14

States should effectively cooperate to discourage or prevent the relocation and transfer to other States of any activities and substances that cause severe environmental degradation or are found to be harmful to human health.

PRINCIPLE 15

In order to protect the environment, the precautionary approach shall be widely applied by States according to their capabilities. Where there are threats of serious or irreversible damage, lack of full scientific certainty shall not be used as a reason for postponing cost-effective measures to prevent environmental degradation.

PRINCIPLE 16

National authorities should endeavour to promote the internalization of environmental costs and the use of economic instruments, taking into account the approach that the polluter should, in principle, bear the cost of pollution, with due regard to the public interest and without distorting international trade and investment.

PRINCIPLE 17

Environmental impact assessment, as a national instrument, shall be undertaken for proposed activities that are likely to have a significant adverse impact on the environment and are subject to a decision of a competent national authority.

PRINCIPLE 18

States shall immediately notify other States of any natural disasters or other emergencies that are likely to produce sudden harmful effects on the environment of those States. Every effort shall be made by the international community to help States so afflicted.

Appendix B

PRINCIPLE 19

States shall provide prior and timely notification and relevant information to potentially affected States on activities that may have a significant adverse transboundary environmental effect and shall consult with those States at an early stage and in good faith.

PRINCIPLE 20

Women have a vital role in environmental management and development. Their full participation is therefore essential to achieve sustainable development.

PRINCIPLE 21

The creativity, ideals and courage of the youth of the world should be mobilized to forge a global partnership in order to achieve sustainable development and ensure a better future for all.

PRINCIPLE 22

Indigenous People and their communities and other local communities have a vital role in environmental management and development because of their knowledge and traditional practices. States should recognize and duly support their identity, culture and interests and enable their effective participation in the achievement of sustainable development.

PRINCIPLE 23

The environment and natural resources of people under oppression, domination and occupation shall be protected.

PRINCIPLE 24

Warfare is inherently destructive of sustainable development. States shall therefore respect international law providing protection for the environment in times of armed conflict and cooperate in its further development, as necessary.

PRINCIPLE 25

Peace, development and environmental protection are interdependent and indivisible.

PRINCIPLE 26

States shall resolve all their environmental disputes peacefully and by appropriate means in accordance with the Charter of the United Nations.

PRINCIPLE 27

States and people shall cooperate in good faith and in a spirit of partnership in the fulfillment of the principles embodied in this Declaration and in the further development of international law in the field of sustainable development.

Appendix C

URANIUM: KNOWN FACTS AND HIDDEN DANGERS*

URANIUM

What do we know about uranium? Well, uranium is the heaviest naturally occurring element on earth. It is a metal, like all other metals, except that it had no commercial value before the mid-twentieth century. Until the last fifty years it was produced only as a byproduct. Thus the entire history of the mining of uranium has taken place during my lifetime. Moreover, a great deal of it has occurred in my homeland, Canada, which was the first country to produce and process uranium as such.

The first uranium processed by Canada was used to produce nuclear explosives for the atomic bombs dropped at Hiroshima and Nagasaki in 1945. Indeed, the beginning of the nuclear weapons program marked the beginning of the uranium industry. By 1956, uranium had become the fourth most important export from Canada, after pulp, lumber and wheat;

*Invited address by Dr. Gordon Edwards at the World Uranium Hearings, Salzburg, Austria, September 14, 1992. http://ccnr.org/salzburg.html. Used with permission from Dr. Gordon Edwards Canadian Coalition for Nuclear Responsibility.

and every ounce of it was used to produce A-bombs and H-bombs for the American—and, to a lesser extent, the British—nuclear weapons programs. It was the only use uranium had at that time.

Today, Canada remains the world's largest producer and exporter of uranium, ostensibly for peaceful purposes; that is, as fuel for civilian nuclear reactors. Canada is also one of the very few countries in the world in which uranium mining is currently expanding. In the province of Saskatchewan, there are environmental assessment hearings going on now, this year, having to do with the potential opening of five new uranium mines. This, despite the fact that the price of uranium is lower today than it has ever been. The price has been falling steadily for more than fifteen years, and is now at an all-time low.

I hope that those attending this conference will write to the Prime Minister of Canada (c/o House of Commons, Ottawa, Ontario, Canada, K1A0A6) and to the Premier of Saskatchewan (c/o Saskatchewan Legislature, Regina, Saskatchewan, Canada) asking them not to continue the expansion of this industry. Why? Because uranium is the deadliest metal on earth. As you will see, the scientific evidence fully bears out this conclusion. I would now like to explain why.

Both the commercial value and the dangers of uranium are based on two extra-ordinary characteristics which it possesses. First of all, uranium is radioactive. Secondly, uranium is fissionable. These are two quite different properties, however, and they should not be confused.

RADIOACTIVITY

The phenomenon of radioactivity was accidentally discovered in 1896 when Henri Becquerel put a rock in a drawer. The rock contained uranium, and the drawer contained a photographic plate, which was well-wrapped and shielded from the light. Some weeks later, when Becquerel unwrapped and developed the plate, he found rays of light on the photograph emanating exactly from the point of contact where the rock had been resting on it. Being a scientist, he was astounded. He could think of no possible way in which an inert rock could spontaneously be releasing energy—especially such a penetrating form of energy. Moreover, the energy release had taken place in total darkness, in the absence of any external stimulation—there was no chemical reaction, no exposure to sunlight, nor anything else. Becquerel had discovered radioactivity.

Marie Curie decided to pursue the mystery further. She got some uranium ore from the Erz Mountains, not very far from here. She chemically separated the uranium from the rest of the crushed rock (she had to crush the rock and dissolve it in acid to get the uranium out, which is what we still do today in mining uranium) and she found that even after the uranium had been removed, the crushed rock remained very radioactive—much more so than the uranium itself. Here was a mystery indeed. Why is it that eighty-five percent of the radioactivity stays behind in the crushed rock?

Starting with many tons of rock, Madame Curie proceeded to separate out all the chemical elements she knew. It was painstaking work. Finally she was left with a small beaker of concentrated, highly radioactive liquid. By evaporating the water, she felt sure she would discover whatever was causing this intense radioactivity. But when the liquid was evaporated, the beaker was, apparently, completely empty. She was deeply disappointed. She couldn't fathom what had gone wrong. But when she returned to the laboratory late at night, she found the beaker glowing brightly in the dark, and she realized that it wasn't empty after all. In this way, Marie Curie discovered two new elements: radium and polonium. We now know these are inevitable byproducts of uranium.

By 1906, all the basic facts of radioactivity were known, except for the central mystery as to "why"; this we do not understand. Indeed, science doesn't really understand why anything is the way it is. All science can do is describe how things behave. Science tells us, for example, that all material things are made up of tiny atoms. The atoms found in most substances are remarkably stable, but in the case of radioactive materials, the atoms are unstable.

Consider the water in this glass. It is made up of stable atoms. Pure water is made up of hydrogen and oxygen atoms, and these atoms are, as far as science can determine, eternal and unchangeable. The very same atoms of hydrogen and oxygen that are in this glass of water were around, in some other combinations, in the days of the dinosaurs.

But radioactive substances have unstable atoms which can and will explode microscopically, and when they do, they give off a burst of energy. This process is called "radioactive disintegration" or "radioactive decay." When radioactive atoms explode, they give off highly energetic charged particles of two types: alpha and beta. These are particles, they're not invisible rays. They are like pieces of shrapnel from an explosion. And this microscopic shrapnel does great damage because of the high energy of the particles which are given off.

DECAY PRODUCTS

When a radioactive atom explodes, that atom is changed permanently into a new substance. And radium turns out to be one of the results of exploding uranium atoms. So wherever you find uranium on the earth, you will always find radium with it because it is one of about a dozen so-called "decay products" of uranium.

To be more precise, when uranium disintegrates it turns into a substance called protactinium, which is also radioactive. And when that disintegrates it turns into a substance named thorium, which is likewise radioactive. When thorium disintegrates it turns into radium; when radium disintegrates it turns into radon gas. And when radon gas atoms disintegrate, they turn into what are called the "radon daughters," or "radon progeny," of which there are about half a dozen radioactive materials, including polonium.

Finally, in this progression, you end up with a stable substance, which in itself is highly toxic: lead. But because the radioactivity of the other materials is so much more dangerous than this toxic heavy metal, people don't even talk about the lead at the end of the chain. They think that once all the radioactivity is gone, what's left is perfectly safe. It isn't—but the lead that remains is just a whole lot less dangerous than the radioactive materials that produced it.

So all the radioactive decay products of uranium remain in the crushed rock when uranium is separated from the ore. That's why Marie Curie found most of the radioactivity left behind in the residues, including all the radium and all the polonium.

RADIUM

Well, how did the story of uranium progress? Because uranium was less radioactive than its daughter products, it was not valued commercially. But radium was. And radium began to be used principally for two purposes. One was to burn cancerous growths. I should tell you that both Henri Becquerel and Marie Curie suffered grievous burns which were very difficult to heal and which left permanent scars just as a result of handling radium. Other scientists got the idea that if they embedded a needle containing radium inside a cancerous tumor, it would burn the cancer—and indeed it did. That was the beginning of cancer therapy using radiation, wherein the harmful effects of atomic radiation are directed against cancerous cells instead of healthy cells. Of course, atomic radiation does similar damage to healthy cells.

Now, the other main use for radium was as a luminous paint, because of the glow-in-the-dark phenomenon that Marie Curie had observed. Believe it or not, the price of uranium in the 1920s was $100,000 a gram— and this is using dollars of the twenties! It was a very expensive commodity, but only very little was needed for any given purpose. Some of it was used to make luminous paint, with which they would paint dials so they could be read even in the dark.

Now the young women who painted these things began to get sick. This was first reported by an American dentist called Blum, who said that he had some very young women—19 years old, 18 years old, 20 years old—coming into his dentistry office. Their teeth were falling out, their gums were badly infected and bleeding profusely, they were anemic, their bones were soft, and in some cases their jawbones had spontaneously fractured. Some of them died of severe anemia.

The only thing these women had in common was that they worked in a radium dial painting factory in New Jersey. Blum called this phenomenon "radium jaw." A few years later, the women who had recovered from these symptoms started developing problems in the rest of their skeleton. They suffered weakening of the bone, spontaneous fractures of the hip and of other bones, and growths—tumors, some of which were cancerous—in the bones themselves. Now, bone cancer is such an exceedingly rare disease, that there was little doubt that this cancer was caused by exposure to radium.

It was discovered that simply by wetting the tip of the brush in order to get a nice clean figure on the dials, these women were ingesting minute quantities of radium. And that was sufficient to cause all these symptoms. When autopsies were performed on the corpses of these women, doctors discovered that in their entire skeleton there were only a few micrograms of radium. This quantity was so small, that no conventional chemical analysis could detect it. Nevertheless, this tiny amount of radium had distributed itself so thoroughly through their skeleton, that you could take a picture of any one of their bones just by laying it on a photographic plate in a dark room. It is called an auto-radiograph—that is, an x-ray picture with no x-ray machine.

So this was our first introduction to the harmful effects of even minute quantities of such substances. By the way, many of the women who survived this phase of the assault later on developed cancers of the head— cancer of the sinuses, cancer of the soft palate, and other types of head cancers. We now know how these were caused. Remember, radium is radioactive—even inside the body. As I told you earlier, when radium atoms disintegrate, they turn into radon gas. So radon gas was being produced inside the bodies of these women. In fact, one test for radium contamination is to check a person's exhaled breath and see if it has radon gas in it; if it does, that person must have radium in his or her body. In the case of the radium dial painters, the radon gas was being produced in the bones, dissolved in the blood, and pumped by the heart up to the head where it collected in the sinus and other cavities. And there it was irradiating the delicate living tissues and causing head cancers.

RADON

Now, it so happens that for hundreds of years, going back to the 15th century, there had been reports that miners working in the Erz mountains had been dying at a tremendous rate from some unknown lung disease. We're talking here about 75 percent mortality in some cases. It wasn't until the late 19th century that the principal disease was diagnosed and found to be lung cancer. At that time, lung cancer was virtually unknown among the surrounding population; yet these miners were experiencing in some cases up to 50 percent lung cancer mortality. The other lung ailments were not lung cancer, but other types of debilitating lung damage.

By the 1930s it had been established that this epidemic of lung cancer and other lung diseases was caused by breathing radioactive materials in the atmosphere of the mine. In animal experiments, radon gas was identified as the main killer.

Appendix C

Uranium finally acquired commercial value in 1942, when we discovered that we could make atomic bombs with it. Only then did we start mining uranium for itself and not as a byproduct of something else. A few years earlier, in 1938, it was discovered that uranium is not only radioactive, it is also fissionable, which makes it unique among all naturally occurring radioactive materials. When uranium atoms undergo the fission process, large amounts of energy are released. Unlike the process of radioactive decay, which cannot be turned on and off, nuclear fission can be controlled. The energy release caused by fission can be speeded up, slowed down, started or stopped. It can be used to destroy cities in the form of nuclear weapons, or to boil water inside a nuclear reactor.

Suddenly, uranium was in demand. We sent miners into the mines in North America at a permissible level of radiation exposure which was comparable to the levels that those miners in the Erz mountains had been getting back in the 19th century. And of course, the results were entirely predictable: an epidemic of lung cancer and other lung diseases. One has to ask therefore: Why were these consequences not predicted and prevented?

RADON DAUGHTERS

The answer is, in part, that the scientists refused to believe that such a small amount of radon gas could cause such a huge increase in cancer. As it turns out, the scientists were wrong. One of the basic things they overlooked, is that if you take a sample of radon gas—right now, if I filled a tube with radon gas in front of your eyes, and measured the radiation in that tube—within three hours, the level of radioactivity would increase by a factor of about five. Why?

As the radon atoms disintegrate, they produce other radioactive substances. And so, in fact, you have a multiplication of new radioactive materials which weren't there to begin with. This is one of the things the scientists overlooked. So that when the miners go into a mine where the radon has been collecting for several hours, it's five times as radioactive as radon in the laboratory. And those other substances—the radon daughters—are extremely dangerous. The worst of the radon daughters, by the way, is a substance called polonium—the same polonium that Marie Curie discovered so many years ago. Recent scientific evidence

221

shows that polonium is, in many circumstances, at least as toxic as plutonium, and in some cases more toxic.

NUCLEAR FISSION

Now, what is that property that made uranium commercially valuable? It's
called fissionability. More precisely, uranium is called a "fissile" material.
Let me explain what that means.

Yes, uranium atoms are radioactive, and so they will disintegrate if
you just leave them alone; but what happens if you poke them? What happens if you bombard uranium atoms with tiny particles called neutrons? It
turns out that in that case, you can force a much more violent disintegration of the atom, which is called fission. When fission occurs, the uranium
atom doesn't just disintegrate, it actually breaks apart into two or three
large chunks. In the process it gives off some extra neutrons, and it also
gives off about 400 times as much energy as is produced by a radioactive
disintegration event.

Now, the fact that fission is triggered by a neutron makes it quite different from normal radioactivity. Radioactivity is not triggered, and therefore science does not know how to control it. We have no mechanism for
speeding up, slowing down, starting or stopping radioactivity. That's why radioactive wastes are such a problem. But with fission, we can start it, stop it,
and control it, just by maintaining control over the extra neutrons that are
produced at each stage. Starting with just one neutron, we can split one uranium atom, and the extra neutrons can go on to split two more uranium
atoms, giving even more neutrons which can then split four atoms, which
can then split eight atoms, and so on. In this way, forty quintillion uranium
atoms can be split with only sixty generations of splittings, all triggered by a
single neutron. (A quintillion is a billion billion, or a million million million.) This whole "chain reaction," as it is called, takes place in less than a
thousandth of a second. That is really what constitutes the atomic bomb.

FISSION PRODUCTS

You may now realize that all of the radioactive materials which escape
from an atomic bomb when it explodes are basically the broken bits of

uranium atoms. These are new radioactive materials, called "fission products," which are created by the splitting of uranium atoms. There are hundreds of them. They all have different names, and different chemical and biologically properties. Most of them did not exist in nature before the advent of nuclear technology.

You see, uranium travels in many disguises. In every sample of uranium ore, one finds radium—but radium is, in a certain sense, just a transformation of uranium. Speaking loosely, one could say that it is a disguised form of uranium. It is just one of the many elements in the chain of decay. Similarly with polonium. Similarly with radon gas. These are all just different manifestations of uranium, so to speak, resulting from radioactive decay.

And similarly with the fallout from atomic bombs; all those radioactive materials which are released by nuclear explosions—such as iodine-131, strontium-90, cesium-137, krypton-85, and all the rest—they are all broken bits of uranium atoms. They are additional disguises for uranium, resulting from nuclear fission.

The radioactive poisons that were released from the Chernobyl reactor are also broken bits of uranium atoms. Incidentally, 80 percent of the total radiation dose delivered by the Chernobyl accident worldwide was caused by the escape of just a couple of kilograms of radioactive materials from the damaged nuclear plant. It doesn't take much. . . . To this day, the sheep in Wales are unsuitable for human consumption because of contamination by one particular by-product of the Chernobyl accident called cesium-137. But every atom of cesium-137 from Chernobyl started out as an atom of uranium.

These radioactive materials, which are called fission products—the ones in bomb fallout and in nuclear reactors—should not be confused with the other radioactive materials I told you about earlier, which are the decay products of uranium. The decay products of uranium are due to radioactive disintegration. They are about two dozen in number, and they occur in nature because uranium does. When you talk about fission products, however, you are dealing with completely different substances. They are created only inside nuclear weapons and nuclear reactors. They are the leftover pieces of uranium atoms which have been violently broken apart by the fission process. There are over 300 of them altogether, when you consider that—being radioactive—each of the fission products also has its own decay products!

Appendix C

HEALTH EFFECTS OF RADIOACTIVE MATERIALS

And so this one material, uranium, is responsible for introducing into the human environment a tremendously large range of radioactive materials which are all very inimical to biological organisms. These are not invisible rays, they are materials. They get into our water, our food, and the air we breathe. They're exactly like other materials except for the fact that they're radioactive.

Take, for instance, radioactive iodine. It behaves just like ordinary iodine, which is not radioactive. Why is there iodine in our table salt? Well, it's one of the few examples of preventative medicine we have. The iodine, when it's eaten in the table salt, goes to the thyroid gland, and there it helps to prevent a disease of the thyroid gland called "goiter." Radioactive iodine does exactly the same thing. If a child or an adult gets radioactive iodine in the diet, the radioactive iodine goes to the thyroid too, and it also helps to prevent goiter. But while it's there, the atoms explode, and the shrapnel rips through the cells of the body, and in the process breaks thousands of chemical bonds randomly.

It's like throwing a grenade into a computer. The probability of getting an improvement in a computer by throwing a grenade into it is very small, and similarly with radiation events and human cells. Now, the cells that die are really no problem, as long as not too many of them die. They can be replaced. The ones that are particularly dangerous are the ones that survive. Those damaged cells can develop into cancers. You can also have damage to germ cells—eggs and sperm—leading to genetically damaged children, grandchildren, or great-grandchildren.

As Alice Stewart mentioned in her talk, there are two categories of human illness that everyone agrees can be caused by exposure to atomic radiation even at very low levels. They are (1) cancers of all kinds, and also (2) genetic mutations—which can be caused right down to the lowest levels of radiation exposure. Most scientists believe that these harmful effects are linearly related to the dose, so that if the dose is doubled, the number of cancers and genetic defects will also be doubled, and if the dose is cut in half, only half as many cancers and genetic defects will be seen. It is important to realize that if a damaging dose is spread out among a very large population, so that each individual receives only a very small portion of the total dose, the number of cancers and genetic defects is in no way diminished. Thus, in the case of radioactive pollution, dilution is no solution at all.

However, there is one other effect of radiation at low levels which wasn't mentioned in the previous talk, and I would like to just mention it here. It has now been confirmed by the scientific community—only in recent years, by the way—that mental retardation is caused by radiation exposure in the womb. This type of biological damage also seems to be linear, that is, proportional to dose, right down to the lowest levels of exposure. There doesn't seem to be any cut-off point. And so we have now discovered yet a third category of documented and scientifically accepted harmful effects of radiation and that is mental retardation in children who were irradiated while still in the womb.

URANIUM TAILINGS

Now, if I could just wrap up, I have to tell you something extremely important. The title of my talk was "Known facts and hidden dangers." I've told you a bit about the known facts. Now for at least one of the hidden dangers.

When we extract uranium from the ground, we dig up the rock, we crush it and we leave behind this finely pulverized material—it's like flour. In Canada we have 200 million tons of this radioactive waste, called uranium tailings. As Marie Curie observed, 85 percent of the radioactivity in the ore remains behind in that crushed rock. How long will it be there? Well, it turns out that the effective half-life of this radioactivity is 80,000 years. That means in 80,000 years there will be half as much radioactivity in these tailings as there is today.

You know, that dwarfs the entire prehistory of the Salzburg region which goes way back to ancient, ancient times. Even archaeological remains date back no further than 80,000 years. We don't have any records of human existence going back that far. That's the half-life of this material.

And as these tailings are left on the surface of the earth, they are blown by the wind, they are washed by the rain into the water systems, and they inevitably spread. Once the mining companies close down, who is going to look after this material forever? How does anyone, in fact, guard 200 million tons of radioactive sand safely forever, and keep it out of the environment?

In addition, as the tailings are sitting there on the surface, they are continually generating radon gas. Radon is about eight times heavier than air, so it stays close to the ground. It'll travel 1,000 miles in just a few days in a light breeze. And as it drifts along, it deposits on the vegetation below the radon daughters, which are the radioactive byproducts that I told you about, including polonium. So that you actually get radon daughters in animals, fish and plants thousands of miles away from where the uranium mining is done. It's a mechanism for pumping radioactivity into the environment for millennia to come, and this is one of the hidden dangers.

CONCLUSION

All uranium ends up as either nuclear weapons or highly radioactive waste from nuclear reactors. That's the destiny of all the uranium that's mined. And in the process of mining the uranium we liberate these naturally occurring radioactive substances, which are among the most harmful materials known to science. Couple this with the thought that nuclear technology never was a solution to any human problem. Nuclear weapons do not bring about a sane world, and nuclear power is not a viable answer to our energy problems. We don't even need it for electricity. All you need for conventional electricity generation is to spin a wheel, and there's many ways of doing it: water power, wind power, geothermal power, etc. In addition, there are other methods for producing electricity directly: solar photovoltaics, fuel cells, and so on. What we have here, in the case of nuclear power, from the very beginning, is a technology in search of an application.

So, I think that we as a human community have to come to grips with this problem and say to ourselves and to others that enough is enough. We do not want to permanently increase our radiation levels on this planet. We have enough problems already.

Thank you.

Appendix D

ENVIRONMENTAL HEALTH COMPETENCIES IN THE NURSING CURRICULUM*

The level of the program of study, for example ADN, BSN, or MSN, will determine the level of concentration possible in environmental health. However, the goal of content in environmental health should include the following four areas:

1. Nursing and the Environment

    Ecological principles and theories in defining environment

    Examination of biogeochemical cycles

    > air, water, soil

    > disruptions and contamination of the cycles

    The impact of the environment on human health, mental health

---

*Adapted from Pope, Snyder, and Mood, 1995.

Role of the nurse as provider of care, manager of care, member of the discipline

    environmental advocacy

    environmental justice

    environmental ethics

2. Overview of Regulation and Legislation

    Environmental Health Regulatory agencies: EPA, OSHA, NIOSHA

3. Exposure Assessment

    Basic toxicology

    Routes to exposure to environmental hazards

    The role of time and dose

4. Health Consequences

    Basic knowledge of most prevalent conditions: lead poisoning, pesticide poisoning, asbestos

    Reproductive toxicants

Appendix E

GRASS ROOTS ORGANIZATIONS

John Platt, Policy Manager
Columbia River Intertribal
    Fisheries Commission
729 N.E. Oregon, Suite 200
Portland, Ore 97232
Tel: 503-238-0667

Steven Rugg, Community
    Development Specialist
P.O. Box 739
Redwood Valley, CA 95470
Tel: 707-485-0084

Martin Topper, National Indian
    Program Coordinator
Environmental Protection Agency
401 M St. NW
Washington, DC 20460
202-260-5051

Global Alliance of the Indigenous
    Tribal Peoples of the Tropical
    Forest
c/o Environmental News Network
1442 a Walnut St., Suite 81
Berkeley, CA 94709
510-525-0796

Tom Goldtooth
Indigenous Environmental Network
P.O. Box 279
Red Lake, MN 56671

Calvin Waln, Secretary
Inter-Tribal Agricultural Council
100 N 27th St., Suite 450
Billings, MT 59101
406-259-3525

Joanne Reynolds, Program Manager
Inter-Tribal Timber Council
4370 NE Halsey St.
Portland, OR 97213
503-282-4296

John Persell, Director
Minnesota Chippewa Tribe
    Water Lab
P.O. Box 217
Cass Lake, MN 56633

Samuel Winder, Executive Director
National Tribal Environmental
    Council
1225 Rio Grande NW
Albuquerque, NM 87104
505-242-2175

Don Warton
Native Rights Fund
1506 Broadway
Boulder, CO 80302-6296
303-447-8760

Gail Small
Native Action
PO Box 316
Lame Deer, MT 59043
406-477-6390

Pam Kingfisher and Lance Hughes
American Indians for a Clean
    Environment
Route 3, Box 834
Tahlequeah, OK 74465
918-458-4322

Ron Skates
Native American Fish and Wildlife
    Society
750 Burbank St.
Broomfield, CO 80020
303-466-1725

Wayne Skenandore
ORTEK/Oneida Environmental
    Laboratory
PO Box 12435
Green Bay, WI 54307-2435

Alaska Indigenous Council for the
    Environment
P.O. Box 10000454
Anchorage, AK 99500

Apache Survival Coalition
P.O. Box 11814
Tucson, AZ 85734
602-475-2361

Columbia River Defense Project
P.O. Box 184
The Dalles, OR 97058

James Bay Defense Coalition
310 West 52nd St.
New York, NY 10019
212–765-9731

American Natives for a Clean
    Environment (NACE)
P.O. Box 1671
Tahlequah, OK 74465
918-458-4322

Prairie Island Coalition
P.O. Box 174
Lake Elmo, MN 55042
612-770-3861

Western Shoshone Defense Project
General Delivery
Crescent Valley, NV 89821
702-468-0230

White Earth Land Recovery Project
P.O. Box 327
White Earth, MN 56591
218-473-3110

Research and Information

American Indian Law Alliance
488 Seventh Avenue, Suite 5K
New York, NY 10018
212-268-1347

American Indian Movement
2300 Cedar Avenue South
Minneapolis, MN 55407
612-724-3129

Appendix E

Indian Law Resource Center
601 E Street SE
Washington, DC 20003
202-547-2800

International Indian Treaty Council
710 Clayton Street #1
San Francisco, CA 94117
415-566-0251

Native American Council of New
York City
404 Lafayette Street
New York, NY 10003
212-765-9731

Solidarity Foundation
310 West 52nd Street
New York, NY 10019
212-765-9510

Southwest Research Information
Center
Southwest Indigenous Uranium
Forum
PO Box 4524
Albuquerque, NM 87106
505-265-1862

Traditional Circle of Elders and
Youth
PO Box 1388
Bozeman, MT 59715
406-587-1002

Issue-Oriented

Alaska Indigenous Council for the
Environment
PO Box 1000454
Anchorage, AK 99500

James Bay Defense Coalition
310 West 52nd Street
New York, NY 10019
212-765-9731

Leonard Peltier Defense Committee
PO Box 583
Lawrence, KS 66044
913-842-5774

Native Americans for a Clean
Environment
PO Box 1671
Tahlequah, OK 74465
918-458-4322

Prairie Island Coalition
PO Box 174
Lake Elmo, MN 55042
612-770-3861

Wewah and Barcheeampe
404 Lafayette Street
New York, NY 10003
212-598-0100

Wounded Knee Survivors Association
PO Box 952
Pine Ridge, SD 57770

Urban Indian Centers

American Indian Community House
404 Lafayette Street
New York, NY 10003
212-598-0100

Minneapolis American Indian Center
1530 East Franklin Avenue
Minneapolis, MN 55404
612-871-4555

Women-Specific

American Indian Family Healing
Center
1815 39th Avenue
Oakland, CA 94601
510-534-2737

Akwesasne Mother's Milk Project
Priscilla Worswick, R.N.
Environmental Office
St. Regis Mohawk Tribe
518-358-2272

Flowering Tree Project
Oglala Lakota Tribe
Box H
Pine Ridge, SD 57770
606-867-5904

Indigenous Women's Network
PO Box 174
Lake Elmo, MN 55042
612-770-3861

Loud Thunder International
PO Box 601
Great Falls, MT 59403

Native American Women's Health
Education Resource Center
PO Box 572
Lake Andes, SD 57356-0572

Native Youth

Akwesasne Freedom School
c/o Akwesasne Nation
Hogansburg, NY 13683
518-358-2073

Heart of the Earth Survival School
1209 4th Street
Minneapolis, MN 55414
612-331-8862

Sapa Dawn Center
1013 Crystal Springs Road
Yelm, WA 98597
206-458-7610

Education

DQ University
PO Box 409
Davis, CA 95617
916-758-0470

Institute of American Indian Arts
College of Santa Fe Campus
St. Michael's Drive
Santa Fe, NM 87501-9990
505-988-6440

Learning Alliance
494 Broadway
New York, NY 10012
212-226-7171
(tapes available from forums)

Native American Educational
Services (NAES) College
2838 W Peterson Avenue
Chicago, IL 60659
312-761-5000

Oglala Lakota College
PO Box 490
Kyle, SD 57752
605-455-2321

Organization of North American
Indian Students
Box 26
University Center
Northern Michigan University
Marquette, MI 49855
906-227-2138

Standing Rock Community College
HC #1 Box 4
Fort Yates, ND 58538
701-854-3861

Economic Development/
Self-Sufficiency

Ramah Navajo Weavers Association
PO Box 862
Ramah, NM 87321
505-775-3342

Seventh Generation Fund
PO Box 10
Forestville, CA 95436
707-887-1559

The Weaving Project—Women in
Resistance
The Survival School
1142 Guerrero Street
San Francisco, CA 94110
or

2150 47th Avenue
San Francisco, CA 94116
800-876-7420
415-821-9167

Periodicals

The Circle
Minneapolis American Indian
Center
1530 East Franklin Avenue
Minneapolis, MN 55404
612-871-4555

News from Indian Country
Rt. 2
Box 2900-A
Hayward, WI 54843
715-634-5226

Appendix F

WORLD WIDE WEB ADDRESSES

http://www.indians.org/welker/canada.htm	Aboriginal Peoples of Canada
http://www.pitt.edu/~lmitten/indians.html	American Indian SITES
http://web.maxwell.syr.edu:80/nativeweb/	Welcome to NativeWeb
http://www.santacruz.k12.ca.us/vft/arctic .html	Arctic Resources
http://www.yahoo.com /Regional_Information/Regions/Arctic/	Arctic Resources
http://galaxy.einet.net/galaxy/Community /Culture/Native-American.html	American Indian
http://www.powerplace.com/atpost /nativeam.html	American Indian Links
http://www.codetalk.fed.us/tribcoll.html	Information on Tribal Colleges
http://bioc02.uthscsa.edu/natnet/archive /nl/9612/0023.html	Indian Tribal Colleges and Universities
http://www.fdl.cc.mn.us/aihec/	The American Indian Higher Education Consortium
http://www.cs.org/	Cultural Survival

BIBLIOGRAPHY

Abzug, B. (1997). Address to World Breast Cancer Conference, Kingston, Ontario.

Ackerman, L. A. (Ed.). (1995). *A song to the creator.* Norman: University of Oklahoma Press.

Adamson, J. D., Moody, J. P., & Peart, A. F. (1949). Poliomyelitis in the Arctic. *Canadian Medical Association Journal, 61,* 339–348.

Alexander, J. S. (1989). Patricia Benner. In A. Marrine-Tomy (Ed.), *Nursing theorists and their work* (2nd ed., pp. 186–192). St. Louis: Mosby.

Allen, P. G. (1991). *Grandmothers of the light: A medicine woman's source book.* Boston: Beacon Press.

Alt, & Hyndman, D. (1986). *Roadside geology of Montana.* Missoula: Mountain Press.

Baer, L.-A. (1992). The game rights of the Sami. *Nordic Sami Institute Newsletter, 1.*

Bagley, C., Wood, M., & Khumar, H. (1990). Suicide and careless death in young males: Ecological study of an aboriginal population in Canada. *Canadian Journal of Community Mental Health, 29,* 127–142.

Beach, H. (1993). *A year in Lapland.* Washington, DC: Smithsonian Institute.

Bellack, J. P., Musham, C., Hainer, A., Graber, D. R., & Holmes, D. (1996). Environmental health competencies: A survey of U.S. nurse practitioner programs. *Journal of Nursing Education, 35*(2), 74–81.

Bellanger, P. (1993). Statement. In J. Walters (Ed.), *Women of the native struggle.* New York: Orion.

Berkow, R. (Ed.). (1992). *The Merck Manual.* Rahway, NJ: Merck Research Laboratories.

Big Crane, R., & Smith, T. (Directors). (1991). *The place of falling waters.* Pablo, MT: Salish Kootenai College Teleproductions Center.

Billson, J. M. (1995). *Keepers of the culture.* New York: Lexington Books.

Bibliography

Boswell, M. (1993, Fall/Winter). Native land issues: Honor land acquisition program. In *Mino-Bimadiziwin, White Earth land recovery project* (Newsletter). White Earth, MN.

Bowerman, R. (1996). Case control study of cancer risk factors in the Alaskan Arctic: responding to village concern about environmental radiation. *Arctic Medical Research, 55,* 129–134.

Boyd, M. (1983). *Kiowa voices.* Fort Worth: Texas Christian University.

Brody, H. (1987). *Living Arctic: Hunters of the Canadian north.* Seattle: University of Washington Press.

Brown, J. E. (1989). *The sacred pipe: Black Elk's account of the seven rites of the Oglala Sioux.* Norman: University of Oklahoma Press. (Original work published 1953)

Brown, N. J. (1996). *The Navajo economy and the environment.* Unpublished manuscript.

Bryan, W. L. (1985). *Montana's Indians.* Helena, MT: Montana Magazine.

Bullard, R. D. (1994). *Unequal protection: Environmental justice and communities of color.* San Francisco: Sierra Club.

Burger, J. (1990). *First peoples: A future for the Indigenous world.* New York: Doubleday.

Cajete, G. (1994). *Look toward the mountain: An ecology of Indigenous education.* Durango, CO: Kivaki Press.

Canoe, L. (1993). In J. Walter (Ed.), *Women of the native struggle.* New York: Orion.

Carson, R. (1962). *Silent spring.* Boston: Houghton Mifflin.

Caufield, C. (1989). *In the rainforest.* New York: Knopf.

Chernousenko, V. M. (1991). *Chernobyl.* Berlin, Heidelberg, New York: Springer-Verlag.

Chessworth, J. (Ed.). (1996). *The ecology of health.* Thousand Oaks, CA: Sage.

Cinebell, H. (1996). *Ecotherapy: Healing ourselves, Healing the earth.* Minneapolis: Fortress Press.

Coats, P. (1984, Fall). Project chariot: Alaskan roots of environmentalism. In *Alaska history.* Anchorage: Alaska Historical Society.

Cohen, B. (1995, October 25). Suzy Yellowtail, the voice of a reluctant rebel. *Missoulain.*

Colburn, T., Dumanoski, D., & Myers, J. P. (1997). *Our stolen future.* New York: Plume Books.

Colomeda, L. (1996). *Through the northern looking glass: Breast cancer stories told by northern native women.* New York: National League for Nursing.

Conrad, M., Finkel, A., & Jaenen, C. (1993). *History of the Canadian peoples: Beginnings to 1867.* Mississauga, Ontario: Copp Clark Pitman.

Coyhis, D. (1996, Summer). *The seasons of change: Winds of change.* Colorado Springs: White Bison Press.

Daily, J. S., Maupin, J. S., Satterly, M. C., Schnell, D. L., & Wallace, T. L. (1989). Martha Rogers: Unitary human beings. In A. Marrine-Tomy (Ed.), *Nursing theorists and their work* (2nd ed., pp. 402–412). St. Louis: Mosby.

Dann, C. (1993). In J. Walters (Ed.), *Women of the native struggle.* New York: Orion.

Bibliography

Dankelman, I., & Davidson, J. (1993). *Women and environment in the third world*. London: Earthscan.

Debo, A. (1983). *A history of Indians in the United States*. Norman: University of Oklahoma Press.

Deloria, V. (1973). *God is red* (2nd ed.). New York: Fulcrum.

DeMaille, R. J. (1979). Change in the American Indian kinship systems, the Dakota. In R. Hinshaw (Ed.), *Currents in Anthropology: Essays in honor of Sol Tax*. The Hague: Mouton.

Doig, F. (Ed.). (1989). *Tonga Maori*. Sydney: Australian Museum.

Doudarev, A. A., Mitretsky, G. I., & Popov, A. O. (1996). Radioecology and the health of the Indigenous inhabitants in Chukotka. *Arctic Medical Research, 55*(Suppl. 1), 32–34.

Dunne, A. (1993). Before the beginning. In *Mino-Bimadiziwin, White Earth land recovery project* (Newsletter). White Earth, MN.

Dunne, A. (1994, Fall). When earth was new. In *Mino-Bimadiziwin, White Earth land recovery project* (Newsletter). White Earth, MN.

Edwards, G. (1992). *Uranium: Known facts and hidden dangers*. Paper presented at the Uranium Hearings, Salzburg, Germany.

Eichstaedt, P. (1994). *If you poison us: Uranium and American Indians*. Santa Fe, NM: Red Crane Books.

Eikjok, J. (1992). The situation of men and women in reindeer herding society. *Diehtogiisa: Newsletter from the Nordic Sami Institute, 1*.

Eisler, R. (1990). The Gaia tradition and the partnership future: An ecofeminist manifesto. I. Diamond & G. F. Orensteins (Eds.), *Reweaving the world*. San Francisco: Sierra Club.

Elkin, B. T., & Bethke, R. W. (1995). Environmental contaminants in caribou in the Northwest Territories, Canada. *The Science of the Total Environment, 160/161*, 307–321.

Feit, H. A. (1991). Gifts of the land: Hunting territories, guaranteed incomes and construction of social relations in James Bay Cree Society. *Ethnological Studies, 30*, 223–268.

Feshbach, M., & Friendly, A. (1991). *Ecocide in the USSR*. New York: HarperCollins.

Fixico, D. L. (1997). The struggle for our homes. In J. Weaver (Ed.), *Defending Mother Earth*. New York: Orbis.

Fonow, M. M., & Cook, J. A. (1991). *Beyond methodology: Feminist scholarship as lived experience*. Bloomington: University of Indiana Press.

Frey, R. (1987). *The world of the Crow Indians*. Norman: University of Oklahoma Press.

Frost, R. (1964). *The complete poems of Robert Frost*. New York: Holt, Rinehart and Winston.

Gaard, G. (1993). *Ecofeminism: Women, animals, and nature*. Philadelphia: Temple University Press.

Bibliography

Garro, L. C. (1988). Suicides by status Indians in Manitoba. In H. Linderholm, C. Backman, N. Broadbent, & I. Joelsson (Eds.), *Circumpolar health 87: Proceedings of the 7th Annual Conference on Circumpolar Health* (pp. 590–591). Oulu, Finland: Nordic Council for Arctic Medical Research.

Gomez, J. (1993). http://www.greenpeace.org/~thome/mercury.html.

Gopher, M. (1993). In J. Walters (Ed.), *Women of the native struggle*. New York: Orion.

Greenpeace International. (1997). www.greenpeace.org.

Grinde, D. A., & Johansen, B. E. (1995). *Ecocide of Native America: Environmental destruction of Indian lands and people*. Santa Fe, NM: Clear Light.

Hansen, R. D. (1997, July 23). Indian burial grounds for nuclear waste. *The Circle*.

Hansen, W. C. (1993). Radioactive contamination in Arctic tundra ecosystems. Arctic research of the United States (Workshop). *Proceedings of the Interagency Arctic Research Policy Committee, 8*, 198–206.

Head, S., & Heinzman, R. (Eds.). (1990). *Lessons of the rainforest*. San Francisco: Sierra Books.

Hill, H. (1996). *Shaking the rattle: Healing the trauma of colonization*. Victoria, BC: Orca Book.

Honko, L., Timonen, S., Branch, M., & Bosely, K. (1994). *The great bear: A thematic anthology of oral poetry in the Finno-Urian languages*. London: Oxford University Press.

Hoxie, F. E., & Josephy, A. M. (Eds.). (1992). *America in 1492: The world of the Indian people before Columbus*. Thousand Oaks, CA: Vintage Press.

Hughes, J. D. (1975). *Ecology in ancient civilizations*. Albuquerque: University of New Mexico Press.

Hutchinson, W. H. (1972, October). Dissenting voice against the myth of the Noble Savage. *Westways*.

Keane, C. (Producer). (1997). *The river that harms*. Sponsored by University of Southern California School of Journalism.

Kelsall, J. P. (1968). *The migratory Barren-Ground Caribou of Canada*. Ottawa, Ontario: Canadian Wildlife Services.

Kersaw, A. (1997, July 14). Study documents serious health risks facing Northern youth. *Queens' Gazette, 28*(12), 1.

Kleffel, D. (1991). Rethinking the environment as a domain of nursing knowledge. *Advances in Nursing Science, 14*, 10–51.

Kleffel, D. (1994). The environment: Alive, whole, and interacting. In E. A. Schuster & C. L. Brown (Eds.), *Exploring our environmental connections*. New York: National League for Nursing.

Koithan, M. (1996, December). *The human-environment connection: The relationship between nursing and environmental sciences*. Unpublished paper delivered at the Nursing Conference in Polar Twilight: People, environment, and health, Rovaniemi, Finland.

Bibliography

Lee, G. (1994, June 20–26). A potential killer's modus operandi. *Washington Post National Weekly Edition.*

Lee, R. E., & Schumaker, L. P. (1989). Rosemarie Rizzo-Parse. In A. Marrine-Tomy (Ed.), *Nursing theorists and their work* (2nd ed., pp. 174–186). St. Louis: Mosby.

Lester, S. (1995). E-Link: Doixin exposure in your community. *EnviroNews Service.* (newsdesk@envirolink.org).

Linden, E. (1995, September 14). The tortured land. *Time, 126,* 10.

Liubomiriski, L. (1991, January). Another look at the reliability of official Soviet pollution control statistics. *Environmental Policy Review, 5,* 1.

Lopez, B. (1986). *Arctic dreams: Imagination and desire in a northern landscape.* New York: Scribners.

Lord, M. (1992, November 27). Sequoyah fuels closed. *The New York Times.* (milo @scicom.alphacdc.com).

Lowell, J. (1990). PCBs in Inuit women's breast milk. In M. Crnkovich (Ed.), *"Gossip:" A spoken history of the North.* Ottawa: Canadian Arctic Resources.

Lowie, R. H. (1918). Crow creation story. In *Myths and traditions of the Crow Indians.* New York: American Museum of Natural History.

Lyons, O. (1984, Winter). Our Mother Earth. *Parabola* 7(1).

MacAdams, L. (1996, June 13). Geronimo vs. Chocise. *Rolling Stone,* 736.

Marriott, A. (1977). *The ten grandmothers.* Norman: University of Oklahoma Press.

Martin, L. (1997). dineh@prime.Net.org or www.planet_peace.org.

McElroy, A., & Townsend, P. K. (1996). *Medical anthropology in ecological perspective.* Boulder, CO: Westview Press.

McQuiston, C. M., & Webb, A. A. (1997). *Foundations of nursing theory.* Thousand Oaks, CA: Sage.

Means, R. (1988). Fighting words on the future of the Earth. In J. Zerzman & A. Carnes (Eds.), *Questioning technology.* London: Freedom Press.

Mercer, B. (1997, June 15). Black Hills water in dispute. *Rapid City Journal.*

Merriam, G. (1997). Spirit and healing. *Missoulain.*

Mino-Bimadiziwin: White Earth Land Recovery Project Newsletter. (1993, Winter). White Earth Reservation, White Earth, MN.

Morrison, J. (1996a, October 7–14). EPA is all talk and no action in moves to protect Lake Superior from sulfuric acid. *Indian Country Today.*

Morrison, J. (1996b, October 22–29). Sulfuric acid no longer a threat to Bad River Chippewa Band. *Indian Country Today.*

Morrison, R. B., & Wilson, C. R. (1992). *Native peoples: The Canadian experience.* Alberta: McClelland & Stewart.

Morton, A. M. (1996/1997, December/January). Honoring is the Key to Healing. *Kai Tiaki: Nursing New Zealand.*

Multinational Monitor. (1997). www.monitor@essential.org.

Nelson, R. K. (1983). *Make prayers to the raven.* Chicago: University of Chicago Press.

Bibliography

Ostler, C. (1996). Effects of cyanide poisoning. In R. M. Feartherstone (Ed.), *A guide to molecular pharmacology:* Modern pharmacology series (Vol. 1, p. 99). Books Demand.

Parker, G. R. (1978). *The diets of muskoxen and Peary caribou on some islands in the Canadian high Arctic* (Occasional paper #35). Ottawa, Ontario: Canadian Wildlife Service.

Peart, A. F., & Nagler, F. P. (1954). Measles in the Canadian Arctic, 1952. *Canadian Journal of Public Health, 45,* 146–157.

Penna, S. S. P. (1992, November 16). Uranium mining in Saskatchewan [On-line]. Available: http://bioc09.uthscsa.edu/natnet/archive/nl/9211/0074.html.

Peterson, D. J. (1993). *Troubled lands: The legacy of Soviet environmental destruction.* Boulder, CO: Westview Press.

Petro Canada. (1980). *Getting along in Labrador.* Calgary, Alberta: Author.

Platt, A. E. (1996). *Infecting ourselves: How environmental and social disruptions trigger disease* (World Watch Paper 129). Washington, DC: The Worldwatch Institute.

Pope, A. M., Snyder, M. A., & Mood, L. H. (Eds.). (1995). *Nursing, health and the environment.* Washington, DC: National Academy Press.

Regan, S. (1991). *Rosemarie Rizzo-Parse.* In A. Marrine-Tomy (Ed.), Nursing theorists and their work (pp. 175–186). St. Louis: Mosby.

Reiffel, B., Williams, J., & Petiquan, B. (1993, Winter). Picking medicine plants. In *Mino-Bimadiziwin, White Earth recovery project* (Newsletter). White Earth, MN.

Report stating that 38 people in Tomsk were contaminated after consuming wild game contaminated with radioactivity. (1991, November 13). *Ivestiya,* p. 6.

Roberts, E., & Amidon, E. (1991). *Earth prayers from across the world.* New York: HarperCollins.

Rogers, M. (1988). Nursing science and art: A prospective. *Nursing Science Quarterly, 1,* 99–102.

Rovner, S. (1993, June 29). Many toxins target women specifically. *Washington Post.*

Ruben, B. (1991, July/August). Grave reservations. *Environmental Action.*

Ruben, B. (1993, June 23). A reason for hope. *New York Times,* p. 13.

Rubin, H. R., & Rubin, I. S. (1995). *Qualitative interviewing: The art of hearing data.* Thousand Oaks, CA: Sage.

Ruby, R. H., & Brown, J. A. (1993). *A guide to the Indian Tribes of the Pacific Northwest.* Norman: University of Oklahoma Press.

Sale, P. (1991). *The conquest of paradise.* New York: Knopf.

Sams, J. (1994). *Earth medicine: Ancestors' ways of harmony for many moons.* San Francisco: Harper.

Sams, J., & Carson, D. (1988). *Medicine cards: The discovery of power through the ways of animals.* Santa Fe: Bear & Co.

Scheffer, V. B. (1991). *The shaping of environmentalism in America.* Seattle: University of Washington.

Bibliography

Schmidt, K. (1992). Dioxin's other face: Portrait of an environmental hormone. *Science News, 141*, 24–27.

Shenandoah, L. (1993). In J. Walters (Ed.), *Women of the native struggle.* New York: Orion.

Shephard, R. J., & Rode, A. (1996). *The health consequences of "modernization": Evidence from circumpolar peoples.* Cambridge, England: Cambridge University Press.

Silbergeld, E. (1991). http://www.envirolink.org/seel/rachel/rhwnoloe.htm.

Small, G. (1994, Spring). Environmental justice in indian country. *Amicus Journal.*

Spector, R. (1991). *Cultural diversity in health and illness.* Norwalk, CN: Appleton & Lange.

Standing Bear, Chief Luther. (1993). *Land of the spotted eagle.* Boston: Houghton Mifflin.

Starhawk. (1990). Power, authority mystery. In I. Diamond & G. F. Orensten (Eds.), *Reweaving the world.* San Francisco: Sierra Club.

Steenland, K., & Brown, D. (1985). Silicosis among goldminers: Exposure, risk assessment. *American Journal of Public Health, 85*(10), 1372–1376.

Steingraber, S. (1997). *Living downstream: An ecologist looks at cancer and the environment.* Reading, MA: Merloyd Lawrence.

Steltenkamp, M. F. (1993). *Black Elk: Holy man of the Oglala.* Norman: University of Oklahoma Press.

Stewart, J. M. (1992). The nature of Russia. New York: Cross River Press.

Stone Child College Catalog. (1992). Rocky Boy Reservation: Stone Child College.

Stubblefield, W. A., Hancock, G. A., Ford, W. H., Prince, H. H., & Ringer, R. K. (1995). Evaluation of the toxic properties of naturally weathered *Exxon Valdez* crude oil to surrogate wildlife species. In J. Butler & J. S. Hughes (Eds.), *Exxon Valdez oil spill: Fate and effect in Alaskan waters* (pp. 665–692). Philadelphia: American Society for Testing Materials.

Sukhanov, G. (1996). *Environmental pollution and human health: A new challenge in Murmansk Region.* Unpublished paper presented at a nursing conference in Polar Twilight: People, Environmental Conditions and Health in the Arctic Region, Rovaniemi, Finland.

Thorpe, G. (1997). Our homes are not dumps. In J. Weaver (Ed.), *Defending Mother Earth.* New York: Orbis.

Thurston, H. (1991, January/February). Power in a land of remembrance. *National Audubon.*

Tosee, M. (1996). Summer travels in Indian country explore environmental issues. *Earth Medicine.*

Trask, M. (1994, Winter). Address to Indigenous Women's Network, Conference, Mapelag, MN. In *Mino-Bimadiziwin, White Earth recovery project* (Newsletter). White Earth, MN.

Bibliography

Trujillo, M. (1995). *Trends in Indian health.* Washington, DC: United States Department of Health and Human Services & Indian Health Service.

Trujillo, M. (1995/1996). *Regional differences in Indian health.* Washington, DC: United States Department of Health and Human Services & Indian Health Service.

Turton, C. L. (1997). Ways of knowing about health: An aboriginal perspective. *Advanced Nursing Science, 19*(3), 28–36.

Ulbrich, J. (1991, September 9). Hydro project benefits all except the Cree. *The Seattle Times.*

U.S. Department of Health and Human Services. (1992). *Healthy people 2000.* Boston and London: Jones and Bartlett.

U.S. Department of Health and Human Services. (1993). *Cyanide update.* Washington, DC: Agency for Toxic Substances and Disease Registry.

U.S. Department of Labor. (1993). *OSHA fact sheet* (N-OSHA), 54–96. Washington, DC: Author.

Viola, H. J. (1994). *After Columbus: The Smithsonian chronicle of the North American Indians.* Washington, DC: Smithsonian Institution Press.

Walsh, R. N. (1990). *The spirit of shamanism.* Los Angeles: Tarcher.

Walters, A. L. (1993). *Women of the native struggle.* New York: Orion.

Weaver, J. (1996). *Defending mother earth: American Indian perspectives on environmental justice.* New York: Maryknoll.

Weaver, T. (1997, July). Keeping track, environmental semimonthly, Johannesburg. *World Press Review, 44*(17).

Weir, F. (1991, July 31). Siberian land myth meets reality. *The Guardian.*

Weist, T. (1977). *A History of the Cheyenne people.* Billings: Montana Council for Indian Education.

Worthington, K., & Cary, A. (1993). Primary health care: Environmental challenges. *American Nurse, 25*(10), 10–11.

Wunder, J. R. (1989). *The Kiowa.* New York: Chelsea House.

Young, T. K. (1994). *The health of American Indians.* New York: Oxford University Press.

Zimmerman, M. (1990). Feminism, deep ecology, and environmental ethics. In I. Diamond & G. F. Orenstrin (Eds), *Reweaving the world.* San Francisco: Sierra Club.

INDEX

Index

Index

Index

Index

Index

Index

Index

Tetanus, 28
Therriault, Ron, 27, 48
Thyroid cancer, 113, 201
Topical interviews, 33
Totemic animals, 174–176
Toxaphane, 130
Toxic waste dumps, 27, 79, 90, 187. *See also* Hazardous waste; Super Fund sites
Transcultural Nursing Theory, 12
Trash dumping, 96
Treaty of Paris (1783), 22
Treaty of Waitangi (1840), 170–173
Trends in Indian Health, 79–80
Trephining, 25
Trillium, 25
Tumors, PCBs and, 131
Tunnel vision, 163
Turtle Shell Calendar, 30
2–4-D, 99, 165
2–4-5-T, 99, 165

Unitary Human Being Theory (Rogers), 10–11
United Nations Conference on Environment and Development, Report of the, 209–215
United Nuclear Corporation, 110
U.S. Bureau of Mines, 60
U.S. Department of Defense, 200
U.S. Department of Energy (DOE), 111–112, 114–115, 140, 200
U.S. Department of Health and Human Services, 16, 26
U.S. Department of the Interior, 122
U.S. Office of Nuclear Waste Negotiation, 114
Upper Skagit Tribe:
  description of, 144–149
  gender roles, 149–151
  history of, 20, 144–145, 148–149
  language, 145
  logging industry, impact on, 155–156
  Reservation, history of, 153–155
Uranium, health effects of, 92–93
  in Black Hills, South Dakota, 83–84
  known and hidden dangers of, 217–228
  mining, Navajo Reservation, 104, 107–113
  in Oklahoma, 92
Urseline sisters, influence of, 47

Vainamoinene, 173–174
Vanderburg, Agnes, 46
Vegetation, indigenous healing and, 25
Vikings, 20
Violence, increased rate, 7, 27, 34, 163
Vision herbicide, 99

Walker, Lanette, 76
Waste management, impact of, 6–7

Water contamination/pollution, health effects of, 152, 167
  PCBs and, 131
  in Siberia, 183–184
Weaver, T., 3
Weedone, 100
Weinberg, Alvin, 113
Western Energy Mines, 74–75
Western Shoshone Tribe, 113, 115
Weurthner, George, 4
Whales, environmental impact on:
  Beluga, 130–131
  Bowhead, 20
White, Betty, 48
White Earth Land Recovery Project, 201
White Earth Reservation, 201
White Pine, air pollution in, 101
Wildlife:
  contamination/pollution and, 104, 125
  owls, 191–192
  PCB contamination and, 131
  poisoning of, 60
Wilmer, Mr., 98
Winneboozo, 199
Witch hazel, 25
Women:
  cancer rates in, 80
  dioxins and, 68–69
  Maori culture, 82
  pregnancy complications in, 183, 188
  roles of, *see* Gender roles
Women of the Native Struggle (Walters), 5
Wood, Donald, 122
World Health Organization, vi, 127
World Uranium Hearings (1992), 111
World Wide Web, information resources, 201, 237
Wounded Knee, 83, 85

Xenoestrogens, health effects of, 9, 68

Yakima Reservation, 44, 113
Yakut People, 19, 181–186
Yankton Sioux Tribe, 89–90
Yanomami People, 161–165
Yazzie, Emma, 116
Yellow Horse, Don, 109
Yellowstone Pipe Line, 134
Yellowtail, Suzy Walking Bear, 9–10
Yeltzen, Boris, 182
Yup'ik People, 20, 68

Zaire, mining industry in, 167
Zambia, Africa, mining industry, 166–168
Zemlya, Novaya, 186
Zimbabwe, mining industry in, 167
Zinc, health effects of, 85, 183
Zortman Mine, 59